Steve Chilton is a committed runner and qualified athletics coach with considerable experience of fell running, and a marathon PB of 2-34-53. He is a long-time member of the Fell Runners Association (FRA). In a long career he has run in most of the classic fell races, as well as mountain marathons. He has also completed the Cuillin Traverse. Steve's academic work has been published extensively, particularly in his roles as Chair of the Society of Cartographers (for whom he co-edited *Cartography: A Reader*), and as Chair of the ICA Commission in Neocartography.

His first book for Sandstone Press, *It's a Hill, Get Over It*, won the 2014 Bill Rollinson Prize for Landscape and Tradition, and shortlisted for the Great Outdoors Book of the Year. His second, *The Round: in Bob Graham's footsteps*, was runner-up in the Striding Edge Guides and Places category of the 2016 Lakeland Book of the Year Awards.

RUNNING HARD

The Story of a Rivalry

Steve Chilton

SANDSTONEPRESS
HIGHLAND | SCOTLAND

First published in Great Britain by Sandstone Press Ltd
Dochcarty Road
Dingwall
Ross-shire
IV15 9UG
Scotland

www.sandstonepress.com

Commissioning Editor: Robert Davidson
Editor: Roger Smith
Index: Roger Smith

The publisher acknowledges subsidy from Creative Scotland towards publication of
this volume.

ISBN: 978-1-910985-94-6
ISBNe: 978-1-910985-57-1

Jacket design Raspberry Creative Type, Edinburgh
Typeset by Iolaire Typography Ltd, Newtonmore
Printed and bound by Totem, Poland

To Moira, my running mate

Contents

Part Five: Changes

Part Six: Moving on

List of illustrations

Photo credits

Acknowledgements

There are always many people to acknowledge when a book comes together, some in a huge way and others for very minor, but critical, aspects. First, I must thank Moira Chilton, for everything really. She has been my rock through over three decades of life together, through all the good times and more recently my less good health.

Throughout the writing of the manuscript John Wild and Kenny Stuart have been exemplary to work with, and they, and their families, have been a joy to cooperate with. On being asked, they have provided, and checked, countless facts, anecdotes and photographs.

The fell running community came up trumps, as always, pointing me to important contacts and leads via its extensive formal and informal networks. Similarly, the B&B community of the Northern Lakes provided me with several excellent research trip stopovers.

As always, conducting the interviews in the research phase of the project has been an incredibly enjoyable experience. Huge thanks for their generosity of time and spirit to: Jack Maitland, Hugh Symonds, Dave Hall, Mark McGlincy, Alan Warner, Malcolm Patterson, Joss Naylor, and Billy Bland.

Many people helped with photo searching and provision, especially Dave Woodhead, Steve Bateson, Neil Shuttleworth, Ian Charters and Denise Park. The photos included are credited with copyright details, where known. A good proportion of the images were John and Kenny's photographic prints, and

Richard Fellows and Alun Johns both kindly loaned their scanning knowledge (and equipment) to convert them to digital files.

Dave Spedding went out of his way to arrange a loan of early Keswick AC Pacemaker magazines. Ed Price and Jamie March provided a sounding board for title ideas, when I was thrashing around indecisively.

Friends are a vital support on the roller-coaster ride that is the writing process. Mike Cambray has long been an absolutely top friend, and has always been happy to provide me with accommodation and share his boundless enthusiasm for my writing projects. Big thanks to Hannah Sheridan for straightening out my thoughts on nutrition in the manuscript, and for trying to introduce me to the world of smoothies and beetroot, only one of which went well.

The first time anyone saw this manuscript was when I showed it to a critical friend. Will Morris was that friend and I emphasised that he must be critical, and he was, and we are still friends. His thorough and detailed feedback resulted in significant changes in structure in the re-write. I am sure these have improved things, but any errors or omissions remain my responsibility, as author.

Finally, I would especially like to thank Robert Davidson and all at Sandstone Press for editorial advice, and for being so good to work with.

Glossary/acronyms

AAA – Amateur Athletic Association

ATC – Air Training Corps

BGR – Bob Graham Round, a 62 mile long distance challenge in the Lake District

BOFRA – British Open Fell Runners Association

carbo-loading – A carbohydrate-loading diet is a strategy to increase the amount of fuel stored in your muscles to improve your athletic performance. Carbohydrate loading generally involves greatly increasing the amount of carbohydrates you eat several days before a high-intensity endurance athletic event. You also typically scale back your activity level during carbohydrate loading.

'chase – Steeplechase

DNF – Did not finish

DOMS – Delayed onset muscle soreness

ECG – Electrocardiogram

fartlek – Means 'speed play' in Swedish, is a training method that blends continuous training with interval training. The variable intensity and continuous nature of the exercise places stress on both the aerobic and anaerobic systems. It differs from traditional interval training in that it is unstructured; intensity and/or speed varies, as the athlete wishes.

ECCU – English Cross Country Union

FRA – Fell Runners Association

IAAF – International Association of Athletics Federations

Inter-Counties – The Inter-Counties is one of the major annual cross country races, featuring the leading runners from each county

'Long' – FRA race category, over 20 kms

'Medium' – FRA race category, over 10 kms but less than 20 kms

Mooning – To display one's bottom in public

Mountain Trial – The Lake District Mountain Trial, a long, testing event requiring stamina and good navigation

PB – Personal best (time) for an event

PYG track – The PYG Track is one of the routes up Snowdon. It is possible that it was named after the pass it leads through, Bwlch y Moch (translated Pigs' Pass) as the path is sometimes spelled 'Pig Track'. Or, maybe because it was used to carry 'pyg' (black tar) to the copper mines on Snowdon. Another possible explanation is that the path was named after the nearby Pen y Gwryd Hotel, popular amongst the early mountain walkers.

RAF – Royal Air Force

reccie – Reconnoitre, usually of a race or route

'Short' – FRA race category, less than 10 kms

SUV – Sport utility vehicle

TB – Tuberculosis

Walshes – The Walsh shoe brand. Popular with fell runners

YHA – Youth Hostel Association

Preface

After fifteen races, a hundred or so miles and a huge amount of effort, the 1983 Fell Running championship was decided at the final fell race of the series, Thieveley Pike. It was a thrilling finale to the finest championship ever, with two men going into the last race with a chance of winning. John Wild, the international steeplechaser, needed maximum points whilst Kenny Stuart, the former professional fell racer, just needed to prevent John Wild from winning.

Stuart may have hoped to have it all sewn up before Thieveley, but he was nervous after Wild had won the last two races, and he had to wait for the last race. Kenny Stuart was worried, as he had always had the impression that John Wild was better than him on a course like Thieveley Pike, and he slipped into reassuring himself that even finishing second overall was good enough in this his first championship season. Kenny Stuart knew, 'It was down to that race. People said I had it in the bag before that, but I hadn't. I had to win that to get it. To be honest I would have settled for second place. I kept thinking to myself, "I have done quite well" and John is a damn good athlete.'

There was huge interest in the race, which was held on a fine but overcast day, with just some mist on the summit. Compared to some years it was very dry underfoot, and this and the battle for victory between Stuart and Wild would produce some stunning times.

It was an amazing race to climax an absolutely enthralling season, throughout which the two greatest fell runners of that year had battled to try to secure the title. The championship at that time was much tougher than it is now. After fifteen races the title was decided by just twenty seconds at the final race.

I had been wondering about writing something around the amazing events of the 1983 season's fell running championships for some time when a serendipitous event galvanised me into action. In a moment of idleness, having voluntarily gone down to a three-day working week, I had signed up to a Facebook group (*I am, or was, a runner*) and saw a posting from a 'John Wild'. A reasonably common combination of names, you might think, but the context of the posting led me to believe it might be the noted fell runner of that name. I decided to drop him a private message, pitching my manuscript idea to him in a couple of succinct sentences, with the hope that he might like to cooperate by agreeing to be interviewed. I received a swift response which included the sentiment that John would be 'glad to help and revisit that wonderful time'.

I had already floated the idea to Kenny Stuart when he attended the paperback launch of *'It's a hill, get over it'*, and received what came across as a cautious show of interest from him. I decided to strike while the iron was hot, and phoned Kenny to tell him about contacting John, and asking him to confirm his own cooperation. With those two verbal agreements in the bag I wrote a fuller synopsis and pitched it to my publisher, and all that is herein follows in some way or other from that initial judicious contact via social media.

In my many conversations with Kenny Stuart and John Wild in preparing this book I got a real sense of the mutual respect between these two very different athletes. At various times they both returned to that theme, alluding to each other's strengths, and to how they had pushed each other to the limit in the 1983 fell running championship season that is the core of this book.

As well as having long discussions with the two main protagonists, I was also fortunate to be able to interview many of the main players in the sport from this era. Many of the events are illuminated by the interviews and analysis from these contemporaries.

Looking at Kenny and John's performances over the years, there is a strange symmetry to their peak years as athletes. John Wild came from the Midlands, and competed on the track (reaching the steeplechase final at the 1978 Commonwealth Games) before coming on to the fells seriously for the first time in the 1980 season. He won the British championships for two straight years in 1981 and 1982, before having the almighty tussle with Kenny that is at the core of this book in the 1983 season. Kenny Stuart is from Cumbria and started running as a professional before he was reinstated as an amateur in 1982, before the big year of 1983, and then won the championships convincingly in 1984 and 1985, before taking up marathon running (with an impressive best time of 2 hours 11 minutes). However, their routes to those fell championship triumphs could not have been more diverse, as we shall see. Wild and Stuart's running careers also began to diverge after 1983, but they remained firm friends.

The book is in six parts, which cover: Wild and Stuart's families; their early lives; their racing careers before 1983; the monumental fell championship season of 1983; their later running; and subsequent lives.

Interestingly, Steve Ovett and Seb Coe, the two great middle distance track rivals, were at their peak at the same time as Wild and Stuart. Ovett and Coe only raced each other on the track six times in their whole careers, between 1978 and 1989. Four of these were Olympic Games 800/1500m finals in 1980 and 1984. Wild and Stuart raced each other eleven times in that season of 1983 alone.

The Coe and Ovett story is played out in Pat Butcher's excellent book *The Perfect Distance*, which contrasts their two different backgrounds, which did tend to get somewhat over-emphasised in the media at the time. There are some similarities with the backstory to Wild and Stuart's lives. In other sports there have been some classic two-person rivalries that dominated their respective sports at the time. In triathlon Dave Scott and Mark Allen's story is told in *Iron War* (by Matt Fitzgerald), and in cycling there are two that stand out: Boardman v Obree (described in Edward Pickering's *The Race Against Time*); and Hinault v LeMond (which is told in *Slaying the Badger* by Richard Moore). Reading this latter book was in a way responsible for the idea for this volume.

PART ONE

Families

CHAPTER 1

Gotta keep it loose

We sat overlooking the pub car park, playing a game of *'is that him?'* Eventually a modest Renault Clio pulled in and a casually dressed man got out. He was of medium height, dressed in a rugby shirt but giving the impression of someone who cared for his appearance. We deduced it was our man and I went to meet him at the door of the pub, introduced myself and got the (soft) drinks in.

I had arranged to meet John Wild for the first time in a style that now seems normal for my book interviews – over coffee in some random location, not really knowing what the interviewee looked like. This time it was a large pub just off junction 14 on the M6. We were breaking a family journey to the Lakes to meet John and have a bite to eat. After introducing him to my wife Moira, we sat down and I explained what I wanted to talk about initially. I had a set of prepared questions which were hardly needed, as after a few prompts John started a flow of anecdotes about all aspects of his running life.

Behind his animated, yet relaxed, exterior beats the heart of a man who I later found out had represented his country at the four athletic disciplines of track, road, cross country and fell running, possibly a unique achievement. I realised I was going to like John Wild, particularly when he said, 'I am astounded that you are writing a book about all this. It is brilliant to archive stuff.'

At the time of our meeting Wild had a bandaged hand. He explained that he had recently had a new finger joint. 'It hasn't gone brilliantly. I can't straighten it,' he laughed. John's finger is arthritic, but it isn't painful any more. Over the years he has had to have several operations. On my asking further about it he replied that he probably had, 'a high pain threshold, although I have been doubting that recently.'

I showed my command of technology by failing to get either of my portable audio recorders to work. So I tried to scribble, in longhand, some of the most important responses as John reeled them off. Unbeknown to me Moira had quietly turned on the audio recorder on her mobile phone, so we had a recording to download and transcribe after all. What a star! John provided a foundation for further discussion by providing interesting stories and background information about his running and his time in the RAF.

I got myself a bit more organised and called John again sometime afterwards, with a request to talk specifically about his early days and his family. He agreed, this time meeting me in another pub just off the A5 as I headed to Snowdonia for my son's stag do. More soft drinks, and on this occasion we covered his early life.

John Wild was born on 13 February 1953, and was brought up in a farming family. His parents, Reginald John and Kathleen (nee Yeomans), were both from Findern, in South Derbyshire (near Repton). Wild comes from farming stock, as his father (who was born in 1914) was also a farmer's son, with his mother having been born in 1920. Kathleen had been married before Reginald, but her husband had died, leaving her to bring up their young daughter. In what John Wild describes as the 'heartless old days' she had been married to a another farmer's son, and when he died the family just cast her off, and she had to move back to her own parents with her baby girl. She would do cleaning jobs, having to take the baby around with her, because there was no welfare state then. She got nothing from her deceased husband's parents. When John's father met her, John's grandfather objected and they feuded. By the time John was born his father had already left the family farm at Findern, after a big bust up with John's grandfather. 'When my dad and mum got together my grandfather objected most strongly to taking on someone else's family. My grandfather refused to pay dad a living wage to look after his new family and so dad left and became a farm labourer elsewhere.' John's mother was never really accepted by her family, and John's father rarely spoke to his own father after that.

In a strange turn of events John's dad's last surviving sibling passed away in August 2016. She had inherited everything that might have come to John's dad. John noted that, 'she didn't leave a will. I have been informed that I am now executor/administrator of her estate as next of kin. So, I may get some of what was not gifted to dad over fifty years ago.'

From the earlier relationship John has a step-sister Diane, who is nine years older than him. He also has a biological sister, Margaret, who is four years older than him. He was the baby of the family. He reckons that he was 'very much wanted, but also *not* wanted'. His father wouldn't have chosen to have any more children, but his mother persuaded him on the chance of getting a boy, and it worked out that way.

Diane was born in 1944 and then after his other sister was born in 1949, the family moved to Shardlow, near Derby, where again John's father was a farm labourer. 'We lived in a two-up two-down farm cottage at the end of Wilne Lane, and we were there when I was born in February 1953. We moved to a brand new council house about two miles away about a year later, and by then my father had left farming. When my grandfather got too old to farm it was all sold off and is now a housing estate. He moved to a house in Aston on Trent with my dad's sister and husband and lived there until he died in about 1963-64.'

John took a nostalgic bike ride in September 2014, on which he visited all the places he grew up in, including Findern. He also visited their old cottage in Shardlow and stopped at the village pub. 'Spookily, I met an old chap and got talking and it turned out that he got my dad his first job outside farming - as a dumper truck driver at a nearby gravel quarry. So you see, I never really had the opportunity to carry on the family farm and it was all history by the time I was old enough to understand.' He did meet his grandfather from time to time, but he was anything but friendly, and all John remembers is a grumpy old man. Back in the early 1980s John went to Findern with his mum and his wife Anne and went for a drink in the village pub. 'Mum recognised an old chap at the bar as someone who'd worked on the farm, so I introduced myself. It turned out that he started work on the farm straight from school and his first job was to look after the Shire horses.'

This somewhat dysfunctional family upbringing didn't really have any deep impact on John, who seems inured to it all now, and has a very balanced family of his own. He says now, 'I can't say that it affected me at all, although I was conscious of it affecting dad at times. I was old enough to know that when granddad died, dad received nothing at all in his will and everything went to his sister.' By that time John's father was a fitter at Castle Donnington power station. The family often struggled, but his father was always in work and they were always well looked after.

John says he had a happy childhood with some marvellous memories, including holidays taken in a caravan in North Wales. John reckons he had, 'some great mates, and we were of that lucky generation that had the freedom to roam the countryside. I was an adult before I realised how good the local farmer had been to us. He must have known we were wandering his fields and woods but just left us alone.' However, they caused no damage. They climbed trees, made dens and played football and cricket in the farmer's cow fields. In the winter they would skate on his ponds. 'My best memory is when I had my first bike for Christmas when I was ten. It was second-hand but a total surprise, as it was unexpected. I cycled miles on that little bike.' Their family holidays were always taken at Rhyl in a small caravan (John has bundles of pictures of the family on the beach). Initially they went by coach from Derby, but then his father got their first car. 'He was so proud of that little car and we were about the first on the estate to get one. It was a Morris 1000, registration number TRU 296, which we named *Truie*,' he recalls.

John went to the village primary school in Shardlow. He remembers the transition to senior school. It was the Ernest Roper Secondary School, a brand new comprehensive. 'We were the first year without the 11-plus (that either sent you to Grammar school or Secondary Modern), but a new exam streamed you for the new Comprehensive. I was in the top stream and went to a new school that had been built at Long Eaton a few miles away.' At school he didn't really start running until he was twelve years old. 'It was all about showing off. The furthest you could run was 880 yards. So myself and a couple of others decided to see who could run fastest. I did quite a good time and was put into the district sports and that was the start.' After three years you could elect to go to the grammar school to do 'O' levels, which he did.

Running certainly wasn't John's main sport for many years to come though. 'My mum's youngest brother, uncle Paul, got me into fishing at an early age. I used to go regularly with him and on my own quite a lot. I even went fishing on Christmas Day one year.' He carried on with that until he joined the RAF. He was also mad keen on football and used to play most nights after school. 'A new playing field was created from the farmer's field in about 1965, and it was right behind our house. I also got into rugby when I went to the Grammar School in 1967 and carried on playing both up until about 1971 when running came to the fore.'

It was as a result of the influence of what he describes as a 'brilliant' physics teacher at Long Eaton Grammar School named Ken Bellerby that John got into his first athletics club. John joined Allestree Woodlands, on the fringes of Allestree Park in Derbyshire, which was the venue of the Inter-Counties Cross Country championships in 1974 and 1980, the two years of John's only Inter-Counties victories. In John's view it was a good and friendly club. On club nights they would often go on a long run. But, there was no pressure to do more. 'I do remember when I was younger I used to go out for a five mile run and my mum used to time me on the kitchen clock.'

That the Inter-Counties victories were on his home patch were special to John. 'Especially as my coach Don Woodruff was watching, and in 1980 he was quite poorly. In 1974 Ray Crabb was second in the Juniors and I won the Seniors, and we were training together at RAF Wyton.' He explains the location certainly had a positive effect on his performances, and therefore his victories. 'The venue was local and it was hilly, which suited me. In 1980 Nick Lees raced away at the start and it was only on the last hill I caught him. He was a great front-runner.'

John recalls that at school his best subject was English, although he was deemed to be 'a bit thick' at school. I find this hard to believe. As I have got to know him he seems a very confident and knowledgeable person. As a youngster his athletics prospered. 'We had access to club athletics and cross country all over the Midlands and also of course, the county championships, which were held at Markeaton Park. I won at all age groups over the years at boys, youths, juniors and seniors.'

However, he only competed at the English Schools track championships once, and in the early days he mainly did long jump and 880 yards. For a runner who became so good over longer distances later on it is remarkable that he also only ever ran at the English Schools cross country championships once. In the 1969 English Schools at Leicester John came 12th in the Intermediate Boys, nine places ahead of Julian Goater. He did the steeplechase the one time he got to the English Schools track championships. 'It was at Motspur Park and the race was over 1000m, so I would be a junior. John Wheway won the 2000m senior steeplechase, I remember.'

I asked John what memories he had of turning up for the first time at the Allestree club. 'I had no proper kit, just plimsolls and shorts. One of the Keily brothers had a kit business and I remember buying some Tiger shoes and a track suit at a race and then going out in them again when I got home. I was like a fish out of water I guess.'

At one point I asked John about his early ambitions, both for his life and his running. He considered for a moment before replying, 'I can't really remember if anything specifically grabbed me, even the usual train driver thought escaped me. My RAF ambitions began when I was about twelve.'

Originally John said he didn't know where that spark came from, as there was no military interest in his family. In later conversations he suggested that maybe, 'the initial idea came from boyhood comics like the *Victor* and *Hotspur* that used to run stories of war time aircraft activities, and I was fascinated by the concept of radar.'

John continued, 'I can't say I had any specific ambitions to be a running champion, but I did realise that I was quite good early on and was prepared to train. I think those advising me had a better idea of my potential than me and they encouraged me to get better.'

Expanding on his theme of others recognising his potential and encouraging him, he recalled that through Ken Bellerby he had got to meet someone he describes as one of the most interesting people he has ever met, Don Woodruff. 'He was ahead of his time and he coached and advised me in later years. Ken Bellerby knew him and said he had this young lad who is a decent runner. We ran things like the Lutterworth road relays, county cross countries and so on. Woodruff was a good man, but sadly he died in 1988.'

Don Woodruff used to drive four miles from his house to pick John Wild and another lad up, take them to the club training night and bring them home. 'My parents encouraged me and came to early races. My dad died in 1972, so he missed most of the big occasions, but I do remember when I had done the ATC National championships at Uxbridge and he met me from the station. I had won the half mile. He said "how did it go", I said "not that well" and then showed him the winner's cup and medal! I also remember I won the ATC National cross country championships twice, once at RAF Halton of all places and once on the Epsom Downs racecourse.'

I was interested in why John thought Don was ahead of his time. 'He was talking about e-additives before others caught on. He later worked in a school for difficult kids. He was telling the organisation to reduce the e-numbers and give them a better diet, and importantly more exercise. There was one young guy who was in for arson. Don used to take him running. After a few weeks he said to Don, "I get the same buzz from running as I do from setting fires". So, a result there', John explained.

Later on, Don's coaching became quite challenging. 'When I was in my late 20s he would suggest a double session, like doing two hill sessions on the same day. I would do a hill session at lunchtime, and the same hill session in the evening, and I would do better on the second one.'

There were early indications of John's individuality, independence and also rebellious nature, as the circumstances of his going for an RAF career show, as does his behaviour after being accepted. He joined the Air Training Corps (ATC) to get closer to the RAF. 'My dad used to get the *Daily Mirror* and there was an advert for the ATC. I wrote off, didn't tell anyone, and got in. I just didn't feel the need to discuss it with my parents. When I joined they were right behind me though. My local ATC was in Alvaston, about five miles away, and I was in that for two years. It wasn't an easy place to get to, with quite a remote bus service. I remember cycling, or going on the bus or my dad might take me. My parents used to come to our open days, and watch me in parades in Derby, everything.'

Through the ATC John visited many RAF stations and also had flying and gliding experiences. It really reinforced his ambition to join the RAF. He attended the RAF Youth Selection Centre at RAF Stafford just before his 16th birthday. 'At the RAF selection I always fancied being in radar, because that was a fancy word then. They said "from the test you have taken you are more suited to navigational work". So I went to Cosford on a two-year apprenticeship in Navigational Instruments.' John recalls that he, 'also had access to good competition through the Air Training Corps and won National titles on both track and cross country (in 1967-69).'

He applied for the RAF in February 1969 when he was just sixteen, and still at school. He had a three-day selection interview at RAF Stafford to do an apprenticeship, for which you didn't need any qualifications. 'When I came back to school in February after being accepted for the RAF I just didn't care about school any more. I didn't revise and didn't turn up for two exams and got fined. It was quite right and a stupid thing to do,' he now says. He remained a member of Allestree Woodlands until it disbanded in the early seventies. 'I was still competing for them in various events such as county championships and even one year, Nos Galan, in 1971 I think.'

He joined the RAF in September 1969, and although he flunked his exams at school he did try hard to get some qualifications later, and to prove himself. 'I got to HNC level (Higher National Certificate) in the end and quite a high mark at Maths, later on when I wanted to be an engineering officer. I wasn't focussed at school. The RAF proved I was quite academic. The apprenticeship was classroom based and was quite hard.'

John's wife Anne came from the Isle of Wight, as did her mother. Anne's father was a marine from Blackburn. He met Anne's mother when he was doing cliff-top abseiling, on the Ventnor cliffs on the Isle of Wight, training for the war. He was a Marine Commando, involved in the D-day landings, crossing with the Americans to Omaha Beach.

John met Anne through athletic misfortune, at the Farnham Park rehabilitation centre. 'I got injured in the last cross country race of the 1974 season. I had ruptured my Achilles tendon. I spent several months attempting to get it healed, to no avail. It was that situation where you recover, start running, and bang it goes again. I was coached at the time by Alan Warner, an RAF Engineering Officer who was also coaching Roger Clark, an international runner. Warner was the RAF Cross Country Team Manager when I started in 1971 and throughout my running career. Roger Clark won the Midlands championships in 1968 or 1969, and was third in the 1973 English National at Parliament Hill that Rod Dixon and Dave Bedford turned up for unexpectedly.'

Alan Warner is now a lively seventy-six-year-old (at the time of writing) who still runs every other day, and loved talking through his connection with John Wild when we met over a long coffee. Born in Wolverhampton, he joined the RAF as an Apprentice at sixteen and had a full career as an Engineer Officer, working with aircraft, on three or four different RAF bases. In his later life he was Chairman of British Road Running, and on the IAAF Cross Country and Road Running Committee. He also worked with Dave Cannon (who coached Kenny Stuart for a while) on Road Running team management in his later career.

Warner's own athletics soon reached county schools level, then on to English Schools, but he didn't get to any track finals. When he joined the RAF he ran for them, until he developed a very bad Achilles tendon injury while he was stationed in Singapore. 'That terminated my career as an active runner,' he explained. 'However, since I loved athletics I then started down the admin route. One thing led to another, and I got in to coaching. I had been an 800/1500m runner, fairly successfully, winning a few titles, but I was finished at 22 years old. The highlight was possibly being ranked 10th at the 880 yards, with running something like 1-56.8. I also ran cross country for the RAF.'

John Wild says that Alan Warner knew orthopaedic surgeon Dr John Williams, who was doing innovative tendon operations. Instead of putting you in plaster for a month and letting it heal he would operate. He would strip the tendon of its sheath, sew everything back together and put you in Elastoplast. But, the essential part of his treatment was rehabilitation and starting the patient on exercises straight afterwards. He was also Director of the Farnham Park rehabilitation centre. 'He wouldn't operate unless I agreed to be a residential patient. I got special paid leave from the RAF for me to attend and I was away from duties for seven weeks, one of which was spent in hospital. I went there for six weeks in 1974. From that day I never had any trouble with my tendon. The day after the operation Dr Williams came round to see me and said, "are you all right John?". I said I was a bit sore. He twisted my foot and said "you gotta keep it loose". By the time I came out of there I was doing full blown circuit training, and I was really fit.'

Alan Warner recalls that, 'we went down a path to get John's injury sorted out, which was a challenge for me personally. The Farnham visit was set up through Royal Air Force channels.' I felt it was pertinent to ask Warner, with hindsight of course, whether he felt John had ever over-trained, resulting in injuries. 'The only injury I know well is the Achilles tendon one, and that got sorted,' he replied. 'It is a common injury, it finished my career, so I think it happened and we got it sorted out. Dr Williams did the surgery and was there the next day to initiate the physio.'

Wild went back to Dr Williams and the rehab centre a further three times, the last time in January 1976 which was when he met his future wife, Anne. John had a really good winter season in 1975-76, but then went back to the rehabilitation centre again as he had a bone spur on his ankle. The surgeon eventually diagnosed what it was and John had another operation. 'Anne was there at the rehab centre training to be a remedial gymnast, working in the later stage in people's rehab routine. Someone else would teach patients how to tie knots in string with their feet. She would do the more advanced stuff, from light exercises to supervising full blown circuit training. She was only 17, which I didn't know at the time. She was training before going to University down in Cardiff. We started going out in early 1976.'

The Wilds have two children, Kate (23) and Jack (21). Kate is with the Home Office Offender Management Service, and Jack is in the band of the Irish Guards. Jack was born in Staffordshire, but for the first pregnancy Anne went to stay with her mum in Derby as John was going through Officer training, so Kate was born there. Reflecting again on his family background, John recalled, 'My grandparents had a farm, which is now a housing estate. I rarely saw my grandfather Jack, as he was a nasty piece of work by all accounts. He died when I was 10 or 11. I never met my granny, I believe she had died before I was born. What I do remember about my grandad is that he always ate his pudding before the main meal. My dad said in the old days when you were responsible for feeding the farm labourers you fed them suet pudding before the meat and veg, so they wouldn't eat so much of that.'

Thinking back over his early running, John says he can't remember exactly why he started doing steeplechase, possibly because he was not fast enough at the mile. 'As a youngster, we did no barrier practice, and I don't think the hurdles came out apart from sports day. However, I still hold the school mile record – it doesn't exist anymore.' Then he joined up and didn't do any 'A' levels. 'I got into the RAF side of things quite quickly. I was just doing my own thing fitness wise.'

There used to be a cross country race for apprentices every September called the Hyde Mass. Wild competed three times, and won it each time. 'I remember before they had finish funnels they just stopped you at the end, and in this race it was backed up 50 yards before the line. I don't know why it was called Hyde Mass, probably 'Mass' part from the fact that over 1000 apprentices were forced to run in it! After I won Hyde Mass two years on the trot there was a plot to stop me, but I got wind of it. The senior apprentices were going to kidnap me to stop me winning!'

The first posting he got was to RAF Marham in Norfolk, near Kings Lynn. It was not considered a good posting – there were no women, and it was out in the middle of nowhere. But it was redeemed for John because there were people to train with, including Brian Jeffs. 'One time we put an RAF Marham team in to do the Land's End to John O'Groats Relay, which we did in 84 hours. I didn't really want to do it but was pressured by the station commander.'

'We did it in two teams of four as a rolling relay. Each team would do four hours, roughly ten miles each in two mile legs, ie 5 x 2 miles. We had a RAF bus in stretcher mode which we would sleep in for four hours when off shift. So, four hours sleep and get out and do it all again. You had to eat in the four hours off too. There was some managing of the team required. This was where what you might call "nice bullying" came in. I am glad I did it in the end.'

Subsequently John wasn't happy at RAF Marham, asked for a change and got a posting to RAF Wyton, where he found that Ray Crabb and Brian Jeffs were also stationed. 'I got a job which was not working shifts, and involved fixing electronic boxes. Now I could train in the morning and at lunchtime.'

Reflecting on this period, Alan Warner commented that, 'John Wild and Ray Crabb got together at Wyton, and I happened to believe philosophically that if you got two athletes together and they are both good and moving forward then you have a good thing. I coached the Rimmer twins (Gordon and Steve) and that was just the same.' He also feels that these connections were part of the process of getting a strong RAF team together across its many bases.

As we shall see, the RAF won the Inter-Services championships many years in a row. I asked John if he had an explanation for this continuous run of success. He thinks they just attracted a steady stream of great runners, but weren't actively recruiting on that basis. Mentioning two international athletes, who were also in RAF teams with him, John commented, 'I don't think that Julian Goater joined the RAF because of the athletics! Steve Jones wasn't even a runner when he joined, he used to smoke and drink a bit. He was a *liney*, working on the aircraft. I'd say it was just an outstanding era, like the Ovett/Coe era on the track.'

At this point John did admit to being a high mileage trainer in his heyday. But he says that he rarely performed to the level he should have in the National cross country championships. For the months of November, December and January he was fine, but he seemed to get jaded, which he claims wasn't anything to do with the extra distance of that race.

'I used to keep a training diary. I did 100 miles a week for over two years continuously once, and got up to 120 miles some weeks.' John Wild's 100 miles a week was certainly more mileage than Kenny Stuart normally put in. Kenny was aware that this changed when John came to the fells, as Kenny thought that, 'when John was on the fells it might have been more like 60 miles a week. But it was very technical – incredible stuff, reps twice a week and a long run once a week. Bread and butter training. He was very coordinated.'

John Wild's training load, and where it got him, will be explored in more detail later.

CHAPTER 2

A good constitution for a small fella

I have come to know Kenny Stuart fairly well over recent years, as I have interviewed him on several occasions in conducting my historical research into the sport of fell running. Once he had agreed to cooperate on telling his life story, he graciously invited me back to his cosy family home to hear about his early life. It is a modest house situated in the shadow of Blencathra, which is a mere stroll from the standard changeover point at the end of leg one of a clockwise Bob Graham Round.

Kenny Stuart started his story by saying that he came to fell running by a natural progression, 'from hours spent playing around my village in the late 1960s – games of an athletic nature involving a lot of running at various intensities. "Hounds and Hares" was a favourite, with its chases on the hillsides, as were many games of football and, in my case, hours spent tramping the hills in winter following the local foxhounds and beagles.' As we shall see, he progressed from this to be one of the finest and toughest competitors on the fells, and later also became an accomplished marathoner on the roads. Stuart was born in fell country, and moved from fell to road, meeting and competing in some epic encounters with John Wild, as Wild moved from his Midland roots through track and cross country on to the fells.

Kenny Stuart was born on 25 February 1957, in Penrith hospital, to parents who lived in Threlkeld at the time. Looking at his family background and roots there is not an exceptional amount of athletic prowess there, except maybe from his grandfather.

Going back a generation, Kenny's grandfather Ernest worked in Threlkeld quarry, breaking stones with a hammer. He was born and bred in Threlkeld, and his wife Eva was a local too. In those days you didn't marry far away. In the early days Eva didn't work while her husband was in the mines. But then when things got better in the 1950s, and women started going out to work, she went to work at Keswick Pencil Mill. Kenny chuckles, 'I haven't a clue what work it was, it was on the production line but she loved it. She liked meeting people. She didn't mind the factory environment.'

Kenny describes his grandfather's Ernest's background. 'He was a different breed, and did a bit of fell running. He also played full-back for Penrith football club when they were in one of the Northern Counties leagues, which were a very high standard in those days. He was a fairly talented footballer. He was also well known for being strong, and for his athletic prowess. He was known as Little Gi, because he was a small fella, but very thickset. So he wasn't a big giant he was a little giant. So, it was 'Laal Gi' really, in the Cumbrian dialect.

Little Gi didn't go to the sports as you couldn't travel easily in those days, there were no cars. He worked in the quarries, doing tough manual work. At one point he worked in Greenside Lead Mine. 'He worked at Threlkeld Quarry, and I think he did a spell at Brundholme Mine, and he worked at the lead mines in Threlkeld here, and at Gategill. Woodend Mine it was. He always had a good constitution for a small fella.'

Little Gi used to tell a story of when he first left school and he had to go to the site and start the bellows off to get the air in to the mines. He said it was dark and full of rats and he hated it. Kenny explains, 'He was only like 14 years old. And he used to wait at the entrance until he could hear the miners' clogs coming and he ran back in and started to pump when he knew they were nearly there. It was a rough old time. The pit ponies were stabled down here in the village, at Stable Cottages just below the school, and he used to take them backwards and forwards. They used to pull tubs with all the metal in them on railway lines. They were deep mines too, right into the heart of Blencathra.'

Without doubt those genes gave Kenny a natural advantage in his chosen sport, and the 'good constitution for a small fella' description can equally apply to him. Kenny acknowledges that Ernest used to come to watch him in his fell running days, until he died at 82 years old. 'He had a bit of a stroke and he never really recovered from it. In those days (1986/7) there wasn't the same aftercare and old people's homes where you were kept alive. I think basically he knew it was time to go and he just went, and that was it.'

Kenny's father Fred was born in Threlkeld, and his mother Sheila was from West Cumbria. Fred Stuart was classed as a labourer on Kenny's birth certificate. He worked in various manual jobs, including following his own father into working in a quarry, and for a brief period at Flusco, which was an open limestone quarry just near Penrith - where the Flusco tip is now. 'He also worked on the railway, on the P F and K line here as a ganger. P F and K is Penrith, Keswick and something else! The line went on to Workington.'

Then Fred worked at the Blencathra Sanatorium, which was a TB hospital at the time, for a couple of years. It opened in 1904, away from the town of Keswick, initially catering for 20 patients. It is now a centre promoting environmental understanding and is run by the Field Studies Council, in partnership with the Lake District National Park Authority. Kenny's father worked there as an orderly for a brief spell. When it was an outdoor centre Kenny's wife Pauline came there with her first husband. He was the warden there, so they ran it when it was a youth hostel. 'The Centre is very environmentally friendly now apparently, and has won a lot of awards. They have a biomass heating system and they have a hydroelectric plant up the road.'

Fred played for Threlkeld football club, but stopped playing when he was in his mid-twenties. Sheila looked after the family. Kenny's father spent the last 26 years of his life working at Hope Park in Keswick as a gardener. 'My father died in 2011, and I worked with him for 14 of his years at Hope Park. I was down there 16 years. I enjoyed that job. It was easy going and suited my training regime!'

Kenny has three brothers, all younger than he is. Duncan is two and a half years younger than him, Gary is eight years younger and Colin is ten years younger. Duncan has been a builder all his life and now runs a successful holiday let in St John's in the Vale (just south of Threlkeld). Gary has had various ailments and has not been able to do a lot of work really. I asked Kenny to say more, but he explained, 'I don't really know a lot about it to be honest. He has some sort of arthritic problem. But we are not that close, so I don't exactly know the details.' His brother Colin is also a builder.

Kenny went to the primary school in Threlkeld village and then on to Lairthwaite Secondary School in Keswick, which is now part of Keswick School. All his brothers went there too. Kenny recalls, 'School memories were a little similar to what James Rebanks talks about in his book *The Shepherd's Life*. You went and you tried to cause as much disruption as you could. We would be rebelling like kids do. The headmaster insisted that we didn't speak in Lakeland dialect. So we went out of way to talk in as broad a dialect as we could just to be annoying to the teachers. We just went to put time in.'

His two brothers, Gary and Colin, twice ran in the Ambleside junior guides race, but were really not that interested. His other brother, Duncan, reached district standard at cross country at school. He had limited success on the Guides circuit, not winning any of the races he entered, although obtaining a good number of second place finishes. Joining the amateur ranks in 1981, Duncan had a reasonable amount of success, including a twelfth place in the Half Nevis fell race, and he also dabbled in road racing. Duncan's 1 hour 12 minute half marathon time in the Great Cumbria Run was perhaps a precursor to Kenny's later marathon exploits. Kenny is obviously quite tight with his brother Duncan, seeming keen that I know about his latest efforts. 'He is into mountain biking now, and he has had quite an illustrious career at the local and Vets level. He was no mean runner either. He did 54 minutes for 10 miles on the Derwentwater race, which is quite a good time. He is also a very talented builder. He is doing work on our house now! He has holiday cottages and log cabins in St Johns in the Vale too.' The Helvellyn fell race used to go from Duncan's property back in the day, being organised by him.

When Kenny was at junior school they decided to revive Threlkeld children's sports day, which was held on the recreation field. There was a cross country race for under-12s, which was up a hill. It was the first race Kenny had ever run, and he won it. He can still see the course from his present house in Threlkeld. Later, at secondary school, he competed at cross country running. He was entered into the district championships, and came second. This took him on to his first County championships and he thinks he was about tenth, so was considered for the county team.

Kenny considers that to have been the highlight of his early career. But he didn't go to the Inter-Counties, as he explained, 'There must have been seven runners and two reserves, so I just missed it. I had to wait until I was into my late twenties until I got to the Inter-Counties, when I was moving from the fells to the roads.' It seems that despite multiple appearances each, Kenny Stuart and John Wild never actually ran in the same Inter-Counties championships race.

Kenny explained how his running progressed after they noticed at school that he was good at running. 'I was running for the county still as I approached 16. You then had to decide if you wanted to run as a professional in the local show races or forgo that to run as an amateur. At that stage I got a letter when I was on the verge of turning 16 in February, saying that if I wished to retain my amateur status I would have to stop running in the summer show fell races. There was nothing amateur really for teenagers then. The races at shows were the big thing – Grasmere, Ambleside and also going up to Scotland. When I look back I think it is ridiculous to think that you could have these people in blazers going round checking up on people. It happened at the Ambleside Sports, the main man from the Northern Athletics Association used to sit around in his blazer with his AAAs badge checking up on the 12-, 13-, and 14-year-olds to see what they were running.'

'Because I was into fell running and there wasn't much road running and things up here I decided to go into the Guides race scene.' He had no real idea of the implications of this decision at the time. 'Obviously I wasn't running that well then. I was quite happy to, say, finish 6th in a field of 20. It was the local shows and it was part of my life, and that was it.'

Kenny left school on a Friday and started a job on the Monday. Careers advice was pretty low-key at his school. There was a careers officer at the secondary school but he was a maths teacher. 'He just came in to the class one day and said "there might be a job going if you are interested. Just go down to Hope Park and this is the Head Gardener's name. Go and see him on the Friday after school and see what he says". It was a part-time seasonal job to start with. I went down and he said "start Monday and see how you go". It was run by Lakeland Amusements which was managed by Sir Percy Hope, who it was named after when he died. He had three hotels in Keswick, the Queens Hotel and two others. He was an OK bloke, you know, old-fashioned. People called him Sir Percy, and he was on the magistrates. But from what I can gather, and I never knew a lot of him, I think he was a very fair man. He was also the Joint Master of the Blencathra Foxhounds, when I started. Then after the first year of working I was sent to college.'

When I asked Kenny to describe his whole working career to me he just laughed. 'I have had just two jobs! I did Hope Park for 16 years and then things didn't go very well there and I decided to leave. I thought I might have a better chance of making something at the marathon running world. Initially I was working as well but I decided to go to being a full time athlete, and I had already got a bad viral problem by then. I lost my job and I lost my running career really. So I had to re-train and I went back to college at Newton Rigg, and then they offered me a job there. I have been there for twenty-four years, so apart from that I have done a little bit of self-employed work, but nothing much else.'

It is also worth remembering that in those days the running culture was so different, as Kenny noted. 'If your neighbours saw you going out for a run every day they would think you were crackers. Some also used to say that if you trained too much you would strain your heart. People would say you have to have the winter off to have a rest. To be fair I wasn't doing much training at that time, I was just concentrating on working. In those days you had to work hard to make a living. There have been a lot of good fell runners who were farmers, who were never really able to develop as they should have because they have had to put their work before their running. I used to put it the other way around, running came before everything else. They might say the day job gave them a good aerobic background. It still doesn't get away from the fact that doing things in a more scientific way they could have been better.'

People very rarely went abroad then from Kenny's village. It was unusual to go on holiday at all. Some families went to Silloth, or Scarborough if they were lucky. 'My grandparents went to Morecambe for two weeks every single year, and my grandfather hated it. We thought we were adventurous when the primary school trip went to Grange-over-Sands, it seemed a heck of a long way.'

From his own background we moved to talking about Kenny's own family. His wife Pauline reached the absolute pinnacle of fell running, and their children had great success for a number of years.

CHAPTER 3

Laidback about training

When Kenny Stuart's wife Pauline was seventeen she worked for six months at Wasdale Hostel, and she says, 'that is where I saw Joss Naylor out running. I just thought it looked really good and that is what I did.' She eventually applied for a job at the Blencathra Hostel when it came up and so she moved up to the Lakes, and became an outstanding fell runner herself.

Pauline was born in Northampton, but raised in Southport. Her mother was a Southport girl, who married a Northampton man, but the marriage broke up when Pauline was four years old. Her mother is Muriel Cushnie, and her father is called Tony [*Pauline struggled to remember, as she has had no contact for over 50 years*]. Pauline is eight months older than Kenny. She went to Southport High School for Girls, a grammar school. She left school at eighteen and began training as a nurse, but packed that in to go to work for the YHA. Eventually she ran a Youth Hostel at Llanbedr, down in Wales, after having worked at a hostel for one summer.

Talking further of her own background, Pauline Stuart revealed that she came from a fell walking background, and had been coming to the Lakes from the age of eleven with a Southport fell walking group, who used to do really long walks. 'I was always a very strong walker and I suppose it was a natural progression to run. You had very little spare time at the YHA. You finished at lunchtime and had to be back at work by four. So I just thought, right, I can get further if I run rather than walk. Breakneck descents of Whinrigg were accomplished solely so as not to incur the wrath of the warden for being late back for work.'

The summer of 1974 passed too quickly for Pauline's liking and she, 'swapped wardening for nursing, and the fells for the dingy back streets of Liverpool.' Having got the running bug, she soon learned that is wasn't to be the same back in Liverpool. 'Just a couple of night time excursions along the Docklands and a scary encounter in Sefton Park persuaded me that cycling was a much safer option, although the dual carriageways between Southport and Liverpool were not without hazards!'

Nursing was abandoned basically because Pauline hated living in Liverpool. 'I spent nearly all my days off trying to hitch up to the Lakes. I had decided that was where I wanted to live.' Having worked in the YHA already she had a chance to come back into the YHA service, which she did in 1977. She knew that she had very little chance of a nursing job in the Lakes, and she didn't want to be living in a city. 'Moving and changing careers was a pretty daft decision really,' she recalls. Pauline also worked at one point at what is now the Derwent Independent Hostel, when it was known as Barrow House, and was run by the YHA before it became independent a few years ago.

In that year Pauline entered and won the inaugural Fairfield fell race. As she recalls, 'a taunt of "you'd never make it round Fairfield" was enough to land me on the start line with some exceedingly fit looking individuals sporting Bolton vests and those of Sale Harriers, the majority of whom were from a background of road and track running. The start was a blur but maybe due to my past experience of descending, I ended up in front.' She gradually ran more races, as separate ladies ones were instigated, and duly took the title of British Fell champion in 1980, in the second year of its existence for women.

Pauline Stuart ran the Kentmere race in 1980 in very poor conditions, with the ladies having been set off about fifteen minutes before the men, as was the way at the time. She recalls that she got to the section that traverses after Kentmere Pike before you go on to High Street. 'It was just virgin snow with this incredible gradient and I thought "well I am not going anywhere". I stopped and Jean Lochhead caught me up, and there were about five of us eventually, including Veronique Marot, and we said "we should wait for the blokes". If you had slipped that would have been it really, as the slope was extremely steep with one slip meaning a fall of a few hundred feet. Mike Short from Horwich and Billy Bland were first on the scene and didn't even pause, just galloped along like a couple of mountain goats. We duly followed in their footsteps! I think most of the girls finished, but an awful lot of people dropped out that year. There weren't that many finishers. I wasn't going to drop out, I just didn't fancy going on to kill myself.' The times were about 15-20 minutes down for the men that year, due to the snow.

Pauline then had a couple of years of injuries and operations. She had an operation on her bunion, which had become very painful, and had a heel spur operation as well. 'I had originally carried on and thought they would just go away. It took about four months I think really before it was OK to run on. I then didn't do much in 1982 and 1983, I am not quite sure why now. I came back towards the end of '83 doing a few races. I was too busy I suppose.' Kenny reminds her that she had a really good season in 1984, as she came back to have a go at the British Fell championships, managing to win it that year and again in 1985.

When asked to consider her career, back in 2004, she commented, 'looking back at my diaries confirms Ken's view that I was very laidback about training (actually he used the word lazy, but I refute that!). For me running just happened to be the quickest, most convenient way to get to work, with the route through Brundholme Woods on the lower slopes of Latrigg always a delight. My mileage was low, around 25-30 miles a week, although my frequent racing schedule upped the tempo and miles a little more.'

From 1980 to 1984 Pauline worked at the doctor's surgery on Brundholme Terrace in Keswick, and lived at the Blencathra

Centre. 'It was just much quicker to run direct through the woods or over Latrigg, or round Lonscale. I had different routes depending on how energetic I was feeling, and what time of year it was. When it was dark at night I used to come back along the A66 road. But in the early 1980s there wasn't the traffic there is now. You could run along the A66 at 7-30pm at night with a torch and back up the minor road to the Centre. You didn't have a fabulous lightweight head torch like you have now of course. So you used to have a hand torch maybe.'

When Kenny and Pauline started a family they were looking after a house in Brocklecrag, round the back of Skiddaw. It was a very remote spot just down from Dash Falls, where they were looking after the house for a couple who were away. Their son Matthew was born there, and the other children, Rosie and Emma, were born in their present house.

All three of Kenny and Pauline Stuarts's children showed impressive running abilities early in life. Matthew Stuart competed on the fells for four years from 1996 onwards, and by 1999 was winning some age category races. He came 3rd in the under-12 fell championships in 1998 and 5th in the under-14s in 2000. Unfortunately, he had to stop competing due to knee problems.

Kenny felt it was difficult to say how much their children took notice of their parents' performances - or even their own! 'Matthew won quite a lot of medals and stuff and they are all upstairs in our bedroom. He never seemed bothered about taking them, as though it was by-and-by. He is very laid back is Matthew, nothing seems to bother him. He has my passion for the hunt though. He is still fit but he stopped running when he was fifteen as he had Osgood-Schlatters [*a common cause of knee pain in growing adolescents*]. He looked at what the other athletes were having to do and didn't want to do it.'

The Stuart girls had fairly short racing careers, and the highlights show how good they both were. Emma Stuart started competing as an under-12 in 1999, entering four BOFRA (British Open Fell Runners Association) championship races, including Ambleside Sports, and won them all. She continued running some BOFRA races, before gradually switching to the FRA (Fell Runners Association) events. In 2000 she won the FRA under-12 championships, placing second in the 2002 under-14s, and second in the 2003 under-16s, before winning that category in 2004. She had two brilliant years in 2004 and 2005.

On 14 August 2004, at Grisedale Pike in the trial race for the Junior World Uphill Trophy championships, Emma came third, behind Katie Ingram and Sarah Tunstall. This gained her selection for the England team in the World Trophy in Italy, where she finished 18th. Soon afterwards she reflected on this achievement. 'Running in Italy was brilliant. I'd never been abroad before and certainly didn't expect to make the team. I was really nervous before the race and it was certainly the hardest event I'd ever done in such boiling temperatures, but the whole experience was amazing.' That year Emma also won individual bronze and team gold in the Home Counties International on her home patch. The England team of Dionne Allen, Blue Haywood (who seemed to be running up an age group here) and Emma Stuart took the first three places for a fantastic under-16 team win.

In 2005 Emma moved in to the under-18 age category, and also experimented with running in some Senior races on the fells. In May she was second Senior at Latterbarrow (to young Laura Park), and in June won the Arnison Dash. Back in her age group she came 3rd in the Junior World Trophy Trial race on 31 July at Barrow Fell and Stile End. Now on a roll, in August she came third Senior at Latrigg, behind Vicky Wilkinson, who beat her mother Pauline Stuart's 21-year-old course record. She then came first lady in the 'Short' race at Rusland, actually coming 8th overall in a race in which Kenny Stuart came 2nd, quite probably the only time they raced against each other.

On my mentioning this last race, Pauline burst out laughing and I asked her to explain. 'What a carry on that was. I don't know why on earth Ken suddenly decided he wanted to run.

He had no shoes, and no shorts. I think he borrowed Emma's shorts, which you can imagine, and studded shoes that were too small.'

Kenny came back with, 'I had not been training. When I got there I thought I might as well have a run. I didn't go too badly. It was a short race though. I must admit that when I came back I was 47, about 11/12 years ago now, and I was only doing about 20 miles a week. I was reasonably fit, as fit would go. I found that so much harder than when I was running at a higher level. It was purgatory, terrible.'

I threw out at Kenny his memorable quote from an earlier exchange, which went something like: '...if I am gonna die they are too.' He laughed and came back with, 'Yeh, but in those days I always felt I had this extra gear, most good runners had. But when I came back and tried again that extra gear just wasn't there! It was quite frightening actually. I remember going to Cleator Moor Sports and I was about fourth when I crossed this river back towards the finish line and I was with Paul Brittleton, who was no mean runner himself. I got up behind him after the river and I thought "this is it, I just turn on that extra gear and away I go"! I got beside him and there was nothing there. He looked at me and I just said "get yourself away, I can't go past yer", and he did.'

Emma went on the long haul to the World Mountain Trophy in New Zealand, coming 22nd in the Junior Ladies race and 3rd English finisher, in an England team that came 4th. Being hard on herself she said at the time that she wasn't happy with her performance. Alistair Brownlee was in the equivalent Junior Men's team on that occasion, coming just 27th in his race. His performance may have been affected by the fact that the week before he was representing Great Britain at the World Triathlon championships in Japan and had flown straight to New Zealand to join the team.

After the World Trophy in New Zealand Emma, and sister Rosie, ran in the British and Irish Home International Fell Running championships in Dundalk, Ireland. They both won individual golds, in the under-18 and under-14 age categories respectively. The next year they both competed in the fixture again, this time at Slieve Gallion, on the edge of the Sperrin Mountains. Rosie was representing England, whilst Emma had to compete as an individual having missed out on selection after being injured for much of the season. Rosie had just secured the 2006 under-16 fell title and had a hard-fought race, staying with the top three for much of the race before slipping to 8th place, albeit helping the team to gold medals. Emma was running in the under-18 race and determined to salvage something from the season. She drew on her reserves and produced a stunning performance, pulling away from a strong field on the climb and maintaining her lead to finish 35 seconds clear and retain her title.

Rosie Stuart is three and a half years younger than Emma, and she also started by competing occasionally in BOFRA under-12 races in 2002, before she too moved to the FRA events. In 2003 she won the under-12 championship, and in 2004 came second in the under-14s, to Blue Haywood. In June 2004 Rosie ran in the Black Forest Games trial race at Ilkley Moor, coming second, with sister Emma 9th and just missing selection. The Black Forest Games are for 12- to 17-year-olds, and she came an excellent 3rd overall, a remarkable performance by one of the youngest and smallest competitors. It is worth noting that the uphill only course suited her, being a far better climber than descender. Her confidence and sparky personality showed when she commented that competition for the next year, 'will be even harder as some very fast girls are coming up from the under-12s and my sister is also starting to train properly!' Looking further ahead she commented that, 'in the long run I would like to run in the World Trophy and maybe even win like my Dad did.'

That year Rosie was again part of the English team at the Black Forest Teenage Games, and came away with four medals, two of them gold. She won the 12-13 year age group race and helped the English team to gold, whilst also gaining a bronze medal by finishing 3rd overall in an event open to 12-17 year olds. The next day she helped the English team to a silver medal in the 800m relay.

As we have seen, Rosie was in fine form in 2005/6. Other highlights for her around this time included coming 5th in the trial race in atrocious conditions at Ilkley Moor for the England team. The leading six girls from the trial got to run in June 2005 in the Marco Germanetto Memorial Race in Italy. Because she was in the younger age category the Italian Mountain Federation would not allow Rosie to run in the older age category with some of her team mates so she had to settle for running in the under-15s. However, she romped away from the field to win by an impressive 57 seconds, and take the 100 Euros prize. That year she was also second in the under-16 category in the FRA fell championships.

By 2006 she was experimenting with track running, and the next year expanded her horizons by entering one of the UK Challenge series of cross country races, at Liverpool. In 2008 she ran as a Junior on the fells, and raced over the country at both the English National and the English Schools, finishing in the 30s at both events. In 2008 Rosie went to the World Mountain Running Association Youth International in Susa and came back with a team gold medal, after finishing 7th in the tough three-lap race. In 2009 she won on the fells at Ambleside and Milnthorpe, and was selected for both the English Schools and the Inter-Counties at cross country.

As already noted, Emma did train harder and made the World Trophy, but sadly Rosie did not achieve that ambition, mainly due to the excellent standard of competition in that age group headed by Laura Park, winner of the English Schools and Inter-Counties.

Both girls took the expected route of joining Keswick AC, where their parents had run, but as the club didn't have many other juniors at the time they transferred to Cumberland Fell Runners in 2002. In 2005 Keswick had revived their youngster's setup and the girls moved back there. Because of their performances, and attitude, they both received awards from the John Taylor Foundation for young athletes.

There was a lovely family scene in May 2004 at the champi-' onship race at Helvellyn, which was held from Kenny Stuart's brother Duncan's farm. On the day Kenny was the race marshal at the summit turn (on High Rigg). He will have seen his two daughters both running superbly, with Rosie taking 1st in the under-14s and Emma 2nd in the under-16s.

Kenny and Pauline were encouraging, yet protective, of their own children, being well aware of the pressure they would be under. So, for instance, Pauline went along as a helper on the Black Forest Games trip with Rosie in 2004. Kenny noted (in 2005) that they trained three or four days a week for around 20/25 minutes, usually alone. Telling of this time, he grinned. 'If they trained together they'd be squabbling all the time because of their rivalry.' They were able to run the grassy fell slopes at the bottom of Blencathra from home, and Kenny sometimes took them running along the Glenderamackin river bank. At the time Kenny also noted that, 'they don't do much heavy hill training, but occasionally do a little gym work and twice a week train at Keswick AC under the supervision of Steve Fletcher.'

The girls have moved away from home now. One is in Ulverston and the other is in Leeds. Pauline noted, 'Emma is doing a bit of running now. Rosie has carried on running but not competing. They were both very good Juniors, on very little training. But teaching commitments were becoming a priority, so they stopped competing.' This prompted Kenny to comment on how life has changed since his day. 'I was really lucky because you went to work and did your time and everything else was free time. There was no having to do stuff, weekends were free.'

Both Emma and Rosie felt fortunate to have had the oppor- tunity to compete abroad, with Emma commenting, 'the trips away to Italy and New Zealand were an amazing experience with super memories to look back on. Fell running was a big part of my life for many years. It was an extremely sociable sport and I met many new people, also travelling abroad for the first time. I didn't always enjoy the training as a junior, but I was a competitor and loved to race (even now, I am still hugely competitive in everything I do!). I had always managed to race well on a fairly basic training schedule. An increase in mileage may have contributed to various injuries and due to an illness I wasn't able to run for a while. Unfortunately, other commitments then became a priority.'

Emma adds that she still keeps fit, and that she really misses, 'the competitive side of running and would love to get back on the fell racing scene in the next year or so. Following after my parents, fell running was always my strength and will continue to be my choice of running (whether just for fun or hopefully one day, competing again).'

Rosie also hopes to compete again in the future saying, 'my days as a junior runner were brilliant, it gave me the chance to meet new friends, travel all over the country and abroad, with my win in Germany a real highlight. I still enjoy running though do not feel fit enough to compete again at the moment, but who knows what the future may bring ...'

These are two very talented youngsters, who like many others, dropped out of competitive sport when they were either teenagers or juniors. But it is great to hear that they still have a place in their lives for the joy of running.

PART TWO

Track and pro

CHAPTER 4

Consistency is everything

After being in the RAF a short while John Wild's running took a more serious turn. 'I was out running one night in the dark and I met these guys and I said "could I join you?". They were doing efforts, something like a mile long. After the first one they said "we are doing four you know", as I was up there with them on the first one! This was where I met a guy called Brian Jeffs and he mentioned me within the RAF, which got me noticed.'

Life in the RAF suited John Wild, and up to a point he could play it to his advantage. Although service life was strict, there were sometimes concessions that could be worked for, or in some rare cases granted due to achievements. 'We all did our jobs. Steve Jones had to set the World Best for the marathon before he was allowed to come in at 10 o'clock in the morning [*so he could train beforehand*]. He wasn't in a high profile position, he was servicing Phantom jets. For me, I used to volunteer for Christmas duties to make up for the time I had off.'

Although the RAF environment obviously worked for John Wild, he recalls that a lot of the time the last thing he wanted to do at a weekend was to travel to Oxford or Cambridge to compete for the RAF, but it was expected of you. 'I won't say it was ever a burden, especially when I was made captain. I was the number two runner at the time when Roger Clark was posted overseas, and Alan Warner asked me to be captain, a post I held for 10 years. We had training weekends and all sorts, it was great.'

Wild's first RAF match was against Loughborough Colleges,

at cross country in 1970. They had similar matches against all the top colleges – such as Oxford University, Cambridge University and Borough Road. 'I was a young apprentice and Alan Warner was the Team Manager. It was at Loughborough, so I got a railway travel warrant and ran in the race.' This was the start of a hugely successful RAF representative career.

In 1971 he finished 11th in his first RAF championships, aged just 18. This meant that he was taken to the Inter-Services race as non-running reserve to experience the atmosphere, and they also took him to Germany for a week on an RAF cross country tour. He was learning to relax. 'Out there they gave me two bottles of Dortmund beer and I was legless. They were good days.' That year he finished 5th in the RAF steeplechase championships in 10-12.4.

The track championships were normally held at RAF Uxbridge, which was the home of RAF athletics at the time. The cross country championships were held at RAF Halton, the home of RAF cross country.

When the Allestree athletic club disbanded, John was approached by Derby & County Athletic Club, as most of the Allestree athletes had just transferred over to them. 'I was unsure about whether to join as I was affiliated to the AAA's through the RAF anyway. But, they said I could join for free, i.e. pay no membership fee, and they would only ask me to run in the National cross country and the 6- and 12-stage relays. This naturally suited my RAF commitments as I was RAF team captain by then.'

John recalls with amusement and amazement that he once got a 'No shaving chit' from the doctor, in order to try and look old enough to get served in the pub. 'I got some stinging nettles and a scrubbing brush to create a rash, and went to the doctor and got a three week no-shaving chit, which lasted seven years. I got a new RAF posting once and got promoted to sergeant whilst sporting a beard. I had a couple of hairy moments when I got challenged and had to go back to the doctor, and had to get the rash going again first.'

The years 1972, 1973 and 1974 were a consolidation period for Wild. He finished 3rd in the first two years in the RAF cross country championships and 2nd in 1974, and progressed from 18th to 2nd (twice) in the Inter-Services cross country championships. Meanwhile on the track he recorded an impressive 9-06.0 for the steeplechase, coming 3rd in a representative fixture in 1972 for the Inter-Services team against Scotland in Edinburgh, despite a fall. John recalls that, 'The RAF no 1 at the time was a bit hacked off he couldn't drop me and told me to slow down when I took the lead. I just overcooked it a bit and fell at the water with about two laps to go. I looked later and found that I'd left skin and hair on the barrier!'

John then came 2nd in both the RAF and Inter-Services steeplechase. He had something of a breakthrough in 1973, winning the steeplechase at both the RAF and Inter-Services championships.

Alan Warner thinks that 1973 was the first year that Wild's running was getting much notice outside the RAF. Warner recalls that, 'subsequently my counting athletes for the Inter-Services championships were all international athletes. I was close friends with Roger Clark, and we were both in the RAF and wanted to build a team. I used to go to races with him, he ran for England in the World Cross Country for instance in 1973. I always took an interest in people I saw at races. I saw John Wild run in the National Junior cross country race at Parliament Hill that year, and he finished 6th. I knew he was in the RAF and straight away he impressed me. He ran well on certain types of courses. I started coaching him and it went on from there. Other people that I met, for example Julian Goater and Ray Crabb (who won the Youths race at that National, where John Wild came 6th), ended up in the RAF. We weren't 'recruiting', just talking to people, some of whom joined the RAF, and some didn't.'

John says that, 'Alan actually knew me before that Junior National he mentions. But he did work very hard at getting the teams together. We had such a good team spirit.'

Warner also commented on John's progress at this time.

'Roger Clark was running in the Senior National cross country that year, which was won by Rod Dixon from New Zealand [*running as a guest*], and Roger finished 3rd behind Dave Bedford. So you can see how good Roger Clark was. That year he was 6th in the International Cross Country championships. Later that winter I organised for the RAF team to compete at RAF Bruggen in Germany. John won the race and beat all our fancied runners. So he was talented! What I then noticed was that he was very good on hilly and tough courses. That also stuck in my mind. What impressed me about John was this terrific advance he was making, on a hilly course in Germany. It never surprised me that years later he went on to run so well on the fells.'

John's posting to RAF Wyton in November 1972 brought him eventually into contact with Grenville Tuck, who lived near St Ives (Cambridgeshire), and John did lots of quality work with him. It also put him in the Southern Counties 'set up', which was advantageous for race invites later. He elected to leave Derby and County AC and join Cambridge & Coleridge AC.

John was coached initially by Don Woodruff at Allestree Woodlands and then by Alan Warner for several years in the RAF. He was later advised by Don Woodruff again from about 1980 till he left for Germany in 1986. He really appreciated the coaching he received in his career. 'Don Woodruff sadly died in 1988, and he helped me immensely throughout my career. I owe Alan Warner for so much over the years. Not only was he a first class coach (he coached Roger Clark, Ray Crabb and the Rimmers as well as me), but he was an exemplary Team Manager.'

Wild and Warner had a coach/athlete relationship at a distance. It was done by written schedule, telephone calls and visits. 'He would sometimes come and stay with me,' Alan remembers. 'We would do a weekend of training and maintain contact by telephone afterwards.'

I asked Alan to expand on his training philosophy. 'It depends at what stage you start working with someone. My coaching philosophy was "if you get someone who knows nothing about it, then you try to teach them the principles you believe in." What you also do gradually is step aside. Hopefully they will eventually become self-sufficient. Then you might have a mentor role maybe.'

John Wild was very young, and he was just out of youth training. 'He hadn't done much before the RAF,' Alan points out. 'When he finished at RAF Cosford he started improving. Given the opportunity to get in bigger races he just improved more. He was then my team captain for 10 years. It was the thing he wanted to do, and he was good at it. He was always very enthusiastic. He took that enthusiasm to the fells too.'

Warner also emphasised what characteristics he looked for in a good captain. 'First and foremost is being loyal to our team and I place great stress on loyalty. I had other team members over the years who were internationals who sometimes didn't support the team. But John was brilliant. He was very likeable, and very determined and loyal, as I say. He put RAF running (both cross country and track and field) first. In fairness some others had strong loyalties to their athletic club teams.'

John also brought real strengths as an athlete to the captaincy, as far as Alan was concerned. 'He was a rugged runner, who ran particularly well on tough courses. I could name other runners who had weak spots. Not John, he always peaked when he needed to and always produced the results.'

Alan Warner was quite close to the athletics Promotions Officer Andy Norman, who organised the Coca-Cola meetings at Crystal Palace, so John would get invited when his times became good enough. John used to run at the Southern Counties meetings and Andy used to give him petrol money each week to drive to train with fellow international Tony Simmons in leading coach Harry Wilson's group at Welwyn. He had been posted to RAF Wyton, but he lived in Sawtry, near Peterborough. 'I was prepared to drive 50-60 miles to get in the quality sessions. I don't know who convinced who, but we got invited to the International Athletes Club international cross country race. There was Europe, England, Scotland, Wales, Ireland and the RAF. We won – and I believe the event was discontinued after that.'

John's memories of the specific races from this era are a little hazy. 'We ran at Crystal Palace a few times and I was 3rd one time (Mike McLeod won - Jim Brown just behind me). That was the year the elastic on my inner shorts snapped and I had to run the last three laps with my nuts hanging out and swinging about (painfully). I think that was 1979, as I think it was the first winter I'd moved to Cosford. It was on Grandstand TV too. Also, one year the RAF team didn't run in the main international race but in an area race run on exactly the same course.'

With a glint in his eye, John recalled much more clearly the later sessions working in Harry Wilson's group. 'The Tuesday evening sessions at Welwyn Garden City were fantastic and worth driving the 50+ miles to get there. There was a large number of athletes and we would do a particular effort session such as 8 x 3 minutes with 1-minute recovery. It was good to train with an athlete of the calibre of Tony Simmons, and on occasion we were joined by internationals such as Ian Stewart, who would turn up in his primrose TR6. Harry Wilson talked sense, but he often gave me a bollocking after a superb effort session with him was followed a few days later with a poor track performance. We always finished in the bar afterwards though!'

Steve Ovett wasn't training with Harry Wilson then, but Wild did run against him once in the Inter-Counties. Wild also went on a training camp with Harry Wilson in Portugal once. He also did the infamous Merthyr Mawr sand dune training once when he was posted to St Athan and he won the week-long Tour of Tameside on the strength of that training.

By now a pattern of frequent racing at both cross country and the steeplechase had become the norm for him. But the 1974 track season was blighted by injury, which ruled him out of both the RAF and Services steeplechase championships. John recalls that he won the Derbyshire county cross country championships at Markeaton Park in January 1974, 'then I won the Inter-Counties later in January, from David Slater and Frank Briscoe. It was one of those days when everything clicked. I was 10 yards in the lead and suddenly got scared. I eased up and then I just blew it away.' The *Derby Evening Telegraph* quoted Wild after the race saying that he, 'took the lead at the end of the second lap, then thought that I had done it too early. I made my burst halfway up the hill on the last lap. At the top of the hill I was four yards clear. I knew Briscoe had a good sprint finish and I have seen Slater win with a quick finish.' The newspaper report also noted that the twenty-year-old was putting in over 80 miles a week in training, and hadn't missed a single day's training in 14 months.

In March Wild had a relatively poor run in the National cross country championships at Graves Park (Sheffield), finishing 22nd, but helping his Derby AC team to win the title, twelve years after their hat-trick of National wins in 1960-62. Wild notes that he had been running well all winter. 'I had won an area match. I had beaten Roger Clark in a match in Germany in December, finishing sixth in this big international race. A few days later we had the area match and I won that. I got an England vest out of that, which I got before the Inter-Counties. I was just 20 years old. I got my first England trip the week after that. But the Inter-Counties win was a bit unexpected.'

'So, I had my first race for England, and just got beat by Roger Clark in the RAF championships and the Inter-Services races. In that Inter-Services, the last race of the country season, I put my foot in a hole and stripped my tendon. I struggled all summer trying to get rid of it.' This was the injury that required an operation at Farnham.

In December 1974 he was back, and travelled to France for the Cross Bolbec race. He came 6th in the 9.9 km race, which was won by England's David Black. 'I had already had one race in Chartres [*in the January*]. I went in to the cathedral in Chartres on the morning of the race, an awesome building, to think about my dad, who was on my mind for some reason at the time. In Bolbec I was very relaxed about the race, but the speed at the start was amazing. I couldn't handle it. I was going backwards and then I came through again to finish in 6th.'

Wild explained how these invitations to race abroad, and at Crystal Palace, came about. 'All the overseas races were representative, either for the RAF or for England/GB. The England races were considered good publicity for the RAF and essentially only requiring a Friday and Monday off work to travel. Everything was sorted out initially with your own boss. I never had any problems but then, I also used to volunteer for additional duties such as at Christmas or other bank holidays to make up for this time. RAF athletes also benefited by getting entries in the IAC (International Athletes Club) track meet too. Alan Warner also became a small team manager for the ECCU (English Cross Country Union) and I travelled with him on quite a few England trips, usually to Spain.'

Wild came back well in 1975, taking 3rd place in the RAF cross country championships, but had to retire hurt in the Inter-Services race, which was at Portsmouth. 'I fell and smashed my knee open on a flint.' He flinches even now at the mention of it. He had started young, winning his first RAF championships as an apprentice. Looking at the records, he won the Inter-Services cross country more times than the RAF championships, by 2-1. He admits that he used to peak too early some times. Come March he might not be able to sustain his peak. There were a lot of fixtures for the RAF, and John felt obliged to turn up. 'I set all of my track PBs in RAF fixtures. That tells you a story, as I tended to be relaxed and perform better. But, I was having a tough time in the AAAs steeplechase once and dropped out, and Steve Jones saw me and dropped out too. He always blames me for that!'

You might conclude that Wild might have been someone who had a tendency to over-train at times. I suggested just that to him, or that he just did not stop at warning signs sometimes. His robust response was, 'not really, and there were sometimes I didn't think I trained hard enough. I was briefly at St Athan with Steve Jones, I'd do say 4 x 5 min efforts but he'd be doing 6, or I'd do 6 x 1000m hills but he would do 10. But it's always a question of balance. When I got to the fells my intensity and quantity of training dropped significantly.' Less is sometimes more.

So, was over-racing perhaps an issue (although I can think of even more frequent racers, like Jack Maitland at his peak)? 'Certainly during the cross country season there were many races, especially for the RAF. However, there was never any pressure to race at maximum pace. Neither was there any reluctance at having to go to Oxford or Cambridge at weekends or various other venues midweek for example. We considered it as part of the job. I may have been a bit jaded by the end of the season though as I often didn't perform to expected levels in the National cross country.'

'I trained in the 70s with Ray Crabb, who won the National Youths cross country in 1973, I think it was [*It was, at Parliament Hill*]. I trained with Grenville Tuck who was nearby, so always had a high standard of training partners. I was working to a programme really. I have always said that consistency is everything. If you have your routes and circuits it may be boring but you know where you are. I do have an old diary from the 70s but I am not one for keeping records.'

On 26 April 1975 he ran in the National 12-stage road relay, turning in a 14-20 8th fastest short leg at Sutton Coldfield. Wild bounced back in the summer season of 1975, winning the RAF steeplechase in 9-11.6, and running a spectacular 8-36.85 in the steeplechase on 29 August in the International Athletes Club meeting at Crystal Palace, coming 7th in a class field while still an under-23 athlete. His race results were now starting to get Wild noticed in the wider running world.

In 1976 he was very successful in both cross country and on the track. He didn't compete in the RAF championships in the February because of a second visit to Farnham for a bone spur problem. 'They had you on foot lathes to make candlesticks as part of the rehab. And I also met Anne.'

On 3 March he won the Inter-Services Cross Country championships at Pirbright, from Ray Crabb and Mick Hurd, with a young Steve Jones in 6th. In the summer, now a Corporal, Wild won the RAF steeplechase title for the third time, and then the Inter-Services title in a record time of 8-50.2. He also recorded 5-35.18 for 2000m steeplechase on 26 May as a guest in the AAA v Borough Road College fixture at Crystal Palace. Finally, he came second in the Cross International Ciudad de Granollers in Spain in December of that year, to Haro of Spain. 'This was a small England team, three runners and a manager. We had many races around Europe like this, often with Alan Warner as team manager.'

Wild felt he had an outside chance of qualifying for the Olympics that year. He'd been running and training well prior to the 1976 trials and had run a good PB in a 2km steeplechase in the Crystal Palace evening meeting (noted above). 'I got up for a morning run the next day and was peeing blood. This eased during the day but started again after exercise. I ended up in RAF Ely hospital for a week shortly before the Olympic trials, ending up with an operation to repair a damaged blood vessel between bladder and kidney.'

The Olympic trial race was at Crystal Palace. 'I ran the trials and felt OK, until I cocked up and fell at the water jump. I didn't finish that race. I was completely winded. My mum laughed about it, she was watching *Grandstand* and I was in third. The coverage went off to show the Shot Putt. When they came back they said "and while we were away there has been an accident in the 'chase and John Wild has fallen at the water jump". So at least it wasn't shown on National TV!' His frank conclusion was that he just wasn't good enough.

Around this time an American university tried to poach him, but he wasn't really interested. Top class youngsters, such as Tony Staynings and Nick Rose did take up offers. 'I toyed with it, as the RAF PE instructor was trying to persuade me. I nearly took unpaid leave to take three years out to do it. I got a letter saying 'call collect' and I didn't know what it meant! I had heard bad things about having to race too much. It didn't really pan out, and I was going to be getting married soon.'

In 1977, he came 2nd in the RAF cross country, with Ray Crabb 1st, Julian Goater 3rd and Steve Jones 4th. He was also third in the Inter-Services (this time behind Crabb and Goater), but his track form moved up another notch. He won the RAF 5000m championships in 14-28.2 and also the 3000m steeplechase in 8-35.8 at Crystal Palace on 3 August, in the match between the Inter-Services team, the Southern Counties, Middlesex, and the ECCU. This was as a first year Senior, and turned out to be his best ever steeplechase time, which still ranks him 58th on the UK all-time list (at the time of writing).

Despite that excellent performance, John told me a story that perhaps encapsulates his track career, which seemed to vary considerably in the results he achieved. 'Harry Wilson used to get furious. I didn't have a track mentality. I think the pressure got to me, I don't know. I know I should have been better. I am pleased with a good time I did in the 2k chase. When I set that best time for the steeplechase there were timings being given but I hadn't realised. With about 500 metres to go, John Bicourt said from the sidelines "go on John you can get under 8-30", and I went to pieces! I suddenly felt dreadful.'

As part explanation for some of his performances he said, 'I remember having to get points. It was all about beating the Army for our team managers. I ended up once having to do a 5k and steeplechase double as it was better points that way. But I didn't particularly like the 5000m and certainly didn't like the 10,000m.'

Alan Warner acknowledges Wild's many occasions of running for the team, and agrees the steeplechase was a good event for him. 'John was a tough runner, he was right for steeplechase.' He also feels that his achievements in the steeplechase were lesser than those at cross country. 'What suited John was hills and mud. He was tough as old boots.' However, he struggled to explain this perceived underachievement on the track. 'I was not there [at the Commonwealths] so I can't really comment.

Mentally I can't quite put my finger on it. Only John can say really. I suppose on reflection maybe his flat speed let him down. All the very best steeplechasers had usually run very well at 1500m. They would be good at 3000m too, and I don't think John got under 8 minutes for 3000m.'

Back in January Wild had run well in the Inter-Counties cross country championships, at Leicester, coming 4th in 39-12, behind David Black (38-50), Steve Ovett (39-00) and David Slater (39-03). Inexplicably Dave Bedford was 71st in the race. I have no idea why, as he didn't normally turn up for a race if he wasn't fit. At the time, Ovett was a mere youngster at 22 years old to Wild's 'mature' 24 years, although Ovett had already had a very successful Junior career.

In the next few weeks Wild raced abroad three times, to get more big race experience. He came 3rd in the Cross de San Sebastian. 'I won a motorbike. A 175cc motocross bike. The first two got gold watches. I went up and got this piece of paper which was the logbook. We had a few beers and myself and Nick Lees (a fellow Derbyshire runner, who was a Junior at the time) eventually found out we needed two-stroke fuel, put some in and rode it around San Sebastian. Then I sold it to the hotel porter.'

He also came third in the Fermoy cross country, one ahead of Jos Hermens, who had recently set the world best for a one-hour run. Hermens later became a highly respected athlete manager, with clients that included Haile Gebrselassie and Kenenisa Bekele. Wild also came 5th in the Portuguese championships at Vilamoura, where he was really mixing it – future Olympic marathon Gold medallist Carlos Lopes won, from Tony Simmons and Fernando Mamede.

On 5 March 1977 the National Cross Country championships hosted a really top field over the traditional Parliament Hill course. Wild came 8th, and led his Cambridge and Coleridge AC club mates to second team, behind Gateshead. Individually the first eight were: Foster, Ford, Simmons, Black, McLeod, Smith, Bedford and then Wild, with Goater, Ovett and Crabb taking 12th to 14th places.

But there was a sour note behind his personal success. At that National cross country championships race Cambridge and Gateshead had been considered equal favourites for the team title. 'It was then that a senior member of the Derby club approached me before the start to say that unless I paid them several years back membership fees then they would declare to the authorities that my membership of Cambridge was invalid, rendering any performance I had that day illegal and affect the club's chances. I felt I had no option but to pay this outrageous blackmail in support of the rest of the team. Clearly, Derby didn't like me leaving! Gateshead beat us to the title anyway in the end.'

John Wild didn't let the issue unsettle him, as his running was going really well and he was now in the frame for international recognition.

CHAPTER 5

One serious regret

Throughout 1977 John Wild began to have consistently good results, which resulted in him being recognised and selected for some major events. He was chosen for the 1977 World Cross Country championships, to be held in Germany. 'In all I was selected for the World Cross championships twice and once as a reserve. They usually picked the top nine from the National cross country championships. So, I was picked for Dusseldorf that year, and then again for Glasgow (1978), and later on for New York (as reserve in 1984).'

Wild admitted that he had got one serious regret. 'That was not winning a gold medal with the World Cross England team. It was my fault in Dusseldorf as I had a bad run. It was a great team for that Germany event. There was a big kerfuffle in Dusseldorf after the race, between Dave Bedford, Mike McLeod, Barry Smith and a barman. I was with Dave Black and we were a bit worse for wear. I was trying to speak German and the bar staff were taking the mickey, and the lads defended me and that is how it kicked off. I realised we should probably go. As we went out one door the police came in another. But McLeod, Bedford and Smith weren't quick enough, and were questioned by the police. I had to go back and tell the team manager, Barry Wallman, about the incident. He was a nice man, and was shocked. We had an RAF cross country reunion recently and Dave Bedford was our guest speaker. I reminded Dave Bedford about it and he said "you started it".'

Alan Warner put this in perspective. 'I wasn't there, but I heard it was a bit of a riotous time! However, you can never let the RAF down. So the RAF guys always had to keep that in the back of their minds, otherwise it could lead to big trouble. After the Inter-Services championships, which the RAF won for 19 years, we always used to have a dinner in the Red Lion in Wendover, and John used to love that. We had some great times, but it was all controlled.'

Wild is right to be disappointed. In the team race that year Belgium beat England by just three points (126 to 129), despite England having three of their scorers in the top 10. The England positions were: 5 Bernie Ford, 8 Tony Simmons, 9 David Black, 29 Steve Kenyon, 35 Barry Smith, 43 Mike McLeod, 45 Dave Bedford, 76 David Slater, and 95 John Wild. It only needed either Wild, Slater or Bedford to have finished in the top 40 for the team to have swept to gold. On any other day that surely would have been a given.

Wild was selected for the steeplechase in an international athletics match in Turin in July 1977 between Italy, England and the USA. It was an evening meeting and unusually the steeplechase was the very last event, even after the relays. Wild chose to go to the stadium later by taxi rather than on the early bus and ended up sharing the taxi with Harold Abrahams and a field event competitor. Wild knew who Abrahams was, as he'd been appointed President of the AAA the year before and his schoolboy interest in past Olympics meant he was aware of his 1924 triumph (as depicted in the film *Chariots of Fire*). 'He was very smartly dressed in blazer and white flannels and was wearing a floppy sun hat with the flag of St George on it. He asked us both about our events and wished us luck and I was quite overawed. In the changing rooms, the field eventer said "who the heck was that old fart"!'

Wild remembers that he had a decent run, but still got a bollocking from Harry Wilson. 'Harry often said I should be steeplechasing 10 seconds faster considering my performance at his sessions - and he was probably right.'

At one point in our conversations I started quoting his own track times at Wild. 'You have a better handle on my times than I have! The best 10k was at the IAC/Coke meeting, in September 1977 I think. I got paid to pace the first 3000m because there was Foster, Ford, Simmons, Black and a load of foreign athletes. Foster was going for the British record,' Wild recalled.

The IAC/Coke meeting was one of the big meets at the time, but there was no steeplechase that year and the only way John could get an invite from Andy Norman for himself, and Anne, was to agree to pace the first part of the 10k race. 'I was running OK with Tony Simmons on my shoulder and looked behind me and a gap was starting to grow and Tony yelled "don't give a f*ck about that lot - just keep this pace". My dear old mum was watching and got quite excited at first with me leading! Heady days – I used to love the Coke meets.' Brendan Foster was first in 27-36.62, which was a UK record.

'Andy Norman had approached me about it two weeks earlier at a track meeting at St Ives. If you got on with him he was all right. But if you crossed him he was quite the opposite. Alan Warner had a good relationship with him and we got a lot of deals through that. I first met Norman when we had an annual cross country race against the Police and Fire Service. Norman managed the police team.'

Towards the end of 1977 Wild had experimented with fell running, as we shall see later. In November and December he also ran at Gateshead in the Schweppes International Cross Country (coming 7th) and the IAC/Philips Cross Country at Crystal Palace (11th in a strong international field, including Miruts Yifter who was third). The report in *Athletics Weekly* noted that, 'best finisher of all was John Wild, who broke into an all-out sprint in the last 150m in turning back Siadek [*Ethiopia*] and [*Steve*] Kenyon,' and finish two seconds behind Steve Jones.

Great results in the 1978 cross country season led to John Wild being selected for the World Cross Country team again, for a race held in Glasgow in March. Wild took in two continental cross country races in January, the first being in Portugal (Amendoeiras em Flor, 17th). 'I went on a training week in Portugal with Brendan Foster and Pete Standing. They asked people if they wanted to stay for the international race, which I did. But, I said I am not staying a few days unless you sub me. It cost them about £500. I remember phoning Anne to tell her I was staying a few more days, which didn't go down that well!'

He also went back to the race in San Sebastian (Spain), which this time he won, having come third the year before. 'I still have the gold watch from that one somewhere. I was so pleased to win that race.'

As a break he took in the Hillingdon 5-mile road race on 18 February, finishing second to Keith Penny, although being given the same time of 23-31, which was then the fastest time for the race. Reflecting on the occasion, John commented to me, with a sense of not so much bitterness, more of injustice, 'Keith Penny didn't go into the finish funnel. I was beating him. Three out of four officials got me winning. The fourth was the referee and overruled them. So he won the portable television. Magnificent prizes in those days!'

Wild also won the RAF championships at RAF Halton in that February. The online RAF archive has a report of the event by Alan Warner:

Following the disappointments over previous years, Cpl John Wild (Wyton) finally added his name to the illustrious winners, thereby realising the ambition which has eluded him, despite his recent achievements as one of the countries' leading performers.

Of the principal contestants only Fg Off Julian Goater (knee injury) was missing and as anticipated it was title holder SAC Ray Crabb (Rheindahlen) who set about dominating the 282 strong field from the outset. By 2km, he had drawn rivals Wild and SAC Steve Jones (Lyneham) 20 metres ahead of rapidly improving Jnr Tech Gordon Rimmer (Lossiemouth) and marathon men Cpl Mick Hurd (Wattisham) and Flt Lt George Edgington (Brampton).

Characteristically, Crabb used his front running ability, and liking for the Halton course, to dictate a furious pace throughout the first circuit. Approaching 5km, along the canal bank, the champion relentlessly 'turned the screw' and somewhat surprisingly Steve Jones (still recovering from a family bereavement) the pre-race favourite of many, started to lose touch, although Wild looked calmly confident. As so often in the past the race was suddenly decided on the climb to the top of the course. Wild, reversing the roles from last year, effortlessly changed gear, and Crabb unable to respond, was quickly 30 metres down, a lead which was comfortably trebled by the finish. Steve Jones had the consolation of improving to a best-ever third place and leading the jubilant RAF Lyneham team to a hat-trick of titles.

Handwritten notes on the scanned report record the positions achieved that year in the National Cross Country championships. Wild and Crabb came 10th and 30th respectively in the English National, while Jones won the Welsh National cross country championships. Wild then moved on to the Inter-Services championships on 10 March at HMS Dryad, where he triumphed (his second win) by 15 seconds over Steve Jones, with Reece Ward (of the Navy) third and Ray Crabb fourth.

The National was held in Leeds on 4 March, and John came 10th in another strong field, in a race won by Bernie Ford, from Ian Stewart. Some of those ahead of him were not eligible/available, so Wild was selected for the team for the sixth World Cross Country championships three weeks later, on 25 March. The race was held in Bellahouston Park (Glasgow), and was won by John Treacy from Aleksandr Antipov (Soviet Union) and Karel Lismont (Belgium), with Wild finishing an excellent

15th. A report entitled 'Treacy leaves 'em for dead', in the Glasgow *Herald*, gives a feel for the event.

Through a curtain of rain the binoculars confirmed what the Americans had been saying all week – Ireland's John Treacy was the man to beat.

Spare of frame but strong on speed and stamina, the 21-year-old student from County Waterford (an apt address in the appalling conditions) conquered a field of about 180 runners from 20 countries.

Why should the Americans have so much insight into the lantern-jawed flyer? Simply that for the last four years Treacy has been studying accountancy in the United States and only a couple of weeks ago won their indoor national collegiate three-mile title in the world-class time of 13 minute 10.8 seconds.

Looking through the full results shows some interesting positions in the race from some famous names. In fourth was Tony Simmons, 6th was Craig Virgin (USA), 7th Nat Muir, 11th Steve Jones, 30th Mike Mcleod, 40th Ken Newton, 44th Bill Rogers (USA), 48th Graham Tuck, 62nd Bernie Ford, 67th Frank Clement, 90th John Graham, and 94th Gerhard Hartmann (Austria). In amongst the DNFs were Carlos Lopes (who had won the race two years previously), Fernando Mamede and Jos Hermens (as they 'didn't like the tough conditions' according to Wild). Again he just missed a winning team medal, with the team results exceptionally tight. France won with 151 points, with USA on 156 and England on 159.

In the summer season Wild didn't compete in either of the RAF or Inter-Services track championships. However, he was still concentrating on his steeplechasing, going for qualification for the Commonwealth Games in the trial race at Crystal Palace. The Games were to be held in Edmonton, Alberta, from the 3rd to 12th of August 1978, two years after the 1976 Summer Olympics were held in Montreal, Quebec. The Commonwealths were boycotted by Nigeria, in protest at New Zealand's sporting contacts with apartheid-era South Africa.

Wild was very focused from the start of 1978, and having had a very good winter he organised some warm weather training in Portugal in January with Tony Simmons (and their respective wives). Times were different then so they sought their own sponsorship to defray some of the costs. Wild approached Beach Villas (in Cambridge) and they gave them a free villa and car for two weeks, meaning all they had to pay was their air fares.

'Bernie Ford came out for the second week and we did some excellent training. Under Alan Warner my training was going well and I went into the trial with a fair degree of confidence. I was never an exceptional track athlete and often my perfor-mances didn't quite meet expected levels. As I have said, I think it's telling that most of my PBs are from RAF matches, which I felt less pressure at.'

'I remember the trials quite well as Anne and I stayed at the Union Jack armed forces club, in Victoria, for the weekend. I qualified through the heats on Friday night OK and was quite relaxed for the final. I believe I was fourth behind Dennis Coates, Tony Staynings and Micky Morris, who was Welsh. So, I was third Englishman and just had to wait. I found out on the following Monday afternoon from brother-in-law Graham Tuck that I was in the team as it had been published in the *Evening Standard*. I felt sorry for Micky Morris, as he beat me in the trials. England took me to Edmonton as third string, whilst Wales didn't take Micky.'

John Wild thoroughly enjoyed the whole Commonwealth Games experience, from flying out on a chartered Boeing 707, to flying back early with the swimmers nearly three weeks later. 'We were out there two weeks before the athletics. I got special paid leave as it was good PR for the RAF.'

He had a bizarre experience on the flight out to the Games. 'Midway through the flight, a stewardess came up to me and said that the captain wanted to speak to me in the cockpit. I thought it might be ex-aircrew from the RAF who knew me but when I got to the cockpit, he handed me some headphones and told me that someone wanted to speak to me. It turned out to be one of my RAF Cross Country associates, Arthur Moore, who was flying in his Vulcan bomber over the North Atlantic.'

Wild shared a room with Dave Black, and continued to do quality sessions with Tony Simmons, who was in the Welsh Team. 'Dave and I also took advantage of the trips on offer and went on a tour of the Rockies for four days (whilst still training!). I was rather hacked off that the 'chase heats were on the opening day of the athletics and the final was the next day.'

Wild recalls that in the heats for Commonwealths he qualified in the first three in his heat. There were twelve in the final, with only two having been dropped by the heats.

As we talked about this era, John brought out a brilliant photo of the Commonwealth Games steeplechase heat at Edmonton, with himself and Tony Staynings in mid-air at the water jump. 'The layout was a little weird too. Because of the position of the water jump, the start was midway down the finishing straight with the first barrier at 50m.'

'In the final I didn't perform badly, but should have run better. Times were slow mainly due to the strong wind, but as Tony Staynings recently pointed out, we were at a level of altitude that affected all distance races, but I only noticed the strong wind really. It was my only shot at a major games and that was that. I was England's third string and finished third Englishman, so didn't surprise anybody, but I shouldn't have been beaten by Ian Gilmour. I've only recently seen YouTube footage of the race and it is still great to hear David Coleman saying my name.'

English distance running was in good shape at this time. David Moorcroft and Brendan Foster won the 1500m and 10,000m respectively, and Mike McLeod and Brendan Foster won bronze in the 10,000m and 5000m races. Kenyan distance runners were beginning to show their strength though, taking gold and bronze in the 800m, gold and silver in the 5000m, silver in the 10,000m and a clean sweep in John Wild's event, the steeplechase. But England topped the overall medal table with 16 golds across the men's and women's track and field events.

The Kenyans may not have started dominating the world cross country championships yet, but certainly had at the steeplechase. The final was won by Henry Rono (in 8-26.54), from James Munyala and George Kiprotich Rono. England had three runners in the final (imagine that now – the GB team for the 2016 Rio Olympics contained just one male steeplechaser). Sixth was England's Dennis Coates, 7th was Tony Staynings and 9th John Wild (in 8-57.94).

In October Wild had an outing on the roads, finishing second in the Henlow 10 mile race to Ray Crabb in 49-21 (a 10 mile time beaten by just three British runners in 2015). He also had two fairly unsatisfactory results (by his own high standards) in late year cross country races in Grenoble and at Crystal Palace.

The year turned, and 1979 was a relatively quiet one for Wild. He started the year with three races over the country in Europe, before turning to the Services races. He came third in the RAF cross country and second in the Inter-Services championships (to Steve Jones). That summer he didn't compete in the RAF or Inter-Services matches at steeplechase, although he did win the RAF 10,000m track championships in July at Cosford in 31-26.2.

Wild was posted to RAF Cosford in June 1979 and then decided to join Tipton Harriers. 'I think I joined them in 1980, and was in their team when we won the National cross country championships at Parliament Hill in 1981. I continued to run cross country for them during my fell running days.'

That year was another Olympic year (Moscow, 1980) and Wild was shooting for selection at the steeplechase. 'I trained hard for the Olympics. I trained with Roger Hackney, Ray Crabb and Grenville Tuck, and in Harry Wilson's sessions at Welwyn at this time.'

When John Wild decided he wanted to try a different training approach, it was not a problem for Alan Warner, who had been working with him for several years, as he explains. 'Harry Wilson was National Event Coach at one stage, and he ran a group down at Welwyn which John used to go down to. I coached John for a long time, and I remember distinctly being on a steeplechase course at Crystal Palace and John said he felt he wanted to continue on his own. I accepted that, not worrying about whether he didn't believe in some of my training philosophies anymore.'

John Wild explained the nature of his coach/athlete relationship with Alan Warner. 'It started in the early 1970s. Then we had a bit of a split in 1976 because we were both disappointed that my 1976 season didn't go well. Then I had some problems before the trials and I fell in the trial itself. I got married in 1977. We had bought our first house in 1976 and I think Alan and I just parted company. I got back with him because I wanted to get to the Commonwealth Games and I asked him if he would set my programmes. After the Commonwealths we were together for a brief time and then I looked after myself, along with Don Woodruff a bit. So it was from 1971 for nine years really.'

Alan Warner also notes that he, 'had no input to his [*Wild's*] fell running whatsoever. Although his training would probably have led to that eventually and indeed helped with his success.'

Having been posted to RAF Cosford, Wild was determined to take advantage of the indoor facilities. Under the direction of Don Woodruff, he embarked on some intensive track work such as 2 x 800m flat out with 10 minutes recovery and 20 x 400m. 'In the end I was doing those 800s in about 1m 58s. And the 400s in 61/62. I had a great cross country season too, especially abroad where I won some big races in Spain. However, it was not to be and I had a rubbish track season, not even good enough to get to the Olympic trials. I probably peaked too soon, but that's life.'

John Wild tried for two Olympics. By his own standards he

had a poor track season in the 1980 Olympic build-up, and he now can't remember much of that time. 'It just didn't work out, I probably was over-training. When you are doing 20 x 400m reps in December it is great for cross country. But my season had no end, like any distance runner. A short break after the National and then I started track.' He gave up serious track running after not making the Olympic trials, just doing RAF ones when asked.

'After that, I decided I needed something in the summer to keep fit for cross country and looked to the fells. I'd done a few fell races before and enjoyed the experience and friendliness and resolved to do more. I got hold of a copy of the Fellrunners booklet and wrote the now infamous letter to Andy Styan [*which we will come back to later*]. The rest is history!!'

Alan Warner completely understands this need for change. 'When a sportsperson has achieved what they want, sometimes they need a new challenge. I think John had done it all. He came from small beginnings, he ran the Commonwealth Games steeplechase, and did the World Cross Country championships. If you see another outlet which is allied to what you have done already you go for it. It is a bit like an athlete moving from 5000m to the marathon.' Here Warner gave the example of Steve Jones, who was very good on the track and then set a World Best at the marathon, and was coached by Warner for a time.

In cross country Wild had won an international race in Elgoibar in January, and then won the Inter-Counties for the second time over an icy course at Derby. One time when we were discussing this period John Wild proudly produced a newspaper cutting for the Inter-Counties, which was headlined '*World class Wild*'. In part, it reported:

One of Britain's hardest exponents won in 37 mins 23 secs, judging his running so neatly that he came home with six seconds to spare over his [*Derby*] colleague Nick Lees.

How good was this performance? 'World class', said Brendan Foster, who was lurking just behind this pair for much of the way looking as though he would pounce and win but finally fading back to fourth position behind Dave Clarke, of Surrey. Foster like most of his other track colleagues has the Olympics in mind and on Monday flies to New Zealand for three months training.

For Wild this victory was something of a comeback for he won the Inter-Counties race in 1974 but still has to make the impact in track racing. For most of the three laps, Lees, who is 21, six years younger than Wild and had won a European Junior championship medal, was way out in front. At one point his lead was over 80 yards but Wild knew that he could pull that back and passed Lees on a hill about a mile from home. Lees responded with a powerful finish but it was not good enough to pull him back to first place.

Reflecting back now, John Wild said how much the two Inter-Counties wins mean to him, and he adds, 'Brendan Foster quoting me as world class - that didn't happen often!'

In 1980 Wild also came 35th for Tipton in the National at Leicester, and was in their silver medal team at the 12-stage road relay, running the first leg in 25-49. John enjoyed his time at Tipton, remarking that, 'they have got be the most supporter and family oriented club.'

Wild was 6th in the RAF cross country championships, which was his lowest position since 1972, and 3rd in the Inter-Services. He won the RAF steeplechase championships, and came 2nd in the event at the Inter-Services, losing to Roger Hackney, who was just emerging on to the scene. However, as we shall see, he was now turning his mind towards a possible change of tack, which would lead to him taking to the fell running scene rather more seriously than he had thus far.

John Wild once said that his most satisfying performances were, 'the 1974 and 1980 Inter-Counties cross country wins, and reaching the final of the steeplechase in the 1978 Commonwealth Games.' But that was before he turned to fell running, with all the success that brought him.

CHAPTER 6

Run lighter, run faster

Kenny Stuart didn't win much as a junior, admitting that he was slow at maturing. 'I was pretty small compared to some of the bigger boys who were almost grown men, and I wasn't training much either.'

Kenny's father took him to his first guides fell race as a junior at Thirlspot in 1970, where he came 5th out of 11 runners. His first senior fell success was over a cross country style course near Wigton in 1974. At the time all there was on the fells were short races. It wasn't until the late 1970s that amateur races started up in the Lakes. Locally, the early ones included the Skiddaw race and the Latrigg race. But apart from those there was nothing.

Kenny was running in 'guides races' as a professional. The term 'guides' stemmed from the experienced fellsmen, such as fox hunters and shepherds, who guided the early nineteenth century tourists on lengthy walks and explorations in the mountains. In the early days these guides were often the only fell race contestants, as they raced to prove their superiority, and thus enhance their employment prospects. The races were virtually exhibition events staged for the guides to display their fell racing talents to appreciative gatherings at the shows. Sometimes they took the form of handicap foot races taking place around an undulating course.

Kenny Stuart may not have been setting the world alight with his running, but he planned to change that. Kenny comments that, 'it was becoming a big thing, was the amateur side.' When the running boom was happening in the late 1970s Ron Hill Sports started importing books from America. Kenny was fascinated with the sport and liked to read. He says he bought a few books, which proved ground-breaking for him. He started reading coaching manuals, from which he adopted interval work and fartlek sessions, which he added to his existing endurance sessions. 'These training books were advertised in Ron Hill's *Running Review*. I saw them, sent off and they opened my eyes to what I needed to do. At one stage I got the impression that because I was really thin and small I needed to build some muscle to get more strength. But reading the books also made me think "run lighter, run faster". I started to watch my body weight. I read that 10,000m runners needed to be 10% less than normal body weight, and marathon runners 20% less. So I got to 112 lbs and never varied from that when I was running. Some of the books were from America, but it did include a Lydiard book. I can't remember what it was called. I used to still have it upstairs, but I tend to give these things away.' Because of this self-improvement plan, all the time he was on the fells Kenny was self-coached.

What is the impact of a significant weight change to an elite athlete? As a response to the doping innuendoes aimed at him during the 2015 Tour de France, winner Chris Froome released some of his physiological data in December of that year. According to this data, when the initial tests were conducted Froome's weight was 69.9kg, 2.9kg heavier than his Tour winning weight, with a body fat of 9.8 per cent. Froome underwent several further tests, one of which determined his VO2 max which was recorded at 84.6 ml/kg/min. This is high, but not unheard of. For instance, three-time Tour de France winner Greg LeMond had a higher VO2 max of 92.5 ml/kg/min. VO2 max is just one measure, mind. What was special was that Froome had a very high peak power rating (540 watts) which he was able to maintain even when losing weight for the Tour. He had a supreme power-to-weight ratio, or as sports physician and exercise physiologist at the University of Cape

Town Jeroen Swart put it, 'the engine was there all along. He just lost the fat.'

So, was Kenny Stuart on to something in thinking to lose body weight? Perhaps, but unlike Froome we have no hard evidence as to whether it did or did not affect his strength. We do know that Stuart had a VO2 max of 80 ml/kg/min, but that was measured in 1990, some considerable time after his peak.

Even after all this training, Kenny Stuart was not yet top of the pile. At the time the top pro runners were Fred Reeves, Tommy Sedgwick and Graham Moffat, and by 1977 Kenny was challenging them, but not yet beating them. Stuart reflected on his early attempts at the Grasmere Guides Race. 'I was often beaten; once I was right behind Reeves at the wall and thought I was in with a chance. I was just a young lad and blew a gasket through being over-enthusiastic and he went away. Tommy Sedgwick and Graham Moffat caught me after that and I ended up fifth. It was painful! It doesn't matter how hard you try, you are spent. I was quite disappointed the others had caught me.'

In 1978 he finished 4th in the professional fell runners championship, having been running from a 12-14 year old in Junior Guides races, but never won a lot. 'In fact my brother Dunc was winning more than I was. I felt a fascination for being there, the atmosphere and being a part of it. It was because in those days it was linked to the hunt and the local shows. The hound trails were there, which I have laid aniseed trails for. Wrestling, you were all part of that. You met people and it was what you did round here.'

Kenny went on to explain how to set a hound trail with two 'hound trailers' who run out together. 'We go to a split point in the middle and one goes back to the finish and one comes back to the start. We do about five miles on the fells each, for a ten-mile trail, but it takes us an hour and a half to do that. So it takes us three hours (combined) and the hounds run the ten miles in around 25 minutes. The aniseed smell lasts quite a long time actually. In fact, sometimes they run what they call a 'dead trail', which means one that has gone before.

So they set another lot of hounds off and they pick it up still.'

In 1979 Kenny had improved enough to take second place in the pro championships, with Reeves winning for the tenth successive year. That year Fred Reeves won his eighth (and last) Grasmere victory in a field of 27 athletes, with Kenny Stuart coming 2nd, and Graham Moffat 3rd. 'It was a wet day and the only thing I can remember is that I was second and pleased with that. But I was a helluva long way behind, nowhere near him. I always used to think on when I was a kid running at school and you saw these fell races going. My ambition was to think in years to come when I am a Senior I might be able to sneak a third position in that big race. So second here was very good!'

By now Stuart's reading of running books had started to give his training a new dimension and he had become ambitious and had a long term training plan to match that ambition. By 1980 Stuart comments that his training diary, 'records average weekly mileages of seventy-plus – mostly on the road in the dark! As the 1980 season started my much improved aerobic capacity pushed my capabilities from strength to strength.'

In researching their two lives I found far more written about (and interviews with) Kenny Stuart than for John Wild, this very much being an indication of how Wild was under-appreciated at the time of his career, and even afterwards. One long article (by Jim Johnston in *Northern Exposure*) about Kenny revealed his thoughts on his own training philosophy, some of which are included here:

Throughout his career Kenny's approach to training has more closely resembled that of a cross country runner than a traditional fell runner. This is illustrated in several key areas: Lower overall mileage than most top fell racers; limiting his running on fells to one third of total mileage in order to maintain leg speed; inclusion of regular interval and fartlek sessions on road and grass.

Kenny has never undertaken any formal structured strength training, feeling that his gardening work provided good all-round body strength and mobility (particularly in the hip and pelvic areas). Training for the fells Kenny would generally train twice a day throughout the year. Starting work at 8.00 am, the first session would take place during his lunch break utilising nearby wooded trails.

Finishing work at 5.00 pm in winter generally meant that sessions were on tarmac roads around his home in Threlkeld. At weekends with more time and daylight available Kenny was able to train around the steep grass slopes and rock ridges of the Blencathra range which rise impressively above his home. Winter mileage would generally be around 80 per week.

Showing this to John Wild, I asked him to give his own thoughts. He responded that, 'by 1981-83 I felt I'd had enough of very intensive training, so reduced my output significantly, especially during the summer. I was an electronics instructor at RAF Cosford at the time so my hours were eight to five, but luckily with 90 minutes for lunch, enabling me to get the big session done in the light. However, I always preferred to train early morning rather than in the evening. Obviously living in the flat Midlands I had no fells to train on, so the hills I did were pretty lightweight. I was also doing a small daily routine with dumb-bells, and often did a weekly circuit training session with the Cosford lads (I was coaching Mark Flint and others at the time). In 1980, I'd experimented with doing two interval sessions on the same day, such as two hill sessions, and continued with that occasionally. One particular session I did specifically for the fells was done on a very steep canal cutting where I'd run up and down six times for one effort and I'd do that five times.'

Kenny Stuart adds that, 'my training plans were flexible and varied with the differing demands of upcoming races. The quality of effort was emphasised at all times, hence the road work to maintain leg speed. The hill rep sessions were run VERY HARD and would not be included in the same week as a race. I often felt hangover fatigue from a Tuesday hill session on

Saturday! It took many years to adapt to this level of training, so it was a gradual build-up. The actual pace of the repetitions was difficult to gauge given that they were not accurately measured. However, based on split times achieved in later events such as the Great North Run, I reckon that my mile reps would have been run around 4-20 to 4-30 pace.' A hard trainer then, with significant DOMS (delayed onset muscle soreness) to deal with.

As we have seen John Wild had been doing hard interval sessions since the early 1970s both individually and with groups, so was pretty much used to anything. He says now, 'I'd also never been frightened of training hard and managed over the years to hold my own with anyone I trained with - including the Tucks, Tony Simmons, Dave Black and Roger Hackney (although Jonesy was bloody hard!) I also feel that with my years of running over 100 miles per week I had put plenty in the bank. I guess we would do one and a half mile repetition sessions at 4m 20s per mile pace. Certainly later, when I was training for the marathon, I was running accurate one and a half mile efforts in under 6m 30s.'

Kenny Stuart's results confirmed him as a serious player on the professional circuit in 1980, as he started to run really well then. He took 3rd at Alva, and also won Grasmere that year in 12 minutes 37.5 seconds in appalling conditions, after taking a 30-second lead at the first flag. *Cumbria* magazine quoted at a later date from a contemporary press account that read: '6500 spectators saw Kenny, a gardener, come in about 500 yards ahead – but his time was still sixteen seconds short of thirty-five-year-old Fred Reeves's 1978 record of 12 minutes 21 seconds.' I rather like this more lyrical description (by Tony Greenbank) that was in the same *Cumbria* magazine article which gives a good feel for the event:

The Senior Guides Race always closes the sports late in the afternoon. It is the moment all eyes are trained on the hundred or so runners as they pile out from the arena across the road as police hold back traffic, and up on to the open slopes to the red flag cracking in the breeze near Alcock Tarn, and silhouetted against the sky. It's from here, at nearly a thousand feet above sea-level, the runners descend over rugged terrain so steep that falling rocks can bounce unimpeded for hundreds of feet down.

And it was down this incline Kenny Stuart of Threlkeld came hurtling that day. So fast was his progress you could almost hear an intake of breath from the multitude below intent on watching his descent in case he tripped and went flying downhill among the rocks and boulders.

Leaping and bounding in mid-air Kenny Stuart dashes down the fell side, arms aloft to keep his balance, as the spikes of his running shoes strike sparks on the stones. It still seems miraculous he doesn't fall. At least a trail hound has four legs to stay the course on a steep mountainside, but for a human being with only two it seems a close call. What a setting it was for the Grasmere Sports that day in 1980, following a dry spell of weather. The arena was a hive of activity with a host of athletic events. On this particular day some among the thousands of spectators were complaining of cricks in their necks before they finished.

At the time Stuart told the *Westmorland Gazette*: 'I knew I had to try to burn them off on the way up, so I went hard right from the start. Near the top, I thought I might just have overdone it, but I struggled on all right, and when I looked around I knew I was safe unless I fell.' Reeves, who came third behind Moffat, graciously commented: 'Kenny set a cracking pace, and his time is fantastic considering the damp, windy conditions.' So Stuart had finally won the race at his sixth attempt, which would have meant doing it first in 1975. Kenny clarified the situation, 'Yes, because when you went out of the juniors you would be seventeen years old, so you went in to the Seniors at that age. So yes that is possible, as I was eighteen then. But as a seventeen-year-old, if you look at some of the photographs, I was a very small, and not very well furnished.'

Three weeks earlier Reeves had led Stuart to the summit at Ambleside, but Kenny took him out on the descent, striding out to a clear win. He could win from the front or from behind, then. At Kilnsey Stuart led up and down the crag to win with a time one second off Reeves's record of 8-01.7.

Stuart won eighteen races in that 1980 season to take the professional championship for the first of two occasions. His wins included Malham, Burnsall, Ennerdale and Buttermere. Kenny thinks Grasmere was a big turning point for him. He knew he was good on short pro races like the Ennerdale race. 'That was on a fell they call Herdas, Great Bourne, it didn't go quite to the top but there is a crag just underneath the summit and it went straight up and straight back down. It is not run now, the show isn't there either. Grasmere was important because the time I managed to run was competitive. There was a lot of focus on the Grasmere race. It was the big one in Cumbria. Down in Yorkshire the Kilnsey Crag race was the one for those lads.'

In 1981 he had an even more remarkable season, being pro champion again with an incredible record of 30 victories in total in 32 races, including 28 in a row at one point. However, as champion Guides racer in that year he is reckoned to have won a mere £687 from his racing. He won Grasmere that year in 12-46.1, from Graham Moffat and Tommy Sedgwick. Stuart's wins also included Ambleside, Sedbergh, Dent, Cracoe, Embsay, Grayrigg, Gargrave, Ennerdale, Langdale, Buttermere and Wasdale.

In that year Mark McGlincy was running as a junior in the pro fell races. His first memory of Kenny Stuart is at the Gargrave Fell Race from that year. 'Kenny got out of his dad's Mini Clubman, I think it was, and this slight little fella got out and someone said that is Kenny Stuart. I thought, I didn't really know who you mean. So, we had heard of Fred Reeves and then Kenny came in before him in the race, that was first real sinking in of how class he was. I watched him through that season at various meetings and he was streets ahead. I also remember him winning Embsay in 1981, which is more of a cross country race and it was really wet. Kenny was running up the main street after coming down off the fells and he was caked in mud. It were awesome.'

Mark McGlincy was born in 1970 and now owns his own landscape gardening business. He was originally from Skipton, and now lives in Grassington, having raced as an amateur for the Skipton, Bingley and Keswick clubs. He has run on the fells since he was eleven. We met in the Kong café in the climbing shop/wall in Keswick to chew over his early days, and he gave me an alternative insight into the professional scene and shared his thoughts on Kenny, as both a pro and then as an amateur.

'It was all pro for me in early days,' he says. 'I was deemed a professional and couldn't do amateur races. I tried to enter Burnsall, but my entry was refused. But we sneaked into amateur races sometimes. But I didn't do a lot travelling, because my parents didn't have a car. I relied on lifts off people to a lot of events.'

'Kenny was an idol, who everybody aspired to be, you know. He was seen as one of the greats, just like Fred Reeves was. I was heavily involved in fell running as it was my passion, and he was somebody you wanted to be. As kids a lot of us dressed in red just because Kenny did. Tommy Sedgwick, he was another idol.'

Mark reckons that Kenny's strength was that he was a great all-rounder. 'His strength relied on climbing because of his physique, being such a slight fella. He just let fly on the climbs. He could come down as well as any too. You got the exceptional ones that could come down like a Tommy Sedgwick in his day, or Graham Moffat. When he was coming through Kenny ran against Tommy quite a few times. Tommy won Grasmere in 1982, after Kenny had won it the two previous years, so he was still going well.'

In his career Mark McGlincy has achieved some impressive performances, including being the first Englishman to win the Scottish Open Hill Race title (which is competed for at the Helmsdale Highland Games hill race). He also won the Kendal

Winter League three times, won the Powderhall two-mile title twice, and was a member of the Bingley team that won their first ever FRA fell relay title, in a team that included Ian Holmes and Rob Jebb.

For a while Mark ran on the pro circuit on the Scottish Borders, where you could win around £600 per race. 'When I won the Powderhall two-mile I won £1200. They were handicapped races on grass most of the time, and Keith Anderson was coaching me at the time. That makes a mockery of pro-amateur divide on the fells. It was £30-40 on the fells.'

Another memory Mark has of Kenny Stuart is at the shepherd's meets at the end of the year. 'He liked a bit of a singsong, because he has a very good voice, and knows the hunting songs. Everyone ended up in the beer tent.'

Kenny himself has some marvellous memories of those days as a professional fell runner, which he shared, together with thoughts on his training regime.

CHAPTER 7

Good at climbing, descending, & training

Kenny Stuart was inspired by fell runner Bill Teasdale, and also by running against two of his other heroes – Fred Reeves and Tommy Sedgwick. He says Sedgwick and Reeves were both runners to look up to, and both had relative strengths on different courses. 'Sedgwick and Reeves were already up there because Fred Reeves is around ten years older than I am, and Tommy Sedgwick seven years or so older. Fred was the go-upper, and Tommy was the renowned descender.'

In 1981 Kenny Stuart lowered Tommy Sedgwick's Alva record to 18 minutes 39 seconds. At Kilnsey Crag Stuart smashed the record he just missed the year before, when local runner Mick Hawkins challenged him all the way, resulting in a sparkling 7 minutes 46.5 seconds record, although this was beaten by Mick Hawkins the very next year (when he won the professional championship title). Stuart also set records for the races at Helvellyn and Braemar, where crowds of 25,000 were not uncommon. Kenny says that the races in Scotland were the same as in the Lakes, adding that, 'Braemar had the same atmosphere, short, just 24 minutes running. It was just slightly longer than the conventional guides races in the Lakes. It goes to the top of Morrone. The Queen was there, driving round the grass track ring in a car, and Prince Charles. They sat in this big log cabin which was on the show field.'

At around this time Prince Charles would sometimes come to the farm shop at Rosthwaite that sold Herdwick mutton and all sorts of things. 'He was very friendly with a family in the valley. He was involved with the hunt actually, but it was kept quiet.' Pauline reckoned that he also liked the solitude. 'A few years ago the hunt got an invitation to send a couple of bus loads down to Highgrove, in Gloucestershire to his home. We all went. I have photos of meeting him and having drinks. He served up his organic lamb', smiled Kenny.

At the Ambleside race Fred Reeves took him out on the ascent, but Kenny Stuart swooped into the lead at the start of the descent to win by some 15 metres. Having sprained an ankle at Alva three weeks previously, he was surprised at his victory, having had to have a training break of two or three weeks. He recalls, 'I was trying to keep my weight down at the time because Ambleside Sports was looming up not too far away. I resorted to drinking blackcurrant jam in boiled water - I don't know where that remedy came from! That was rather than eat any meals. I strapped myself up ankle-wise and I beat Fred Reeves at the Ambleside Sports. It was quite a bad injury. It affected me for a number of years afterwards, being somewhat swollen up. I had that and a bit of Achilles tendon trouble and some knee trouble and that was about it. Just niggles really.'

Looking back on his years on the pro scene Kenny reflected, 'I always remember the help both Tommy and Fred gave me in those early years. They were different personalities, but both were very approachable, and I'd like to think I am the same. Once you have been a fell runner, that world is always there. I can't think of any better pursuit to keep you interested, quite apart from all those cracking people taking part.'

In earlier discussions with Kenny Stuart I had broached the subject of betting in the pro side of the fell racing scene. It had started when Pauline Stuart made a comment about betting, which took us briefly into that topic, and Kenny commented that, 'there was a bit of betting. What you got at the big sports shows were hound trails as well, so the bookies were already there. I never once had a bet on myself or on anyone else. Once I had a bloke approach me at Ambleside Sports and he said 'you don't want to win today'. I said 'I have trained all year and have a good chance'. He said 'no, you don't really want to win, do you'. And then I did, and I beat Fred Reeves for the first time. Then the same man came up to me later and said, 'I think you have had the wool pulled over your eyes, I think Fred must have been betting on you'.'

Certainly in much earlier days there was a lot of underhand stuff. It was reckoned to nearly destroy the sport in the 1950s. The old runners used to talk about going to a sports meeting and it being 'your turn'. As Kenny explained, 'it was like six or seven blokes backing this one runner. There are stories of the winner coming in and he wasn't supposed to win because they had all backed the second feller. He had to stumble and hide behind the wall. There was quite a bit of that going on. Another thing that destroyed the whole betting syndrome in the old days was the fact that Fred Reeves and Tommy Sedgwick started to train twice or three times a day, like professionals. Dennis Beavins was supposedly coaching Fred. Because they were training like that they weren't interested in throwing races for a couple of quid, and that destroyed the betting.'

As pros, Tommy Sedgwick and Fred Reeves used to train on courses like the Grasmere Guides one, often doing reps on the course. Kenny Stuart recalls that he, 'went over once and we ran it twice together. On the first I beat them by a mile to the top. The second time I waited at the top for them and they said "we'll have a race down now" and they beat me easy. They were reckless. I couldn't understand why they would need to do that in training. That was the way they were. I had a lot of commitment, mind. I trained hard, but I trained with a purpose. I don't see that in modern fell runners. They train to train, rather than train to race, that is the big difference. You hear, "we had a run in the morning, then someone came round and we went over Blencathra and then back over Skiddaw, and were out for five hours". I am sorry, that is training to go long distances in training. Lads are turning up for races tired.'

Kenny also suggested that was why he never considered doing

the Bob Graham Round, or attempting anything like it. 'I knew that mid-season it wouldn't do me any good. You have to reccie the sections, and I couldn't be bothered with all the organisation. I thought that when I get to about 35-36 I would maybe have a go. It didn't happen, but I don't regret it. From when I was a teenager, with aspirations of one day to maybe be good enough to come third at the Grasmere Guides race, to do what I did as a Senior absolutely surprised me.'

When I spoke to him, Tommy Sedgwick commented that there was a closeness amongst the runners that hasn't been matched since. 'There were some quick guys: Fred Reeves, Kenny Stuart, Mick Hawkins. We had a get together in 2012. Fred Reeves was over from the States, plus Kenny, Pete Bland, Graham Moffat, Steve Carr, William Reid and Roger Gibson. We ran some miles – in the lounge. A great craic,' he smiled, recalling the occasion.

Tommy also said it would have been good to have seen Kenny and Fred race when they were both at their prime. 'Before he was reinstated I ran against Kenny at Wasdale in a short Kirk Fell race. It was steep. I thought he can't run up there. If I could have got him to walk I'd have walked as quick as him. I remember looking up and he was going away. I don't see how anyone could do his level of training and keep doing a manual job.'

Kenny reckons that people from this background had a constitutional advantage, being fit and healthy to start with. 'Bill Teasdale was a guides racer and professional all his life. He was just a Lakeland shepherd but he had the constitution.'

I wondered whether the handicap races in Scotland had interested Kenny because of the potential rewards. 'No not really. I did a bit on the track. I cleaned up a lot, up until obviously the handicappers started to realise and then they put you so far back it wasn't worth competing.'

'I did have a bloke called Jossy Watson, who competed a lot on the track scene on the pro side of things, come to me one October and wanted me to go and stay with a bloke called Ossie Sword who shouldn't have been involved in this sort of thing, as he was doing all the handicapping, but he wanted to train a number of runners to go to do the Powderhall races up in Scotland. So the deal was that I would have to go up there over Christmas to live with Ossie for 2-3 weeks and he would put me through the training for the 800 or 1500m on the track. The deal being that they would get the bets on me, and I would get a percentage of the winnings, if I won. I declined because I didn't want to go away at Christmas, and I wasn't interested to be honest.'

Kenny Stuart's training is fairly well documented and looking at it closely might perhaps cause surprise as the detail is revealed. He trained at a lower mileage than many fell runners, limited his running on the fells so as to maintain leg speed, and included interval sessions on road and grass. All of this was influenced by his having a manual job and limited daylight training hours.

Kenny has a light frame, being just 5 feet 5 inches tall, and weighed just eight stone at his racing peak. Newspaper reports routinely proclaimed him to be either *The Human Whippet*, *the Flying Gardener* or *King Kenny of the Peaks*. The reality is that his height and weight gave him an incredible ability to ascend well. This was one of his greatest assets, and he is reckoned to be one of the very few that could run all the way up Thieveley Pike for instance. He certainly trained hard though, reckoning that his mile reps would have been run at a pace of around 4 minutes 20 seconds to 4 minutes 30 seconds per mile.

In longer races Kenny (along with other fell runners) was developing the obsession with "running light" into a fine art. 'The clothing and gear I used to wear during races in the 80s started with Walsh footwear – either studs (the Walsh PB) or sometimes the Walsh Fell Spike with three spikes in the heel for short, grassier races. Clothing such as nylon jackets and trousers wrapped up into nothing more than a thick waist belt tied with elastic bands were the norm and seemed to be copied from the likes of Billy Bland. In colder weather I used to wear Helly Hansen short-sleeved tops and sometimes their thermal bottoms in addition.'

Kenny regards himself as a racer rather than a runner, and consequently he had only one approach to racing and that was 'all out'. He didn't believe in easy races and began to limit his racing programme to avoid mental as well as physical fatigue (he had to turn down many of the invites to local races which followed his successes). Although successful across all distances Kenny felt he was best at 'Medium' races with steep grassy ascents and descents. He didn't enjoy rocky terrain and had problems navigating in misty conditions in long events.

John Wild also says he regarded himself as a racer and never avoided competition, although he preferred some forms of running to others (he wasn't too enthused about road running). He raced an awful lot, although many RAF cross-country and track races were quite low key and could be used as part of his training. However, he comments, 'I ran to win in fell races. I was confident in my abilities, and would go with the flow. For example, the first time I ran Kentmere I was feeling great and even on a bad weather day, was in the lead very early on. In other races I would let a big lead develop before going up a gear and winning.'

Hearing them both describe themselves as racers, I asked each of them to outline their preparation for races in both the days before, and on race day.

Kenny Stuart had a standard routine for his race preparation. 'Pre-race tapering for a Saturday race would commence on Thursday with two 20 min easy runs (three miles) and one 20 min run on Friday. For important long races the taper might begin a full week ahead and I would also increase intake of complex carbohydrates in the final few days before the race.' In his early days he had problems with muscle cramps towards the end of races which he puts down to inadequate tapering. Kenny is adamant that fell runners should avoid running in the hills in the three days prior to a race.

John Wild tapered down for most races but some he just trained straight through. He also believes he was best at

'Medium' races, but also acknowledges that he, 'had a few good 'Short' and 'Long' ones (and a few bad long ones too!). I did the week-long carbohydrate depletion diet for the first time at Edale Skyline and it worked for me. I also seemed to have the ability to descend at speed, even on rocky terrain and won several races on that.'

Kenny Stuart's pre-race warm-up was quite simple. He would commence about one hour before the start time by getting out of the car and walking and generally getting mobile for 15 to 20 minutes. He would then jog easily for about 20 minutes and follow this by some light (static) stretching exercises. Kenny would then do some fast relaxed strides for five minutes and spend the remaining time staying relaxed and keeping loose. If he had to travel a long distance to a race he would do some flexibility and loosening exercises prior to starting the journey.

On final preparations, John Wild commented, 'for warm up, I'd just do a gentle jog with a few strides unless it was a very short race like Burnsall, or Grasmere, then it would be much more. There were some occasions where Anne and I had a poor night's sleep in the back of the minivan or a long drive up the M6 in the same van. So stiffness was often an issue.'

These routines certainly worked for Kenny Stuart. In the two years that he won the professional title Kenny had swept the board in the races, being virtually unbeatable. But, there were small fields in the pro races, and always the same rivals. Not unnaturally he started looking for further challenges. He was twenty-five years old, and reaching his peak physical age. He was beginning to increase his training and wanted to have increased competition, by competing in the larger amateur fields, over greater distances and to have the option of competing on the roads or at cross country if he felt like it. His also wanted to compete with his brother Duncan for Keswick AC, as they often trained together but were always going to different race venues.

Joss Naylor knew Kenny in his professional days. Joss played a huge part in the early days of fell running, but he shouldn't need much more introduction here, as he is probably the 'face' of fell running to many people, both within and without the sport. He has almost certainly had more written about him than any of the other great athletes who have graced the fells. I have written my fair share about him in my two previous books, but certainly learned more about him when I drove round to Greendale to interview him for this book.

I reminded Joss Naylor of his influence on Pauline Stuart, but he couldn't remember it specifically. But by his words and actions Joss has influenced countless people, being also something of a hero to me. As he acknowledges, when discussing this, it didn't matter whom he met, he used to encourage everyone. Talking about Pauline he commented on *her* influence. 'Pauline worked hard. For a year or two she was practically unbeatable. It was good for our sport. Pauline is a lovely person, and I have got a lot of time for her. She made the other girls work too in races.'

I asked Joss about some of his amazing long distance achievements, and for one particularly strong memory. He is a thoughtful man, and paused for a moment before responding. 'Well, it is difficult to say. When I did my 60 at 60 I was in tremendous nick. The first 10 hours I was just floating along. Then something happened to us when I was going up on to Sail. There was some long heather and my legs kept going from under me. At that time I had been poisoned by organic phosphor sheep dip, which killed a few lads. I lost my power but I could run.' That is just one example of the obstacles that life has thrown at him, but which he has stoically overcome to carry on with his running.

On another occasion, after doing the Ennerdale race and running the Pennine Way his body was, as he put it, 'knackered, my joints were buggered and I was supposed to give up fell running and farming and go into a rehabilitation centre and learn a trade. I had been told that I would never run again. Doing the Pennine Way I went into a hole almost to the top of my leg and came down with such a crack. The next day I was black and blue, and I couldn't run, and struggled to the end. Both my Achilles tendons were blown, they were a mess.'

Joss saw a specialist and the one thing he said was that he could square up the Achilles tendons. He saw the physio every day for a fortnight and it went back to normal, and he had no more problems with them. 'John Wild had the same problem. He had the operation, whereas I was advised against it. John never really got going again after that. But they did try to measure me up for a corset too! They said you will have to wear one of these for the rest of your life, you understand. I was fitted with it, went for fish and chips, and threw the corset in back of car and never put it on again. It just shows, doesn't it?'

However, John Wild points out that Joss is actually wrong there. John had no more Achilles trouble after his own operation. But he did have ankle trouble, as he seemed to twist his ankles regularly.

By the late 1970s, and into the early 1980s, Joss points out that he didn't have time to do many races, 'although I always tried to make time for the Mountain Trial, because it was at the time of the year when I had an easy time on the farm.' He then laughed at memories of his less than normal training and racing regime at the time. 'I often didn't have time to train, but I won some big races by decent amounts. I used to train on the sand at Seascale for an hour when Mary was doing the shopping!' This training was often done with John Kirkbride, the 1972 Olympian (at 1500m) from Whitehaven. Kirkbride was also in hospital with John Wild at Farnham Park in 1974, having the same tendon operation.

So, in 1982 Kenny applied to the Northern AAA for reinstatement to amateur status, in order to pursue these aims. Joss Naylor gave these thoughts about Kenny's ability to cope with a change of code to the amateurs. 'He was a great athlete; he was a front runner was Kenny from day one. He was good at climbing, good at descending, and good at training. He trained very hard all through his career, and put a lot into it. He was just a genuine athlete. You wouldn't come across anyone who worked harder than him, or had more dedication. At the shows, when he was in his peak, there was no-one that could get near him. Fred Reeves had a lot of leg speed. He was a good all-rounder was Fred. Kenny wasn't the best at the longer distance races. But he converted fairly well from the pros. He had that pace to cover the front if anyone broke away. He eventually got the course record for the long Ennerdale race, remember.'

Talking about the change of codes, Kenny Stuart notes, 'I applied in springtime and it came through just before Burnsall in August. I carried on training right through. It got a bit messy during that period because you had the Northern AAAs officials taking names of youngsters competing at the sports, so they could ban them. They didn't have to win money to be banned. They were deemed to be competing as pros. It was ludicrous. A lot of kids were put off by it.' Because of this he missed most of the 1982 season sitting out his 'suspension period'.

Mark McGlincy reiterated that, 'when Kenny went into the Seniors as a pro he was quite mediocre. Then in 1980 he really made his mark. But, he only really had 1981 when he was at the top of pros. It was a bit of a shock for some people when he changed so soon after reaching top of the pros. People expected Kenny to have multiple wins at Grasmere and Ambleside, like Reeves and Sedgwick. After two years he moved to the amateurs.'

'Graham Moffat was expected to take over the pro scene when Kenny went amateur. He was second behind Stuart that day at Gargrave, with Reeves fourth.' However, Moffat went across to the amateur code in around 1984. He did leave one mark on the pro scene though, as he still holds the under-17 record for Grasmere, which has lasted 40 years now.

Kenny's reinstatement came through on 11 August. Looking back now he says that he, 'found that many people in both codes were very negative about my motives for this change, and I know my parents would have preferred me to carry on winning more races on the open [pro] running circuit.'

PART THREE

On the fells

CHAPTER 8

Having the guts to commit

John Wild achieved some pretty impressive marks in the decade of the 1970s on the country, track and roads, but was looking for new horizons in his running. He comments now that the stress of international track racing was huge, and that cross country was actually his favourite surface at that time. Furthermore, looking back he says that when racing on the fells he felt, 'no pressure, like running fete day cross country. I was confident of being good, and that I might win some'.

In early 1981 Wild wrote to Andy Styan (the editor of *The Fellrunner*), saying, 'I hope you don't mind me writing to you specifically, but I need some advice.' He asked some general questions about fell running, in particular about longer races. He also showed a lot of confidence, when he intimated that 1981 was the year that he intended to make his mark in the fell racing scene. Styan (who had come 10th in the previous year's championships, and had been champion in 1979, so no mean fell runner himself at the time) wrote back, although John can't remember exactly what the reply was.

John recalls, 'I think he felt that as a "soft" track athlete, who was I to think I could run the fells. I also recall him publishing details of the letter and had the feeling he didn't take me seriously. Later Styan put a caption competition in *The Fellrunner* magazine with a picture of skin coming off my feet, implying my shoes were no good. I had always liked running in Nikes. When I got on board with Reebok they designed some shoes for me. They were good to me.' John took offence to the shoe caption, as he felt it was implying that his Reebok fell shoes were to blame for the incident. He added, 'There was a dig about me wearing a Reebok Racing Club vest too. Reebok Racing Club was an affiliated club, so I was entitled to wear the vest in races.'

Kenny Stuart's take on this situation was that there was a bit of that sort of stuff going on amongst the fell running community. 'It was moving away from the traditional lines of fell runners serving their apprenticeship on the fells. I was still running professionally and getting *Running Review* at that time, and I recall that I saw reports of this John Wild and the times he was putting up and distances he was beating people by, and I thought he must be one helluva runner. I was to find out how good! Many people thought John wouldn't last the long distances, but he certainly did.' Pauline Stuart comments that, 'there was a bit of jealousy. They should have welcomed someone as talented as John Wild into the sport.'

A few years earlier Wild had run the Stoodley Pike fell race and finished second to Ricky Wilde (who was one of the top fell runners at the time) - on 2 October 1977. John remembers that he, 'had such a good day out at the pub and was so struck by the friendliness of all concerned that I vowed someday to do more. It had just been a question of having the guts to commit myself.'

In the race Ricky Wilde beat off all challengers in a formidable field to win, smashing the previous year's record time by more than a minute, even though the course was treacherous and muddy in parts. He came home in 16-54 and was one of nine runners inside Martin Weeks' record of 18 minutes. Weeks, defending his record, beat his own time but only managed 8th place in 17-16. Ricky Wilde led at the Pike in 11 minutes and held his lead to win by 25 seconds from Wild (then running for Cambridge & Coleridge AC), ahead of Mike Short and Harry Walker. John had a great day, recalling Cyril Smith MP presenting the prizes and being stunned at how big he was. 'My prize was a radio alarm clock!', he chuckled.

That year Wild also won the Worcestershire Beacon race, an event I too have fond memories of running in – partly for the fact that it used to start with a massive downhill section. John recalls, 'I held the record for Worcestershire Beacon too. I won a mirror there, I may still have got it.'

It is worth remembering that at the time of these two fell excursions John Wild was concentrating on his steeplechasing, with the Commonwealth Games (in August 1978) coming up soon, and needing to be qualified for. But he had good memories of fell running's friendliness (and post-race pub action) and vowed to do some more as he waited to have 'the guts to commit himself.' Nearly four years passed before he was ready to make that commitment.

The Fell champion in 1977 was Alan McGee, with Mike Short taking the title in 1978, and Andy Styan in 1979. Then in the 1980 fell season Billy Bland won his only British Fell championships title. That year, of his ten championship races Billy won eight, and he took the title by 13 points from Mike Short.

Billy Bland is something of an icon in the sport, mainly due to his outstanding performance in 1982, when he set the current fastest time for the Bob Graham Round of 13 hours 53 minutes. This is for an endurance challenge over a 62 miles circuit of 42 of the main peaks in his native Lake District. Billy Bland also dominated the long fell races in the Lakes for a period in the 1980s, being virtually unbeatable in races over the Wasdale and Borrowdale fells, which he knew like the back of his hand. He lives in the back end of Borrowdale and trained on the very tough terrain that surrounded him. He regularly raced against Wild and Stuart, so I took a trip to see him on his home patch. I wanted his take on their performances in this period and, as expected, I got some forthright and fascinating responses.

Billy Bland started by prefacing our discussion with a warning. 'I remember the ones [races] that didn't go well. I see bad in somebody before I see good. What that makes us I am not sure!' Leaving any psychoanalysis for later, I asked Bland for his overriding impressions of both Wild and Stuart, and he started with Wild, whom he acknowledged that he hadn't known as well as Stuart, not being a local.

'John Wild was a class runner. He could push himself until he was sick, which I could never do. He was a hard man in that respect. If Kenny hadn't have been about then he would have been way out there, and maybe no-one else could have pushed him like that. I think I am right in saying he won the Inter-Counties cross country championships [*yes, twice*]. Put me in the Inter-Counties and I couldn't have finished in the first half.'

Bland also thought that, 'in a way coming to run in a fell race was a bit of an adventure for John, running amongst plodders. Well not John and Kenny, because they both were very good runners. But fell runners often have very little natural speed. [*Bland then listed all the really good runners at the time, as though to disprove his previous comment.*] Any of about twenty runners were capable of winning a race. Races were harder to win then as there weren't that many and the runners were together a lot.'

Moving on to Kenny Stuart, Bland thought that Kenny didn't push himself as hard as John did. 'I think he would accept defeat before John would, that is my personal thought. But Kenny was a really fast runner.'

I mentioned to Billy Bland that Kenny Stuart had reckoned Billy to be a leader in what might be called the lighter kit movement. Billy laughed as he replied, 'I would have runners come up to me, and they would say "what you wearing today, Billy?". I would think, well what have you got between your lugs. Whether I was too brash I don't know.' But he did agree that he took as little as possible, of what you were supposed to take. 'I could never see if there was a drop of rain about or a laal bit cold then people would start with a cagoule on. Well I could never see the sense in starting in a cagoule because it pulls the juice out of you. Yes, put a cagoule on if you need it.'

Billy then talked of the impact of deaths in the sport. 'It was when someone died that we started to get more complicated kit-wise. Then you start dancing to insurance companies and that. I think in early days it was just left down to you and common sense. I can't remember having a bum bag, it was just like a money pouch really. You could get a Mars bar and a map in, and a compass. It was just like a belt and your cagoule would be tied round your waist and knotted, not stuffed in a bum bag. I remember running round, the day Bob English died I think, in the Ennerdale race with just a Lifa top on, and Tecwyn Davies said to me "you were a hard man". I just looked at him and said, "well as long as you are making body heat, you are fine". I might have put me cagoule on if I was cold.'

Billy Bland was renowned for his ability to route-find in the Cumbrian races but wasn't so sure about both Stuart and Wild's natural abilities in that area. 'Kenny couldn't find his way out of a paper bag if the top was open! I have said it many a time. To a certain extent John was the same. They were both racers and a lot better runners than I ever was, but they weren't mountain men if you know what I am saying. They were what I refer to as proper runners, which I wasn't. But on certain courses we would come together and we were a match for each other - almost [laughs]. Don't get me wrong, they were both fantastic runners, John winning two Inter-Counties and Kenny doing a 2-11 marathon, that is class running from both of them.'

Mindful that Kenny won three fell championships and John two, I asked Billy Bland why he only won the fell championship just that once, and he replied, 'Because I wasn't good enough! I was good on long 'uns. If someone had said 'Right Billy you can pick races this year' I could have won a few probably. You know, some short and rough ones and that.' Bland acknowledged that he rarely could beat Wild and Stuart at their peak, saying that 'against Kenny and John, unless it was a Borrowdale, a Wasdale, a Duddon, or summat, I would never even enter their heads, apart from being a useful guide for a bit early on!'

I left Mountain View with plenty to think on, and further comments from Billy Bland on particular races he ran against both Wild and Stuart, which will be covered later in this story.

John Wild ran his local fell race, The Wrekin, in May 1980 and his time of 34-27 is still the record (he also holds the second fastest time, with 34-36 in 1981). The 1980 race was run on a warm, sunny day and Wild led throughout, to beat Mike Short (who had won the Three Peaks race the week before) and Taff Davies.

Wild's next fell race was the Ian Roberts Memorial Relay in August 1980. The event was held in memory of Ian Roberts, who had been struck by lightning and killed the year before in the Dolomites. Roberts competed on the fells and on the roads, and it was decided by his club, Holmfirth Harriers, to include both surfaces in the race. The first and third laps were four miles on road, and the other two around four miles of country and fell. The hosts came in first, with John Wild's RAF Cosford team just nine seconds behind after 16 miles. The second and third fastest fell legs were from Jeff Norman (22-14) and Harry Walker (22-24), with John Wild over a minute faster (20-58). John noted, 'that was a great day out and quite an unusual event. I won a bolt of cloth for fastest lap!'

In September Wild won the Eccles Pike fell race from Andy Wilton (18-14 to 19-23), setting a new course record in the process. The very next day Wild won the nine-mile Withins Moor fell race. On another clear day he won by two and a half minutes, to set a new course record of 52-58 there as well. Then in October Wild entered the long Three Towers fell race, in which he led Jeff Norman for a while mid-race before losing out by just 18 seconds.

John Wild had one more fell outing in 1980, turning out on 27 December in the short Wansfell race. Although beaten into second place by Kendal's Andy Taylor, he beat many quality fell runners – including Harry Jarrett, Jack Maitland, Colin Donnelly, Jon Broxap, Harry Walker and Mike Short. This prompted Harry Walker (who had placed 9th) to say, 'just watch him go next year!'

Jack Maitland's performance, in coming 4th in this race was pretty remarkable, as he was just eighteen at the time and a student. As far as he remembers this was his first fell race, which seems to be confirmed by scanning through results in *The Fellrunner*. This was him starting to dabble in fell running, after originally being an orienteer. Within a couple of years he was challenging the best in the sport, which obviously included Wild and Stuart.

I decided I wanted to hear Jack's take on the events of that era, so (after a bit of networking) I arranged to meet him in the café of the John Charles Sports Centre, in an industrial estate in southwest Leeds. As I pulled in, a large group of triathletes were gathered, having just finished a morning swimming session. Being slightly early I joined several of the triathletes in having one of the warm home-made cherry scones that seemed to be the (re)fuel of choice. Sitting down with scone and coffee I acknowledged Jack, who was finishing a post-training debrief with one of the athletes.

Jack Maitland is Director of Triathlon at Leeds Beckett University and part of the British coaching team for triathlon, so regularly works with the Brownlee brothers (Alistair and Jonny), who are also based in Leeds and are at the time of writing arguably the two best triathletes in the world. Maitland started running the fells more seriously in 1983, which turned out to be the incredible fellrunning championships season, as Stuart and Wild went head-to-head over 15 races. As Maitland progressed over the next couple of years he became perhaps their chief rival, and eventually succeeded Kenny Stuart as British champion in the 1986 season.

I sat opposite Maitland, watching his craggy face break into frequent laughs as he recalled incidents from his career. He had brought along his own training diaries from the mid-1980s, which proved really useful when we started looking back at races in which he had raced Stuart and Wild in that period. His fresh recollections and pithy diary entries illuminate many of the subsequent events in this story.

In the 1983 season Maitland was consistently third behind Kenny Stuart and John Wild, and he commented that, 'at the time Kenny and John were at their peak I was racing for third place. Maybe I was a better descender than the other challengers like Sean Livesey and Dave Cartridge.' But before getting into detail we talked through his background.

Jack Maitland was born in Aboyne in Aberdeenshire in 1962, and attended Aberdeen University to study Computer Science in 1978-82. He took a year out working at making orienteering maps, by hand as this was before the advent of computer cartography, which allowed him to train for his sport. He went and trained in Norway, then moved to Leeds to do a postgraduate course in teacher training. He made the British Junior and Senior Orienteering squad, so orienteering was his main sport initially. When he went to University he joined the swimming club, the volleyball club and the running club, but really he only did running and orienteering. Meeting Colin Donnelly at the university was something of a catalyst which resulted in Maitland doing more fell running.

Maitland went to New Zealand to make orienteering maps in the winter of 1985-86, and was by then doing mountain running, and thinking about triathlon. Then he came back to Europe and raced the fell and mountain running season. That was the year he won the British Fell championships. After that he did a mix of fell and triathlon races for a few years. At the end of 1989 he did the World Mountain championships and came 10th in an uphill only race. 'I think I knew I wasn't going to win a medal and that I had reached my limit. The Commonwealth Games was including triathlon in 1990 and I knew I could get in the Scotland team. I did, and having done that I thought I would see if I could get in the British triathlon squad. Fell running had seemed a solo thing really and I enjoyed the team aspect of orienteering and triathlon.' Triathlon certainly was the better for his change of direction.

John Wild had already shown some remarkable form prior to writing to Styan to ask for his advice, in order to take his performance up a notch as he concentrated on the fells. He was right to be thinking about the long races, and how he would do in them. Although the opposition may not all have been taking the 1980 year end race (at Wansfell) too seriously, Wild's second place did give an indication of what he was about to achieve in the 1981 season. 'I didn't have any specialist shoes so ran it in road racing shoes, consequently I was all over the place as it was so wet and muddy.'

Part way through the 1981 season an interview [*by Andy Styan as it happens*] with John Wild appeared in the August issue of *The Fellrunner*. He was asked about his move to the fells. 'Once I had made the difficult decision that track would come second this summer, I was able to pick all the fell races I wanted. The thing I like most about the fell racing scene is the hospitality of runners, families and spectators alike. To have such a sociable and friendly atmosphere in a running event is rare in my experience. I can't praise the organisation of the Fell Runners Association highly enough either. No other running body, for example ECCU or RRC [*English Cross Country Union and Road Runners Club respectively*], provide so much advance information.'

Looking back on it now, John remarked that he had, 'trained so hard for the 1980 Olympics and got nowhere in the whole season. I didn't even get a PB, let alone selection. It was soul destroying. I can see no reason for it. I had the indoor stadium at Cosford, I did good winter sessions of 20 x 400m. I was training with Roger Hackney now and again. I was doing hurdle training, to improve my technique. Maybe I peaked too soon, I just don't know. I was being coached by Don Woodruff, so it was a scientific approach. It was all going well, I had won the Inter-Counties that winter. In the end I stopped trying for track in 1981, and I decided to do something different to keep fit for my first love - cross country.'

Mention of hurdle training prompted me to ask John about the current dominant Kenyan steeplechasers, who in many cases have very poor barrier techniques. He responded that it was possible to be good without technique, just by being very fast between the barriers. As an example he gave Dave Bedford, who once beat the British steeplechase record, 'he was not a proper steeplechaser, but just a good runner between the barriers.' I had not known that Bedford held that record and on researching this nugget found that in fact he set a British record in just his second ever 3000m steeplechase race, running 8-28.6 on 10 September 1971 at Crystal Palace.

In February 1981 John Wild led his RAF Cosford team to cross country victory in the RAF championships at RAF Halton. The top five were almost a Who's Who of top athletes at the time. Steve Jones won for the third time in a row, followed home by Julian Goater, Steve Rimmer, Gordon Rimmer and then Wild. Two weeks later those five were joined by Roger Hackney and Ray Crabb at the Inter-Services cross country championships at HMS Dryad. The RAF's running strength was shown by their taking the first four places, in Steve Jones, Julian Goater, John Wild and Roger Hackney, to easily beat the Army and the Navy for the Inter-Services title. Reflecting on this era, John makes this point about his Services commitment. 'I think I'm more proud of the fact that I was captain of such a great RAF team for ten years than anything else. I took the job seriously and was always conscious of looking after the team and of course, the Inter-Service rivalry.'

John was also part of the successful Tipton team that won the National cross country team title that year. In the race at Parliament Hill he came 48th. Tipton Harriers have a comment on that era on their website:

At last in the winter season 1977-78 the clean sweep of all three National titles was achieved, as was every age group in the Staffordshire and Midland cross-country championships. This was followed with victory at the National championship at Leeds. The one remaining peak was almost scaled in 1981 when Kearns, Rushmer, Holden, Milovsorov and Emson just failed to win the European Clubs championship at Varese in Italy, succumbing only to Sporting Club Lisbon, i.e. the Portuguese National Team. With the addition of John Wild their supremacy as a genuine club team was clearly established by their remarkable win, by a margin of 129 points from Gateshead, in the National at Parliament Hill Fields.

Wild recalls, 'I just remember having a good run on a typical Parliament Hill course. The club was so well supported, all the old supporters out with hats and scarves.'

On 4 April 1981 John started his fell season by racing in the 'Short' Pendle race, a championship counter. For this season (and also the 1982 and 1983 seasons) there were fifteen races that counted for the championships. These fifteen races were categorised as five 'Long', five 'Medium' and five 'Short'. (The races chosen varied from year to year.) The athletes scored their best ten events, of which three had to be 'Long', three 'Medium', three 'Short', and an extra one of the athlete's choosing. The scoring was 32 points for a 1st place, 29 points for 2nd, 28 for 3rd and so on down to 1 point for 30th.

After John Wild's startling performances on the fells the year before, and a recent win in the Milford 21 (a cross country race which was a local for him, being on Cannock Chase), everyone was watching him, to see how he would manage in the first championship race of the season. They had their answer 29 minutes 27 seconds later, as John had a new record for the course, getting his revenge for Wansfell over Andy Taylor. After a fast start Taylor and Wild were together at the summit, but John took nearly a minute out of his rival on the descent. Telling me about this, John laughs as he recalls that, 'on top of the moor there is a long climb on a lane and there is a maggot farm on the top. I was retching from the smell of rotting flesh.' Bob Whitfield was quoted at the time as saying, 'none of the first five would finish in the British Fell Running championship top five at the end of the season.' After Taylor in 2nd, the 3rd to 5th places were Colin Donnelly, John Reade and Colin Moore.

This race was the second in Jack Maitland's young career, after Wansfell the previous Christmas, which Colin Donnelly suggested he should come down to. Maitland recalls that he came 23rd out of the 402 that ran that day, and comments that, 'subsequently, I'm pretty sure that I ran all the way up the Big End at Pendle in 1984, when I set a new record of 29-44 [*This was on a slightly longer variation of the course from 1981 when John Wild set a faster time]* which was still printed in the fell race calendar as the record until this year, when I think they finally realised that the course must have been changed at some point in the interim. Harry Walker was a great runner and was definitely my inspiration for doing that – when the record stood for so long I did wonder subsequently if there had been a favourable tail-wind that day.'

Apparently someone had said, 'apart from Harry Walker, John Wild was the only one who can run up Big End', and it was reported in *Athletics Monthly* in the July of that year. John Wild says he heard this comment from Harry himself on a separate occasion. But Maitland's comment would make him the second person to achieve the feat.

The next weekend John Wild ran in the Kentmere fell race. Andy Styan had set the record in this 12-miler in 1978 in snow and mist. It was misty again this time, which caused some amazing problems. Billy Bland, Andy Taylor, Bob Whitfield, Jeff Norman, Mike Short, Colin Donnelly and several others all went off course, going over Harter Fell. Meanwhile, John Wild had reconnoitred the course the weekend before (on the Sunday after winning Pendle) and was on the right course and out on his own. He took it carefully on the run up from the village church via Kentmere Pike, up on to the plateau of High Street. Having passed through the summit checkpoint, he flew back down the Froswick/Ill Bell ridge, taking 30 seconds off the record, finishing over four and a half minutes ahead of Jon Broxap. Twenty minutes later, and more, the wayfarers started coming in, although several (including Billy Bland) actually retired, presumably with hurt pride. John laughs about it now, saying, 'I think that me getting this record was what really pissed off some of my rivals!' John Wild was now showing his potential as a fell runner, and began to mount a serious challenge for the 1981 fell running championship.

CHAPTER 9

An idol and an inspiration

Not only was John Wild making his presence felt in the 1981 championship races, but he was rising to specific challenges that were being put to him. At Easter, John took on the short Rivington Pike fell race, the only occasion he competed in it. John comments on the challenge, 'I met one of my fell rivals, Brent Brindle, at the 2015 Snowdon race gathering (his daughter, Lindsay, was running for England ladies) and he reminded me of some background I'd forgotten. Apparently Brindle, Mike Short and lots of the Horwich lads were fed up with Ron McAndrew constantly bragging about his Rivington Pike record from 10 years earlier and how invincible it was.' An advert was placed in *Athletics Weekly* citing the record, but John didn't see it, he went purely on the say so of the others. 'Both Brent and Mike persuaded me to come up and have a crack at it - so I came up from a holiday and had a go at the record.'

He adds, 'we were on the Isle of Wight on holiday with Anne's parents. I had done some very good long distance training there, and I was quite relaxed.' John was certainly building his mileage in training at the time. The four days before Rivington had been 12, 10, 9 mile days and then a 7 mile taper, with his diary noting that the day after he did, 'a steady 20-mile run on Cannock Chase. New record for time on feet 2 hours 7 minutes.'

Referring to the Rivington Pike race, John added that he was, 'driving a TR6 in those days and we drove up with the roof down on a lovely day. It just went so well. You don't realise what you are doing when you do it, you just run to your capacity, and I took 37 seconds off the record. Later they invited us up for a reunion for the 100th anniversary. The organiser invited all the previous winners back. My daughter was quite young at the time and she was getting quite agitated as she didn't want anyone to beat my time.'

Wild was obviously in sparkling form, although he says, 'when I did my first season in 1981 I kept breaking records. I wasn't trying to, but it just happened.' The Rivington Pike race report notes that conditions were good, fine and sunny with a cool breeze and good underfoot conditions. Bill Smith notes in *Stud marks on the summits* that, 'Wild was first to the tower in 9-48, 22 seconds ahead of Alan Buckley, and swooped down to victory. Long-serving RMI Harrier Cyril Hodgson, who was officiating at the summit tower, afterwards remarked that he'd never seen a fell runner complete an ascent looking so fresh and as unstressed as Wild did.' Andy Taylor overtook Alan Buckley on the descent for 2nd, with Jeff Norman coming in 4th.

Studmarks records the pre-race setup thus: 'An advertisement for the 1981 race in *Athletics Weekly* cited McAndrew's record of 16-30, adding: "Ten years is a long time – can it not be beaten?" A further challenge was extended on the race entry form: "Ron says it can't." Cross country ace John Wild (RAF Cosford) accepted the challenge.' Ron McAndrew came 31st in the race and congratulated Wild at the prizegiving afterwards. Ten years may have been a long time, but over three decades later Wild still holds that record.

Peter Watson's book *Rivington Pike* discussed some speculation that 'Wild may have taken a shorter route on the return journey.' However, he does go on to make two points that mitigate against this idea. 'Firstly, in the year previous, Norman Matthews of the Horwich club had chosen an unusual route and had been quietly reprimanded. One can be fairly sure that at that time the unspoken rule was to keep to the farm tracks and the concrete road. If Wild had transgressed this rule at the quarry he would have been observed by the nearest following runners and by all the spectators at the popular Lower Knoll farm vantage point. The post-race, pre-prizegiving gathering of spectators and competitors would have been full of talk about the line Wild had taken to break the record. Runners present at the time report that no such talk took place.' When I delicately mentioned this to John Wild he confirmed that he knew of no such speculation, and was adamant that he had followed the correct traditional line on his descent.

A week later the Three Peaks race was snowed off. The race secretary noted, 'the road beyond Horton towards Ribblehead had been closed by a general depth of 5 or 6 feet [of snow] and an avalanche had occurred at Selside, and electricity lines were down.' Farmers reported depths of snow up to ten feet, with drifts up to 18 feet higher on the fells. The race was postponed till mid-October. Jack Maitland travelled all the way down from Aberdeen to do the race, but arrived in Settle to find it had been cancelled due to the snow and so travelled back again the same day.

Then on 9 May the third championship race was held at Ben Lomond, a tough 9 miles with 3200 feet of ascent. John Wild won again, this time taking 16 seconds off Mike Short's course record, and finishing over two minutes ahead of Harry Jarrett. Wild had run three races at the start of the season and broken three course records. He says now that he wasn't trying to do so, but that it just happened. 'This was really the case - I'd got no perception of the distance and difficulty, but it was great to run with no pressure and with a degree of confidence.'

'We had one dog at the time, and we used to sleep in a minivan with a calor gas stove. It was an adventure. I remember coming back that first year after I had done the Ben Lomond. We travelled back to the Lakes on the Saturday night and slept in a layby.' These comments show both Wild's balanced approach to life, and also his commitment to leaving no stone unturned in his bid to succeed on the fells, as he added, 'I then did a reccie of the Fairfield, which was the next race.'

So, only a week later it was Fairfield, the third 'Medium' race of the championships, with nearly 300 entered. On a cool day John took one and a half minutes off Ricky Wilde's 1979 record, for his fourth record in four races. He didn't spend much time reflecting on events, as his diary entry for the day contained just eight words: 'Fairfield horseshoe race. First. Darby second. New record.'

On 30 May it was a long category 'A' race – the Welsh 1000 Metres. John recalls that he often used to sleep in a van before the Welsh 1000s, although sometimes organiser Ken Jones would offer a free room. That year John could only finish in 10th place, some 20 minutes off the pace. Mike Short won from John Reade and Jon Broxap, with some of the main players not even being there.

By June, John had won five out of the seven championship races, and may have seemed to have the title sealed. But he had only run the one 'Long', that 10th place at the Welsh 1000s, at which he struggled on the last climb. He was credited at the time with saying: 'I was absolutely knackered at the end and it was all I could do to stay on my feet, let alone run. I just hope the Lakeland ones aren't as tough or as long as that. I'd just hate to have to repeat that exhausting experience. It was also humiliating to say the least for me to be reduced to a wobble and to be assisted over rocks by a hiker at one point.' He concluded that at least it proved he was human. He reminisces, 'I was wasted. Just after the Pen-y-Pass Hostel, I'd actually passed the hiker once, only for her to catch me up again! I ran out of energy and I completely blew. Bonking they used to call it. I had got to Pen-y-Pass hostel and just went back through the field.'

The aforementioned interview with John Wild took place around this time. He was asked what his ambitions were, to which he replied, 'It may sound corny, but honestly all I want to do is go out and enjoy myself. Have a good day, and do well in all the races I run. I thought I would do well in some of the more 'runnable' events, but I didn't expect to be running as well as I have been.' In particular, he didn't know how good he'd be at descending – it turned out that he was really quite good.

Asked which races he had enjoyed, his response (in 1981) was, 'collectively, I've enjoyed them all, even though I've been knackered at the end of them all, despite people saying I look good at the finish. I have raced them all very hard. Picking one or two out – I enjoyed Kentmere because I felt so good that day and I managed to get round in spite of going off course three times. It's lucky that there were hikers about. I enjoyed Ben Lomond because the weather was so good and the views from the top were the best I've seen anywhere.'

As to the rest of the season: 'I hope I can keep my present form on the fells, although there is a long way to go yet. I intend to do some track races, in fact I've recently run 8-55 for 3000m steeplechase and 5-47 for 2000m steeplechase, so I could surprise myself this year.' Asked about long Lakes races, Wild said: 'I intend to run the Wasdale and Borrowdale. Unfortunately I will be overseas for the Ennerdale for an RAF fixture. I don't know how I'll go in the longer ones because I've never done anything like it before. The longest I have ever been on my feet is just over two hours. I am just going into it with an open mind – and a Mars bar.'

That last comment led to me asking both Wild and Stuart about their diets. John Wild had what might be called an uncomplicated diet. He says he, 'used to eat anything and everything. My diet didn't change for the fells, as it was always varied beforehand. By today's standards, it was probably considered unhealthy (especially all the beer!).'

Kenny Stuart explained his views on diet at this time. 'My racing weight was very consistent and didn't vary much between 110 lbs and 112 lbs. My diet was, by today's standards and fashions, slightly higher in fat and protein value for an athlete and I always ate a decent percentage of meat and cheese protein to cope with my daily high intensive work loads. My employment as a gardener was also of a physical nature so my energy expenditure was very high at times. When I was in full training my alcohol intake was also moderate and I only drank an odd night at the weekend or perhaps a "blow-out" after a big race.

Preparation for the long races never involved the full carbo diet, but in the three or four days preceding a competition I would eat plenty of complex carbohydrates, finishing off with sweets, syrups and fruit sugars. I very rarely ate or took anything during a long race apart from water or occasionally glucose tablets – it was always my belief that one's body shuts down to such an extent during this type of physically intense effort that at times even water is not utilised by the body to its fullest extent but just causes excess sweat which helps to deplete electrolytes.'

Both Kenny and John admitted that they didn't really receive any nutrition advice back in the day. I wondered how their stated diets stacked up against current nutrition advice for endurance athletes. Having been shown the two paragraphs above, the following are the thoughts of a sports nutritionist on current theory and practice. Hannah Sheridan, who works with elite athletes at The University of Birmingham *High Performance Centre,* commented: 'Athletes will hopefully choose to have a high protein diet. Good quality protein sources with each meal, plus protein in snacks also help continual recovery throughout the day. Red meat, like Kenny said, is a good protein source for athletes, as it also provides iron. Iron is often something which endurance athletes are low in because of the damage that the impact of running can have on red blood cells, because of restricted diets and small losses of iron in sweat. An athlete's most important energy source is carbohydrates, therefore heavy training volumes call for a high carbohydrate and high protein diet to provide energy, training adaption and repair and rebuilding of muscles. Moderate fat intake, coming from good healthy unsaturated fats is fine. Fat intake should never compromise the proportion of carbs and protein.'

John's worry about long races continued, as in June he had passed on one more 'Long' race at Ennerdale, and in July he would fail to finish at Wasdale. This situation meant that he would have to compete in both the Borrowdale and Moffat Chase 'Longs' later in the season in order to get his quota of long races in. In between the Ennerdale and Wasdale dates John ran in the Butter Crag race on 21 June. Butter Crag was his second 'Short' of the championships. Due to fixture clutter there was a smaller field than might have been expected, but there was one entrant who had travelled up from way down south.

In researching this book, I looked back at my own running efforts. It was classy enough at the front end of the race, but I see from my own training diary I was running what was my first fell race that day, and significantly off the pace I was too. At the time I was just getting more serious about my running, and had completed the first ever London Marathon in what my diary recorded as an 'easy seeming' 3 hours 5 minutes three months earlier. I guess I was exploring what other events running had to offer, as the diary records that the next two races I did after Butter Crag were a half marathon and then a one-mile track race. One memory I have of the Butter Crag race is hitting the wall, literally. On the way out of the field, to get on to the real climbing you had to mount a dry stone wall. It was something of a shock to me so soon into the race. It was each to their own, and if you didn't make it at your first attempt there was every chance of some studded Walshes landing in the middle of your back as you were used as a stepping stone by more experienced fell runners. I also recall the damage to the wall being rectified by one of the leading athletes straight after the event. I have no recall of who it was, but in my mind I like to think it was Billy Bland, a man with considerable walling experience, and who was competing that day.

Back to the race, and Mike Short was first to the summit on this steep climb (900 feet in just three quarters of a mile), but John Wild put 11 seconds on him on the descent, to take another win. Sean Livesey showed some of his potential, beating Billy Bland into 4th place. As to myself I ran like the novice I was, finishing well down the field. I went OK uphill but was somewhat phased by the breathtaking descent, which had caused ladies winner Ros Coats to take a bad fall on her way down.

Two days after Butter Crag John Wild was racing in the RAF track championships at RAF Cosford. Sgt Wild, as he was at the time, won the 10,000m race in 29-29.6, with Junior Technician Al Jones 2nd in 31-13.6. A week later Wild won the RAF steeplechase title in 9-07.6.

Wild was back on the fells for the Wasdale race on 11 July, but as mentioned already, he dropped out. His wife had gone up from Wasdale Head to Black Sail pass with some *Accolade* drink, but he didn't make it round, and the race was won by Billy Bland. Wild's form either side of this date suggests that he was very fit. I naively assumed he had problems with either navigation or dehydration. John candidly told me the reality. 'I just got embarrassingly pissed in the Wasdale Head Inn the night before and had a dreadful hangover. I got real grief from Anne too, as it made it a "wasted" weekend, not to mention the pointless hard walk she'd had.' Being mindful of the life of the partner of a fell running obsessive, he also recalls that one year there was a thunderstorm in the night and Anne was frightened witless that they would get struck by lightning as they lay in their little tent.

Joss Naylor recalls that the Wasdale race was held on a really hot day that year. 'I think a lot of them went off too fast. Then your legs would suffer on the steep downhills. There was a big up on to Seatallan, you had to be careful there.'

On 18 July it was the Snowdon race, which has 3300 feet of ascent in its five uphill miles. Although it was a British championship race, there was also a strong Italian entry. It was a very busy day in the fell running calendar, causing the talent to be spread around the races a little, with Billy Bland winning at Kinniside, Colin Donnelly at Slieve Donard, and Bob Ashworth at Ingleborough.

John Wild comments, 'I was laid back. I was confident, verging on over confident. I let the Italians go as I thought I would get them on the descent. I felt they weren't going to be any trouble. I had heard rumours that they weren't so good going down, and they were quite some way ahead at the top.' Wild reigned supreme, beating Rovedati by 13 seconds, with Lazzaroni three minutes behind him in 3rd.

Running in his second 'serious' fell race that day was Malcolm Patterson, who went on to become a major player on the fells in the years of Wild and Stuart's big rivalry. Patterson was born in Manchester in 1958 and moved to Yorkshire when he was three. He made international standard as an orienteer, which was his original sport. Explaining his background to me, he notes that, 'I competed for GB at orienteering, but my major aim was to get selected for the World Championship team, which I never achieved'.

His parents took him fell walking, and invariably up to summits, right from birth. 'So I always loved to climb, but wasn't so keen on descending! We used to spend every other weekend in the Lake District. I used to see men running on the fells and sometimes went to Ambleside Sports – though the day that I heard some bookie screaming: "who'll give me 5 to 1 on Patterson?" when Patterson was a shy young lad about my age rather put me off!'

Malcolm Patterson started orienteering, and running as training, seriously in 1976. Later he did the occasional local fell race, such as Guisborough Moors, as training. He recalls that, 'one of my first fell races, done with fellow orienteers Chris Hirst (who won) and Robert Bloor (son of Three Peaks Winner, Jack), was the Marsden to Edale Trog in January 1980. Then it was Angela Carson (now Brand-Barker) who persuaded me to do one of her local fell races - Snowdon - in July 1981.'

Commenting on the Snowdon race, in which he finished 10th behind John Wild, Patterson remarked that, 'this inspired me to switch from orienteering to fell running for the 1982 season - when I had my first serious go at the British championship - and thereafter, apart from a couple of years where I tried to combine both sports, I was hooked! This was also my first encounter with the mighty Wild! He gave an impressive speech at the prizegiving, which he was wont to do. Then showed his arse shortly afterwards, as he was wont to do without prompting! It was my first big fell race and I enjoyed the whole experience immensely, well apart from seeing the Wild arse!'

Before he took fell running seriously, Patterson was already aware of, and inspired by, recent fell champions, particularly Harry Walker, Mike Short and Billy Bland. 'But from the moment I met him, John Wild became an idol and great inspiration. Later I added Kenny Stuart to that list and then the Italian Fausto Bonzi.' Within his club (Dark Peak Fell Runners) he had several mentors who he acknowledges gave him much valuable support. 'The club as a whole gave me a great bunch of friends and training/racing partners, but in particular it was Andy Harmer whose performances inspired me, and the late Tony Trowbridge who gave me many wise words on how to train and race smarter.'

Patterson is a librarian by training and worked in libraries of one sort or another until 2001. Since then he has been a self-employed researcher and editor. In addition to this he has worked part-time for Scottish Athletics since March 2014, as a Coach Mentor for Hill and Mountain Running. He explains, 'I am based in Glasgow, and am part of the performance development team, working to improve athlete performance across all athletic disciplines. As well as working with the top senior and junior hill runners in Scotland, I work with coaches and their clubs by supporting them in developing their athletes.' As we will see, he had a good view (often from close behind) of Wild and Stuart's battles over the years, and often has a view to add to the story.

A week after Snowdon John Wild missed the 'Short' Melantee race in Scotland, and then he headed back to the Lakes for the 'Long' Borrowdale race on 1 August. Billy Bland showed his mastery in his local race, winning in a new course record, almost nine minutes ahead of Bob Whitfield in 2nd. John Wild lost out in a three-way tussle for 3rd, with Harry Walker and Mike Short just beating him home. Billy had been mischievously asking if there was a bookie to take bets on Billy against the field. Afterwards Billy Bland was prepared to give John Wild credit for his effort, especially after he failed to finish at Wasdale earlier – a race won by Bland.

I prompted Billy Bland with the bookie comment, and he came back on it. 'If my memory serves me right to win the British championships, I think John had to be 4th. I believe he ran that race just to be 4th, and didn't really compete. I did say when I was interviewed after that I was disappointed in John. Who knows, he might have beaten me.' John Wild is adamant that he wouldn't have had that attitude. 'If I could have won Borrowdale I would have bloody tried for it', he says in response.

John had a routine victory at the short Burnsall race in August, by 16 seconds from Mike Short, with Harry Walker 3rd. Ben Nevis on the first weekend in September didn't go so well. He slipped to 9th, as Bob Whitfield won from Billy Bland. Whitfield missed the course record by two seconds (Bland had missed Dave Cannon's record by a mere second the year before). This was John's first race for Cumberland Fell Runners. 'I was second claim to them because Danny Hughes kept badgering me (nice man though). I ran for them in fell races.'

Joss Naylor recalled this happening, explaining that, 'Danny Hughes was a shift manager at Calder Hall power station, and he was good at organising. He put a lot into fell running. I used to have some rare battles with him too.' Joss also commented that like Danny Hughes, 'John Wild was one of those sort of people that would help anybody. John was a very interesting bloke too. He left a tremendous name for himself.'

John Wild needed one more 'Long' race to complete his counters, and this was the 20-mile Moffat Chase on 4 October. Colin Donnelly took the victory, 2 minutes up on John. His long race performances were getting better though. He had not won one yet, but here he saw off Maitland, Bland, Reade and Broxap, among others. Having won three 'Shorts' already, and having four 'Mediums' in the bag he therefore didn't need to run the last 'Short', which was the Blisco Dash – very late in the year (on 14 November).

This situation gave John the chance to enter a long non-championship race to experiment with his approach to a tough 20 miler. He chose the Category 'B' Three Towers fell race on

18 October. 'You parked your car at Ramsbottom cricket club. A bus takes you to the start, and it finished in Ramsbottom. Many cross country runners ran it (like Dave Lewis)'. Wild was worried about it, so started cautiously. Running alongside him, Harry Walker said, 'what are you doing here with us plodders? Get up there.' This John did, eventually beating a good standard field by nearly a minute.

In the fell running championship John Wild succeeded Billy Bland, whom he beat by 37 points. It was a strange result in some ways. Mike Short was on the same number of points as Bland, but had gained his by competing in 13 of the championship races, but only his best 10 across the three categories counted. Billy, however only competed in nine races over the season. Furthermore, he only completed one 'Medium' (Ben Nevis). Theoretically he could have run two more races, and one can easily speculate that two further 'Medium' wins would have given him the necessary points to have retained his title. There is no point saying, "but Billy could only win Longs". In his winning 1980 season he won four 'Longs', but he also won two 'Mediums' and two 'Shorts', coming second in the other 'Medium' and the other 'Short'. So, an almost perfect season that year.

I wondered if John had any idea why Billy Bland didn't do a full complement of races that year, and defend his title better. 'I have no idea. He didn't like to go out of the Lakes much, and he may not have agreed with the format. He was a purist fell runner.'

Also, what of Bob Whitfield's prediction about the first five runners in the first race of the season NOT finishing in the top five in the championships? Well, he was obviously very wrong about John Wild, but not so far out on the others. John Reade managed 5th at the end of the season, but Donnelly was 20th, Taylor 37th and Moore down at 47th.

After the long fell season Wild still had the drive to have a couple of road outings. Just before the last fell championships race (Moffat Chase) he ran the Benson 7, coming 2nd to Lunnon (from Bracknell), their times being 35-09 and 35-23. After the season had well and truly finished, on 18 November, he won the Henlow 10 in 51-19, from favourite Steve Jones in 51-44. This is an important RAF event although it is an open race, and the first ten that day were all servicemen, and all with times of 53-14 and under. John Wild pointed out that, 'Steve Jones was just coming through then. I remember him being at a race at Gateshead around this time, for one of his first vests for Wales. It was lovely to see the excitement on his face as he mixed with all these internationals. No-one knew then how good he was going to be. He had been a smoker and drinker until a guy called Bob Wallis got hold of him.'

John Wild ended the 1981 season a convincing championship winner, which gave him considerable confidence to take into the 1982 season.

CHAPTER 10

Young, lean and hungry

Kenny Stuart was thinking of switching to the amateur code in 1982, and joined Keswick AC at the beginning of that year. He reduced his pro racing commitments, trained even harder, and used a couple of races early in the year to test his endurance.

Some fell runners used the 22-mile Buttermere Round road race as a low-key training run, taking place as it does in January when not much else is going on. Kenny Stuart competed in the race in 1982, 'to see what distances I was going to be able to cope with. I ran all the way with Jon Broxap.' There was no entry fee or prizes, but the two of them did record a new fastest time of 2-05-30.

Early in the year Kenny Stuart won a cross-country race in Scotland. He opened his professional season at the Rusland May Day race, which he duly won. Then on 8 May he (very unofficially, and not commented on in *The Fellrunner* report) ran in the Duddon fell race – a Category 'A' 21-mile race with 6500 feet of ascent. He came in to the finish field together with Billy Bland, and just managed to outsprint him, to win in 2-46-10. A contemporary report notes, 'not yet a competent navigator, nor sufficiently familiar with the route, Kenny stayed with Billy almost to the end, a technique which he has since perforce employed on several occasions.'

Kenny recalled, 'Well yes, I ran Duddon. I met the bloke who organised that, Ken Ledward, two days ago in Penrith – and he recalled the occasion. He is a nice bloke, and did a lot in a roundabout way to get the sport amalgamated. Duddon was like a race with no rules, if you like. I think Joss was running as well. They invited people to take part with professionals and risk being banned. Nobody dared say anything about it.'

Joss indeed ran in the first two or three Duddon races, but it was a bad time of year for him with lambing and having two jobs. 'Amongst the runners there was no animosity, and we welcomed people like Kenny', Joss says now.

Kenny laughed at the comment noted above about following Bland. 'Billy didn't like that! Billy spent a lot of time on these courses perfecting his own routes. Joss did the same. It was obvious that to beat Billy you would have to go with him to find out the best routes. I look back at Duddon and think that now I would be different, maybe. Having won the races I have won, I might now say "let's run in together". But I was young, lean and hungry and Billy Bland was a good scalp and I don't regret it.'

Billy Bland recalled the occasion when I mentioned it to him. 'Kenny was on my shoulder all round, in racing parlance 'you couldn't get him off the bit'. I remember coming in to the Three Shires Stone and I saw Ann there and I stopped, and Kenny stopped too! On the second half of the race he was still there and I could see top of Caw and said "left of that bump" (we were both in Keswick AC at the time) and I said "if I am with you on that top, I will beat yer", and finally I told him to go, as I knew he was capable of winning it. On the way down he was pissing about and I caught him. He beat me by a second on the run in.' After a pause Billy conceded that the best man won.

Billy Bland also stated that he was never bothered by the possibility of being banned. 'Ken Ledward thought it was all stupid. Professionals were making a pair of shoes out of it. It all came together in the end.'

Despite wanting to retain his fell title in 1982, John Wild still competed in the RAF and Inter-Services cross country championships early in the year. On 10 February Wild was only able to finish 11th in the RAF cross country championships, as he was suffering from a heavy cold. Julian Goater won the race from

Steve Jones. Wild had obviously recovered by March when the Inter-Services championships were held. This was won by Steve Jones from Roger Hackney, with Wild just beating Julian Goater on this occasion, giving the RAF the first four places. Wild also came 26th in the National cross country championships, which were held that year in Leeds.

The first championship race of the British Fell championships for 1982 was the 'Long' Edale Skyline. An anonymous correspondent in the Keswick club newsletter commented that there were, 'fifteen races chosen and forced into a season from the beginning of March to the end of September.' The format and scoring was the same as it had been for the 1981 season (illustrated earlier).

John Wild's distance training and new confidence were both in evidence as he stormed to a new course record of 2 hours 35 minutes 16 seconds in the Edale race. Just two weeks later John was at it again, smashing his own Kentmere Horseshoe record. Conditions were dry and fast, helping him beat Jon Broxap by three minutes and take four and a half minutes off the record. In retrospect Billy Bland's 11th place here turned out to be the main reason he didn't seriously challenge for the title, as it turned out to be one of his scoring events, as he only did two other 'Medium' races.

Interestingly, the Edale race was the first time John Wild tried the carbohydrate depletion diet and he reckons it worked for him. Wild comments, 'I followed the Ron Hill method that many guys had been introduced to in the 1970s. I had a long run seven days before the event and avoided carbohydrates for 3.5 days and then loaded for 2.5 days. The third day of the bleed out phase was hard, especially as I was still working as an instructor. The young technicians I was teaching used to wave Mars bars in front of me! I found all foods tasted bland during this phase, although the load phase was great, chip butties and Guinness at the pub! In the race, I didn't feel great for the first 8 miles or so, and said this to Don Woodruff who was watching. He said don't worry as it will kick in - and it did. At 12-15 miles I felt great and finished with ease, and with lots to spare.'

As someone who used a full depletion diet for marathons (successfully as it happens), I fully appreciate Wild's thoughts about the bleed-out phase, where I used to have all manner of weird feelings of worry about energy levels.

Edale was Malcolm Patterson's first British championship race of the 1982 season, and it was also an iconic race for Dark Peak club members. Patterson had, 'prepared as best I could, by running round the route (in sections) beforehand and consulting the wise old men of Dark Peak – like Mike Hayes and Chris Worsell – as to the best route. I was at the front, proudly, nay arrogantly, pushing the pace, much to the consternation (or was it bemusement) of the wise old hands like Andy Darby and Bob Whitfield. I had a big reality check somewhere between Mam Tor and Brown Knoll when the two Johns (Wild and Reade), Andy and Bob pulled away. I hung on grimly for 5th. At least I had the consolation of being first Dark Peaker, ahead of Ray Aucott and John Blair-Fish (who have both sadly passed on).'

Between these two races was Pendle, which Jack Maitland came down for (still being a student at Aberdeen at the time), coming 2nd to Malcolm Patterson. Maitland recalls that, 'it was Colin Donnelly that got me to come down to England to race. I did Ben Lomond that year, and as I remember John Wild won.' Maitland also came down to do the Ennerdale Horseshoe and Buckden Pike.

For Patterson, Pendle was his first big win. He won in 29-51, a minute ahead of Jack Maitland, who he already knew well through orienteering. Reliving it vividly, he says, 'I still have the pressure cooker that was first prize! I remember it as just a blast, I think I was in the lead most of the way, and I loved the Big End. I took my mum, who was always my most loyal supporter, to the race, and I remember we got lost on the way and arrived so late that I just rushed into the registration area, grabbed a number and ran off. Some minutes later my mum wandered into the registration area, now empty of runners. She went up to the lone official at the desk and said "I need to pay for my son's entry". "Too late, I'm sorry" the official replied. Mum pointed up the hill and said proudly, "that's my son in the green shorts at the front, but he hasn't paid yet".'

The Three Peaks, on 25 April, was not a championship race but John Wild had his eye on it, having been disappointed at the cancelled event the previous year, due to massive snow-drifts on the approach roads and on the fells. At the time the Three Peaks race was sponsored by the *Daily Mirror*. In 1981 the sponsors had requested a photo of John, and went down to RAF Cosford to meet him. They wanted him with a kit bag in front of the jets or something. They put some spiel in the paper and then it was cancelled because of the snow. They came down in 1982 having said, 'what are you going to do if you win?' John said, 'have a beer', and the newspaper guy was there at the end with a pint of beer.

This year it was completely different, the weather being sunny with a coolish breeze. Wild was perhaps the favourite in a fairly strong field. John Reade took an early lead going up Pen-y-Ghent, followed by Mike Short. At the summit these were joined by three others, including former British fell champion Alan McGee, with Wild not far behind. Mike Short lacked fitness and soon faded, whilst Wild joined the leaders on the way to Whernside. Then Wild took the race on and won in a new record of 2-37-30, having taken five and a half minutes out of Alan McGee in second place. The picture of him with his pint was on the back page of that Monday's *Daily Mirror*. 'It was quite weird seeing my picture in a national newspaper, but my mum loved it. I was in the Guinness Book of Records for this race.' In his files John has a copy of that Monday's *Daily Mirror*. Whilst the back page has his photo in the report on his Three Peaks win, the front page has a headline that scream "IT'S WAR – says Argentina", with a subhead saying that Britain had taken back South Georgia.

In May and June there were championship races at Ben Lomond, Fairfield and the Welsh 1000s. John Wild was having an amazing streak and won them all, giving him a run of five consecutive race wins in all to start the season.

Malcolm Patterson describes Ben Lomond as a big adventure for him. 'I had never been there before, had only rarely been to Scotland (I was living in Sheffield at the time). I was also full of confidence, having won at Pendle and Kinder Downfall in recent weeks and was thinking that if I could finish 5th to Wild in a long race like Edale, I could do even better in a 'Medium', straight up and down race like Ben Lomond, which played to my strengths. It was a calm sunny day, though there was snow on the summit ridge. I started confidently, with scant regard for the fact that Wild was the best fell runner in Britain, not to mention the course record holder from the previous year! I was indeed first to the top, and able to judge how far I was in front of Wild by passing him on the return journey along that summit ridge. I thought the descent was going well, with no sign of my pursuers, until suddenly, about three-quarters of the way down, Wild and Donnelly passed me in quick succession. I couldn't close the gap and had settled for 3rd when, coming along the road and up the slight rise to the finish I was amazed to see Donnelly almost at a standstill. I was able to get past him and grab 2nd spot, albeit half a minute behind Wild, who lowered his own course record to 1-02.17.'

In June John Wild chose not to run in the long Ennerdale race, relying on Wasdale and Borrowdale to add to his two first places in 'Longs' so far. Billy Bland duly took the Ennerdale victory, from Bob Whitfield and Hugh Symonds. What many find astonishing, but which Billy himself plays down, is the fact that exactly seven days later Bland tackled the Bob Graham Round and came home in a fantastic time of 13 hours 53 minutes, which no-one has got anywhere near since. (For details see: *The Round: in Bob Graham's footsteps*, from Sandstone Press.) Kenny was his pacer on the first section, from Keswick to Threlkeld, his patch really. 'I used it as a long run as part of my training for that week. I was already bloody tired. I got to the end of my leg and Billy went on and I thought "blooming heck, he is going at helluva pace, because I am knackered". I could tell he would go very well, OR blow up. There were no mobile phones in those days so you couldn't keep in contact with people, so I didn't know until the next day that he had run that time.'

In an earlier conversation Billy Bland had explained the setup. 'We were out of Keswick at 5am. I have still got a card with the times on. Kenny [*Stuart*] was on that leg – the little bugger could run. We departed Threlkeld 7.16am. It took 53 minutes to top of Skiddaw, 1-20 to Calva, 1-59 to Blencathra, and 2-13 to Threlkeld, and back out in 3 minutes. I only had Kenny on that first leg.'

The short Buckden Pike race took place on 19 June. Hugh Symonds, who along with Jack Maitland, was regularly Stuart and Wild's closest challenger, recalls that it was, 'the first fell race I ever won, breaking the course record.' Jack Maitland was 2nd at the summit, but was overtaken by Bob Whitfield in the latter part of the race. Hugh Symonds also told me a story of a much earlier fell race experience. 'I ran Burnsall in the early 1970s. I remember Jeff Norman took me there but couldn't take me home. There was a Sale Harrier there who had a Mercedes who said "I will take you home as long as you don't beat me", but I did beat him - as a teenager! That was probably my first ever fell race. I joined the FRA very early, and I am member number 126.'

Hugh Symonds was born in Berkshire in 1953, where he lived for two years before his parents moved to near Altrincham, and he went to school at William Hulme's Grammar School. 'There I played rugby which I decided wasn't for me when I was about to score a try and I got tackled and got hit in the testicles. I went to ground and felt sad, and thought what sort of sport is this? On the way home I was on the bus and chatting to someone and they said have you tried running. You just do it he said, we go round Alexandra Park.'

Soon he was winning school races, and his father encouraged him and thought he should be doing more, and he found out about Altrincham and District AC and Hugh went along. He was inspired by the club's Olympians, Alan Blinston who went to Mexico in 1968, and Jeff Norman who went on to run the marathon in 1976. He recalls that they were very inspirational and helpful. 'It was quite something for a youngster to train alongside them. Running became part of my life. I would say it helped me discover who I was. Before that I was maybe the sort of person who was timid and sometimes got teased. Running gave me something tremendous.'

Then he went to Durham University in 1972 to read Mathematics. 'But I wanted less track and more off the beaten track. Whilst I was at University I did the Three Peaks race, badly, maybe coming about 30th. I know I had been hoping to do well as I had done a marathon in about two and a half hours. I had a latent interest in fell running, although I had no success yet. I just thought I want to do this. I loved running around on the hills.'

He recalls a really memorable day where he went with Jeff Norman and some others to reccie the Three Peaks course. 'The big question mark was how to get from Pen-y-Ghent to Ribblehead. We ended up at the Hill Inn and bumped into Joss Naylor, who was also doing a reccie. He seemed to be dressed in a sack held together with safety pins, and had hair all over the place,' Hugh chuckled.

After teaching in India for a while Hugh got a job back at the school he had previously attended. Then he and his wife were expecting their first child, Andrew, in December 1980. They began to think they would like to live somewhere more rural than South Manchester. Hugh spotted a job in Sedbergh at the school, teaching maths. 'I came for the interview and while there I went for a run up Winder and I thought I want this job, I want to live here.' Fortunately, he got it, as it was a life-changing experience for the whole family. It also had a profound effect on their three children.

'In August 1981 I had just run the Lancaster to Morecambe marathon and sort of enjoyed it. But I was transitioning to fell running in that autumn. I joined Kendal AC and they were very welcoming. I did some cross country and road races for them. I realised I might have talent for racing on the fells when I ran Ben Lomond in 1982, when I think I came third. I thought wow I can race these people.' Having had good races at Ben Lomond and Ennerdale, and won Buckden Pike in a new record, Symonds was established as one of the top fell runners at the time.

However, I was interested in his thoughts on why he never won the British Fell championships. Hugh laughed gently as he responded, 'first and foremost I think there were runners better than me. I would say that Kenny Stuart and John Wild were better runners than me. I'd say to be British champion you had to specialise and say "they are the races I want to do". Around this time there was a championship called 'All the As', and one year I am pretty sure I won that.' He did, in the 1983 season. Symonds also ploughed his energy into being Editor of *The Fellrunner* for two years, after Andy Styan and before handing over to John Reade. All this backstory emerged from a fascinating morning's chat in Sedbergh in the middle of the floods that ravaged Cumbria, including closing the bridge between Sedbergh and Kirkby Lonsdale.

I was interested in how well Hugh Symonds knew Kenny and John. 'I know Kenny pretty well, having travelled to international races with him. I don't know John Wild very well at all, but recall he was a bit of a joker.'

So what of their personalities and abilities? 'I was amazed that John Wild was as good as he was at fell running when he primarily lived in the Midlands. Staggering. You could imagine training to ascend not living in the hills, but training to descend is another matter. He could do it. He was obviously very talented physically. John was highly competitive, really driven. Kenny lived at the bottom of Blencathra, an out and out Lakeland man. He came in through the short Guides races of course. He won Ennerdale, but I don't think he won Wasdale, and may never have run that race [*he didn't*]. There is an analogy I can think of between cycling and Kenny Stuart, going from short to long. Bradley Wiggins was a track man, in a four-minute event, who then later won the Tour de France (a three-week event).'

'Kenny Stuart and John Wild were both very fluid runners. Beautiful style. Relaxed and natural runners, yet so different. Both were really strong mentally. Kenny was really light, and I was taller and a stone and half heavier. On the uphills I used to feel this was a disadvantage to me, it was like I was carrying a rucksack.'

Both Kenny and John were obviously very strong mentally, and gave their thoughts on this vital aspect of athletic performance. Kenny thinks that, 'during long races it is very important to maintain a positive attitude to help block out the inevitable pain. Try to stay in a good mood by focusing on pleasant thoughts such as the pints of cold beer that you'll drink in the pub after the race! Don't show discomfort when you are under pressure, always look like you're in control. I am convinced that I have won races against stronger opponents when feeling awful simply by looking like I was stronger than my rivals!'

John also tried to disassociate, recalling that, 'my international career had taught me all about pressure, especially at big track events and I can honestly say I didn't feel any pressure at all during my time on the fells, even for a race to try to seal one of the championships. I was just confident in my abilities and the outcome was never that important.'

In the first weekend in July it was the Skiddaw championship race, which Wild was running for the first time. In driving rain, a low mist and a cool wind Wild followed closely behind Malcolm Patterson to the summit, which he reached in 42 minutes. Wild closed the gap and shot down in 21 minutes 38 minutes. The only time there had been a faster descent had been in 1969, when Jeff Norman had done it in a stunning 20 minutes 55 seconds. Wild chuckles, 'The descent was so wet and greasy I fell down more in that one race than I did in the whole of three years of fell racing!'

Malcolm Patterson very nearly didn't get to the race at all. He was driving a hire car with three friends as passengers, when the throttle jammed and he was forced to stop. He wasn't known for his car maintenance skills but, desperate to make the start, he managed to locate the problem and to fix it. Of the race itself he remembers the wind being really strong on the summit ridge. 'Being in the lead and completely alone in the mist, I took the decision to drop off the ridge on the return journey and so I never saw who was behind me or by how much [*in fact, he reached the summit about 30 seconds ahead of John*]. With difficult conditions as John describes, I just focused on keeping upright on the fast descent, until I was startled, somewhere on Jenkin Hill, by the commotion caused by the "Wild locomotive" as he steamed past me not to be seen again until the finish, where he was waiting calmly with a cheeky grin and outstretched hand.'

The next championship race was Wasdale on 10 July. John Wild had a nightmare race, being ten minutes off the pace by Pillar. By the end Wild was in 20th place, some 20 minutes or so behind second placed Bob Whitfield, who was similarly 20 minutes behind the winner. When asked why he had such a poor run John's disarming response was, 'it may have had something to with the Theakston's Old Peculier.' Billy Bland looked comfortable all the way round and knocked a massive four and half minutes off Andy Styan's record from 1979. Remember, this was just three weekends after he had set the Bob Graham Round record. We talked about his performance and John rued, 'I didn't learn my lesson from the year before. I always needed some anaesthetic to sleep in the van or a two-man tent. I found Wasdale possibly the hardest race I did. I did it because if I had never done Wasdale I would have felt incomplete. I needed the respect, I tried it.'

Billy Bland says he can't remember John Wild in that race really, and acknowledges that Wild never ran well there. He then revealed that he was disappointed that Kenny Stuart never ran Wasdale. 'The chance of me ever getting a victory over Kenny in them days was fairly remote. That would have been one of my chances. At Borrowdale he won once and once he got beaten, and didn't come again', chuckles Bland.

When we talked about Billy Bland winning Wasdale so soon after his amazing Bob Graham Round record, Joss Naylor gave his thoughts on Billy's abilities and slightly unorthodox training. 'Billy had the legs for them sort of races. He trained hard on them, on the rough ground and that. I don't think there was anybody trained harder on that sort of ground. But anybody who had the legs on a decent bit of running ground could handle Billy. However, his concentration was also very good, and he wouldn't put a foot wrong coming down. I have heard his cousin Chris saying that when they were doing building work say at Ambleside that he would get out of their transport at Dunmail and run home [*over the tops to Borrowdale*]. All those races near where he lived he would know the ground so well.'

One week later Wild was back on form, running in the non-championship Snowdon race. Once again there was a strong Italian presence, with Pezzoli and Bonzi leading the climb and reaching the summit in 42 and a half minutes, with Wild 13 seconds behind. Wild chased the two Italians and caught them on the steep stretch to Clogwyn Bridge, taking a further half minute out of them for a convincing win. An article by Hugh Symonds in the Calder Valley Fell Runners Newsletter commented that Wild:

'... returned to Llanberis dropping 3,300 feet in five miles in a time of 22 minutes to win by more than 30 seconds. This is a speed which would be hard to match on a flat road course. Naturally, gravity is doing some of the work but it's not everyone who can take advantage of this, as the runner still has to be able to keep the legs moving at speed in addition to finding a sure footing. Some liken the skill of descent with that of a ball game player. It requires quick reactions, good balance and fast leg cadence. Ace Lake District runners such as Billy Bland and Bob Whitfield can pick their way down through rough mountains and can maintain their speed whether the surface is rough and rocky or smooth and grassy.'

The race report commented that, 'it is a shame that this race up Snowdon was not considered for the 1982 championship. Many people thought that the record was there for the taking, with the improvement of the path combined with John Wild's good form.' John himself mentioned that, 'Ricky Wilde said he could never understand why I didn't beat his Snowdon record, because I descended so fast. I used to know I could let the Italians go and catch them on the way down. That is the way I ran the race.'

But why did John do these non-championships races? 'The Snowdon race was just a fantastic social event, mostly from the hospitality of Mr Snowdon himself, Ken Jones. He looked after the athletes with such great deals on accommodation. I think Anne and I got it free most years. I must admit to some boorish antics too that have been well documented.'

One such occasion was noted by Malcolm Patterson, when apparently John let off a fire extinguisher in the hotel at Snowdon. John Wild doesn't deny it being let off by him, and cheekily added, 'I once played the piano naked, with just a tie on. When I went to Snowdon last year for the anniversary (they invited all the previous winners) the piano is still in the same place. It was a joy to see Ken [*Jones, the former Snowdon race organiser*], and was a great weekend.'

On the next two weekends Wild ran in two more non-championship races. First he won the eight-mile category 'B' Turnslack fell race. He destroyed a good field to set a new course record, finishing just over two minutes ahead of Jeff Norman. Then he won the five-and-a-half-mile uncategorised Mow Cop race, having to receive treatment for blisters after the race. Wild's local paper, the *Evening Sentinel*, reported:

As he took off his running shoes he peeled back the skin from the whole of his heel and waited for a first-aid official to cut it away. The athlete from RAF Cosford had suffered badly from blisters, following a race the previous weekend and said every step over the five and a half miles of road and footpath around Mow Cop had been agony.

He added: 'This run was a lot harder than I thought it would be. Although I had been told before about the 600ft climb, it did not sound as bad as it was when I came to run it. It was very tough going, with two very big climbs, the one on the second lap being the most difficult.'

The Mow Cop fell race was the day after a championship race at Melantee, which Wild and many others didn't run in. Melantee must have been one of the smallest ever fields for a British championships race, with just 43 runners. Wild's comment on not going to Melantee was, 'the Scottish races were always a logistic challenge especially as our transport was an old minivan (we used to kip in the back of it). The Melantee was tailor-made for Kenny Stuart, and not my kind of race at all. I only ran it in 1983 so people would not accuse me of trying to avoid him.'

John recalls, 'I seem to remember that the Mow Cop was soon after Snowdon and the blisters I'd encountered in that race were ripped off the soles of my feet. The fast, hot Snowdon descent had caused the original blisters.' He added that, 'the other non-championships races were done for fun. As I have said, I found international athletics, especially track, quite stressful and so to run these races free and easy was a great relief.'

John now needed to let his foot heal, and get back to racing championship races if he was going to retain his title.

CHAPTER 11

He came to beat me that day

John Wild needed to run well for the rest of the 1982 season to maintain his championship challenge. He next ran the challenging Borrowdale fell race on 7 August, hoping to erase his 20th place in the Wasdale race from his scoring races for the season.

On the day the Borrowdale tops were hidden in cloud and several runners had navigational problems. Billy Bland knew his local course better than anyone and had no problems finding his way round. Wild tried to stay with him, but was dropped beyond Great Gable, lost his bearings and did not finish. Wild said that he, 'got totally lost and finished up way down Honister Pass, but managed to trot back up the pass to the hostel at the top.' Billy Bland beat Bob Whitfield by nearly 16 minutes in the end, with his brother Stuart Bland having a great race to take third.

Sitting in his garden discussing the occasion, Billy Bland felt that John DID come for a race this time. 'I am absolutely sure he came to beat me that day. Away I went, and I remember as we were going towards Highhouse Tarns I told him to shut up. I like talking during a race like, but I was not recognising for a couple of hundred yards exactly where I was. It turned out I was only the width of this garden out, but I wasn't sure. So I said "shut up John, we are not reet here". A hundred yards on I said "reet, we can talk again now". We got to the top of Scafell Pike and I am thinking I have got to get rid of him along the corridor route, otherwise I am in trouble, and he will beat me. I didn't get rid of him, and going up Gable, and I always remember this, I could hear him breathing [*grunts several times for effect*]. He was cracking, he might say different, but he did get to the top with me, and we just left the top in mist still and he fell in the stones, I think because his legs had gone. Anyway, I heard him fall and shout out. I said, "are you all right, John?". He says, "yeh". I thought that'll do me! If he had shouted "no", I would have stopped. He lost us in the mist and 400 yards or so on he was going way off course. He dropped out eventually. I reckon he came to beat me, but I reckon I had him anyway, although I couldn't say for definite.'

John Wild agrees that he was very determined that year. 'I was hanging on, so I didn't get lost. I say this with hand on heart, if I'd have managed to hang on to him I would not have tried to outsprint him at the end. I couldn't have lived with myself if he had shepherded me round just to be outrun. As it happens I didn't get that opportunity!', he chuckles.

I asked John how he got on with Billy Bland in situations like that. He replied quite unequivocally, 'he knew the course like the back of his hand. I was trying to hang on to him, but couldn't keep up and he was off. I had no hope really, I would never have beaten him in a sprint finish. He was on his home ground, he did what he needed to do, as he wouldn't want me as a passenger. I would have hung on if I could. I went the wrong way in the mist towards Honister Pass. I deserved that. None of us were as good navigators as Billy and Joss. It is no good having a map and compass if you don't know where you are.'

Malcolm Patterson remembers vividly the first steep and loose climb at this race, on the direct route to the first checkpoint on Bessyboot (since discontinued because it was getting so eroded and dangerous). 'I think Billy and John managed to get a lead here, and I never saw them again. Meantime myself and a whole bunch of other runners emerged onto the misty plateau and, bearing in mind that Bessyboot is merely the highest of 1001 similar looking knolls, spent what seemed like a lifetime running like headless chickens from knoll to knoll looking for the checkpoint marshals. Eventually we gave up and ran off! [*It later turned out that the marshals hadn't been able to find Bessyboot either*]. The racing line around Glaramara wasn't so well established in those days, and being an orienteer, I decided to use map and compass to guide me. This had the immediate effect of gathering a bunch of about 20 runners behind me. About 10 minutes later I had the bizarre experience of running down a narrow valley and being confronted by Pete Haines, another orienteer, running towards me, map and compass in hand, with a similar group of devoted followers. Both confident of our route finding, we simply carried on straight past each other, though some of our followers did switch allegiance at this point! The rest of the race was painfully slow for me, far behind the leaders. I do remember finishing just behind Duncan Stuart, Kenny's brother, as well as a good three minutes behind my orienteering rival, Pete Haines!'

The next championship race, the short, steep Burnsall race on 21 August, was notable for two reasons. It was the centenary race, with sixteen previous winners invited back, nine of whom competed. Equally importantly, it was the first time Wild and Stuart raced each other, and what a race it was. Wild commented that, 'the situation in pro and amateur races was all too silly. I think I won more money in a race abroad than he [*Kenny Stuart*] did in his whole [*professional*] career.' It was just a week before the Burnsall race that Stuart was informed that his application for reinstatement had been approved.

It was reported that there was a bad vibe about Kenny as he prepared to move to the amateur code. He says, 'to be honest it was reported like that, but I don't remember hearing many comments at the time. There was tittle tattle in the background. Looking back now I just can't understand what that was all about. This thing about professionals earning loads of money is rubbish. I won more as an amateur, I mean I got money going to Houston to run a marathon.'

Joss Naylor felt it was a good thing for the sport when Kenny got his amateur status, 'and I know Chris Brasher fought hard to get it sorted out for him. It was just at that awkward time, when the changeover was going through, and a lot of these old boys in London were a bit outdated I think. Once the orienteering side got set up, then the fell running side got sorted as one sport.'

Joss recalls that, 'there were one or two people who weren't happy. I thought, here were some great people, who were putting the work in to run professional or amateur, and it would only help our sport along if it combined. There was no animosity as far as I was concerned. When Pete Bland did his first Ennerdale [*after his reinstatement*] there was one or two that didn't want him to run, and I said "it is going to happen, it may as well happen today".'

Billy Bland can't particularly remember bad vibes at the race. He thinks now that it might have been the attitude of some of the older people who had been pros, maybe. 'The star man [*Kenny*] was leaving them and that. But, the first and second man in the race were clearly the best. But, there's no need to overplay the situation. They were not competing for the crown jewels were they!', was Bland's take on it.

On the day, the weather was grim, with clouds on the tops and drizzle making the descent slippery. Wild took a decisive lead on the steep part of the ascent, having a handful of seconds on Stuart at the turn, and extending it on the descent to win by 33 seconds. Stuart had just been reinstated as an amateur and was reckoned by some to have lost some fitness in the waiting period. Kenny counters, 'I hadn't lost any fitness, but I had lost a bit of race experience and race fitness. To be honest on Burnsall I would have to be at my very best to beat John on a course like that, he was brilliant.'

Stuart had chased hard, but he said at the time, 'there was no chance of me catching him coming down.' Reflecting back on the situation now John Wild comments that he had, 'taken to Kenny straight away and couldn't understand the hostility he was getting from some quarters. My wife Anne even remembers a group of runners discussing Kenny the "professional" and I berated them for making stupid comments.' Stuart was even heckled as he collected his second place prize (a silver tray) at the presentations afterwards.

Burnsall that year was a high standard race, with Billy Bland, Andy Styan and Jon Broxap filling the 5th to 7th places, for instance. When I asked Billy Bland if he had a chance at Burnsall, he replied 'Yes and no. Anything of that length with anybody good in it and they would beat me.' The result also served notice of the coming battles that were to ensue between Wild and Stuart over the next couple of seasons. Kenny summed it up. 'We weren't dissimilar runners really. Willing and able to take it out fast and sustain it. Quite often John would go out really hard and not last, and my strength would take me through to win. But if he was at his best he could sustain it right through. He had this desire to finish first and you could not beat him.'

Malcolm Patterson had come 4th, beating Billy Bland by 3 seconds. 'I enjoyed Burnsall. It is one of my favourite races, especially because of all the tradition and history behind it, and the atmosphere and tension on that start line. It's the nearest most fell runners will get to feeling what it is like to line up in the Olympic 100m final! I was very pleased with my race, though annoyed to be overtaken on the easy lower half of the descent by Bob Whitfield. But it also sticks in my mind because it was Kenny's first race as an amateur and the first time I met him. I was delighted and excited - and my first impression was of a friendly and modest man that I immediately warmed to - but not everyone felt the same, sadly.' Patterson explained the last remark by adding there that he felt there was some animosity towards Kenny as a pro turned amateur, not to him as a person.

Several of the pro runners came from the Gargrave Show, which was held on the same day, to witness Kenny race that day, knowing it was his first official race as an amateur. 'That was why we were there,' says Mark McGlincy. 'It is a classic race too. Witnessing him running the Burnsall Sports, and seeing the calibre of athlete [*Wild*] that could beat Kenny was an eye-opener. In 1982 it was still a split sport, so I couldn't compete in the Junior race at Kenny and John's first event at Burnsall. Fred Reeves did run in the race though, having turned to the amateur code.'

McGlincy admits that he didn't know John Wild that well. 'My view of John was that I got to know the name through the Burnsall Sports really. When Kenny made the transition to the amateur scene then John's name came to the fore. "Who is this guy?" some thought. You were brought up thinking Kenny is number one, and you thought he would still be number one on a short course like Burnsall. Then Wild beat him, gosh. There was a bit of a divide between pro and amateur. I think some of the amateurs were a bit scared of Kenny. Only thing I can remember as a spectator is that many who knew Kenny were behind him. There might have been a few there but I never came across it personally. If there was booing at the presentation that was not sporting, especially when you have seen two athletes giving it all to put on a good show. Nobody deserves that.'

Wild dropped a bombshell though, by announcing that he was to have an operation on a muscle subacromial decompression in his left ankle the following Tuesday, which would obviously put him out of action for a while and jeopardise his championship chances. John explained the detail behind that situation. 'The RAF surgeon was a Belgian who'd had experience with Tour de France cyclists and he gave me the confidence to go ahead rather than leave it to potentially get worse - certainly a risk but it paid off. I've never been afraid of surgery to correct problems and I've had more than ten operations in the past to resolve injuries. There were certainly some rivals who seemed pleased that Bob Whitfield might win the championship instead of me!'

Revelling in his new freedom to race, Kenny Stuart competed in the Sedbergh Hills Race the very next day. He and the previous year's winner, Bob Whitfield, took it out, with John McGee chasing them. McGee dropped off the pace and Stuart pulled away on the last descent to beat Whitfield by 27 seconds.

'The novelty of being reinstated meant I just wanted to race in these great races. I had never been on the Sedbergh course. The same thing happened again, as I waited till I knew where I was and then took off.'

After his operation Wild obviously missed the next championship counter, which was the Ben Nevis race two weeks later. In his second championships race Kenny Stuart was strangely identified as unattached in the results, despite clearly being a Keswick member since his reinstatement. 'I don't understand why they said I was unattached at Nevis – maybe when I entered the race I was unattached. I suppose I hadn't got my registration sorted.'

Kenny Stuart was first to the top of the Ben, with Billy Bland soon catching him on the scree descent, but Stuart came back again to win, Bland having taken a fall near the Red Burn crossing. Bob Whitfield came through from 8th place at the summit to a solid 3rd place. Stuart remembers that it, 'was horrendous the speed he [Bland] came down. He caught me on the mad descent, on the boulders and scree, and he was jumping everything that he came across. I was trying to stay with him, but was on a knife edge. I couldn't think of anything else but to not let that string break. Luckily when we got to the Red Burn he was slightly in front and when he hit the grass he did a belly flop and I went straight past him. I thought he was going to come back past as it was steep again. I think he was a bit shocked and his legs were affected and he didn't.'

Billy Bland remembered it well. 'The reason I fell was because I was knackered. It happened to me Ben after Ben, actually. The year I won [1978], I didn't expect to win, so didn't go out as competitively. I obviously ran a lot more sensibly, got to the top maybe two minutes down on Mike Short, and won it by two minutes if I remember rightly. I became a better runner after that and never ran as fast again! I got sick of going there. My legs used to go to nothing because I had a year's training, on better ground than any of them, but I was too competitive on the way up. If I had given Kenny three minutes at the top there I believe I could have caught him still. But I was trying to race him up there, and I shouldn't have been. I should have saved my legs for coming down. The same happened when Colin Donnelly won it in 1979.'

Showing me the scars on his elbow, Billy Bland concluded, 'I ended up in hospital having bits of stones taken out of the wound, before having it stitched. I missed the presentation, so I never got to meet Kenneth McKellar, not that I was bothered! I got up and finished 2nd, but I was dripping blood.'

Stuart was unusual in the fact that he was one of the few who could win the Ben Nevis race at their first attempt. He recalls that he, 'went with no expectations really. I had never been over the whole course. The day before I went up to the Red Burn and had a look around. I had a general idea where I was going to come back from.'

Malcolm Patterson felt quite detached from the mighty battle up front on this occasion, as he finished in 12th place. 'You've got to remember this was my first time up the Ben – I'd stood at the bottom of the mountain on at least two occasions as a child, crying because my mother wouldn't let me go up because of bad weather, so I still held it in awe. I think the build up to the race had used up all my nervous energy and the race itself rather overwhelmed me. After my strong climbs at Ben Lomond and Skiddaw I was shocked and appalled when I began to struggle halfway up the climb. I just hadn't factored in that extra 20 minutes of climbing time. After that, the descent was a nightmare! It was a humbling experience.'

Kenny Stuart's navigational skills were challenged the next weekend when he could only achieve an 11th place finish in the Vaux Mountain Trial – a 17-mile orienteering style event, won in rough conditions by Billy Bland. 'I had no idea where I was going or anything. It was held at the west side of Thirlmere. It was a novelty for me. I had read about the Vaux and thought I would enter that. You went off at intervals and if you got behind a slower runner and didn't know where you were going it could cost you. It was misty and I had no chance, I was out for about five hours.'

At this time the long-standing Langdale fell race was going through a difficult time, and a scathing unattributed report appeared in the December 1982 *Fellrunner*, listing the organisers' faults. This year a revised course just to Scafell Pike and back, via Mickleden, Rossett Ghyll and Esk Hause, was used and provided another tough win for Stuart. Kenny commented, 'The organiser hadn't got things in place, not enough marshals and it wasn't good. This year it went to the top of Scafell and back, up Rossett Ghyll. I won it but it was quite a struggle. I went into the race feeling tired, and it was a Billy Bland kind of race. I couldn't get away to get a lead at the top and was still with him at Rossett Ghyll. I got nearly to the bottom and my legs were getting tired and I clipped a stone and went over. I was lying on these rocks and a hiker picked me up. I went back to him and nearly caught him and did the same blooming thing again and took a chunk out of my hip. I hung on and hung on, then on the mile and half run-in I took him, quite easily. I felt good at the end and then had to sit down as I started feeling funny, with delayed shock.'

As evidence of their respective capabilities over different race distances and course types, Billy Bland just noted that, 'Kenny never ran the full Langdale race, even though he won the shortened one.'

A couple of weeks passed and John Wild came back after injury for Thieveley Pike, as he had only bagged two 'Short' races so far and needed to score at this and/or Blisco later on. It turned out that he had lost some fitness and probably shouldn't have even been running, but he still managed a gallant 6th place. Ahead of him Kenny Stuart was looking imperious on this warm September day, being the only one able to run every step of this tough little course (a legacy of his professional days on such courses). He beat in-form Hugh Symonds by 32 seconds in a new course record, showing the way home to some class fell runners. I wondered why John ran when he could have relied on Blisco (guessing he wanted four scoring 'Shorts'). 'I needed the race fitness and to test the ankle without consequences,' he replied.

Four seconds ahead of Wild was Malcolm Patterson, who claims he doesn't remember much about this race, despite it being the only occasion he beat John Wild. 'I knew he was coming back from his ankle operation, so beating him didn't really mean much. I was quite pleased with my race, but somewhat overawed to be so well beaten by Kenny (I was over a minute behind), not to mention Hugh and the Andys (Darby & Taylor). As an aside, I do remember us runners getting frustrated on the start line at having to wait until the last poor sheepdog penned his sheep – the shepherd was none too pleased with us for whistling our encouragement.'

On 2 October Kenny Stuart had a run out in a non-championship race as part of his continuing education on different courses, this one being the inaugural Tour of Pendle, a test over 17 miles with 4200 feet of ascent. He won by more than two and a half minutes from Dave Cartridge. Billy Bland was third, ahead of young Sean Livesey and Jeff Norman. Stuart remembers that his wife Pauline, 'also ran and won. It was the same thing again, I didn't have a clue, I just wanted to explore. The longest professional race was about 50 minutes running time, the Helvellyn race, which is no longer run.'

The next championship race was at Butter Crags on 10 October, being the fourth amateur race over the historic Grasmere Guides Race course. The course was muddy in some parts, but this didn't stop Kenny Stuart leading all the way, winning in 12-55. For discussion on the merits of times on the Guides versus the amateur courses see 'It's a hill, get over it' (from Sandstone Press, 2013), although it is worth noting that Stuart beat second placed Bob Whitfield by 33 seconds on a mile and a half race. Third was Hugh Symonds, followed by Billy Bland, and John Wild in 5th, still getting back his fitness after his short break. 'It was on a really bad day, with the mist down. Pete Bland was on the summit blowing a rescue whistle to make sure people found it', Kenny recalls.

For Hugh Symonds this was his last championship race of that season. He had also gone to the States earlier that year and run the Pikes Peak (on 22 August). 'I came second in 3 hours 50 minutes 23 seconds to an American Indian called Al Waquie. I missed a lot of championships races that year due to being away a lot.' Despite this Symonds did manage fourth place in the British championships that year.

Malcolm Patterson did this iconic race just the once. To him, 'it is a lot like Burnsall, and I should have enjoyed it for the same reasons, but I had a bad climb and by halfway to the top my race was effectively over. I was in awe of Kenny that day, and spent the next few months trying to work out what he had that I hadn't. I remember over-simplifying the gap by concluding that it was because he could descend so much better than me, whereas in fact there were many other reasons why he was so much better.'

A week later John Wild went to defend his Three Towers fell race title, enjoying a 20-mile 'training run'. Although there were a good few fell runners in the field, it was two runners more noted for their cross country exploits who took first and second places. Three-time National Cross Country championship winner Dave Lewis [*1985, 1989, and 1994*] beat another cross country exponent, Bob Treadwell, by exactly one minute. Wild was almost another minute down, in 3rd place. John sums it up, 'I loved the Three Towers, especially with my connection to Rivington Pike. It was a great day, finishing at the cricket club for pie and peas and it was just like tough cross country.' Jack Maitland was down in 11th place, but he was just warming up for a win in the Elite class at the Karrimor Mountain Marathon on Dartmoor the next weekend, with John Baston.

It is a challenging point-to-point race, which Malcolm Patterson enjoyed. 'Not to mention the pie and peas, and I enjoyed racing on the fells against some big names like Lewis and Treadwell. I was bitterly disappointed with my result though. My excuse was a navigational error which took me into deepest darkest Darwen, but really I didn't have the speed endurance to stand a chance against those guys on that course.'

The fifteenth and final race in the 1982 championships was

Plate 1. John Wild winning the Derby Youths cross country championships in 1967

Plate 2. Kenny and Duncan Stuart at the 1971 Threlkeld Sports

Plate 3. John Wild steeplechasing at the 1973 RAF Command championships

Plate 4. John Wild winning the 1974 Inter-Counties cross country
championships in Derby

Plate 5. John Wild at the 1978 Commonwealth Games at Edmonton, Canada

Plate 6. Kenny Stuart leading at the 1980 Grasmere Guides Race

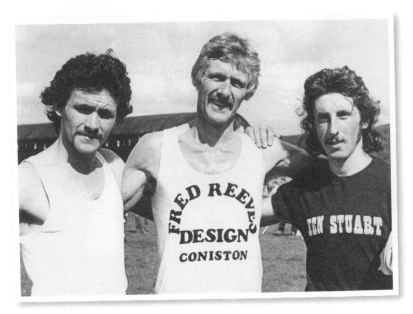

Plate 7. After the 1980 Benson Knott fell race
(l to r Graham Moffat, Fred Reeves, Kenny Stuart)

Plate 8. John Wild winning for England the 1980 Elgoibar International
cross country, Spain

Plate 9. John Wild winning the 1980 Inter-counties championships at Derby

Plate 10. John Wild holding the trophies after winning the
1982 Three Peaks race

Plate 11. Billy Bland and John Wild after the 1982 Wasdale fell race

Plate 12. John Wild shows his foot problems after the 1982 Turnslack fell race

Plate 13. Kenny Stuart leading at the 1983 Blisco Dash

22	30 2nd Stuart.	11	11
23	M Steady / Steady	4 13	17 28
24	T Steady 3x R) 5~30, 5.17, 5.2. 4x Up & Down Canal 2.52, 2.49, 2.43, 2.32 (5)	4 6 5	15 43
25	W Steady / Steady / Steady	4 6 9	19 62
26	Th Steady / Steady	9	18 80
27	F Steady 6 x R 2.53, 2.52, 2.52, 2.50, 2.50, 2.43. 3x Up & Down Canal (5) 2.42, 3.10(6) 2.51	4 7 5	16 96
28	S Steady	15	15 111
29	Su Steady (start diet)	18	13 18
30	M Steady / Steady	4 9	13 31
31	T Steady / Steady	4 10	14 45
1	W Steady / Steady	4 10	14 59
2	Th Steady / Steady	4 8	12 71
3	F Steady / Steady	4 3	7 78
4	S Race. watch 1000m Peaks 1st - Kenny 2nd Record - 3 hr - 26.33.		22 22 100

Plate 14. Two weeks of John Wild's training diary (May 1983)

Plate 15. Kenny Stuart leading John Wild at the 1983 Fairfield fell race

Plate 16. John and Kenny ascending Snowdon towards the end of the
1983 Welsh 1000s fell race

Plate 17. Hugh Symonds leads the 1985 Three Peaks race

Plate 18. John and Kenny sharing a drink with Jon Broxap after the
1983 Kinniside fell race

Plate 19. John Wild leading at the 1983 Burnsall Classic fell race,
with Kenny Stuart in third

Plate 20. Jack
Maitland at the 1983
Ben Nevis race

Plate 21. Kenny Stuart following Mike Bishop in heavy snow at the 1984 Blackstone Edge fell race

Plate 22. Pauline Stuart on her way to winning the 1984 Ben Nevis race

Plate 23. International Mountain Race at San Giovanni,
Italy, in 1984 (l to r Kenny, Jon Broxap, John, Shaun Livesey)

Plate 24. Kenny Stuart in second on a tough ascent in the 1985 Ennerdale race

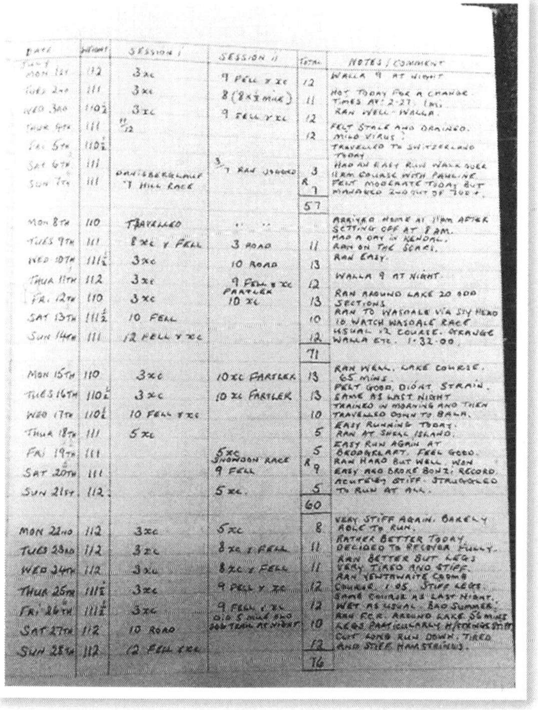

DATE	WEIGHT	SESSION I	SESSION II	TOTAL	NOTES / COMMENT
JULY MON 1ST	112	3 xc	9 FELL + xc	12	WALLA 9 AT NIGHT
TUES 2ND	111	3 xc	8 (8 x ½ mile)	11	HOT TODAY FOR A CHANGE. TIMES AT: 2-27 (av)
WED 3RD	110½	3 xc	9 FELL + xc	12	RAN WELL - WALLA.
THUR 4TH	111	11/12		12	FELT STALE AND DRAINED. MILD VIRUS?
FRI 5TH	110½				TRAVELLED TO SWITZERLAND TODAY
SAT 6TH	111		3/7 RAN JOGGED	3	HAD AN EASY RUN WALK OVER 11KM COURSE WITH PAULINE
SUN 7TH	111	DANISBERGALUF 7 HILL RACE		R 7	FELT MODERATE TODAY BUT MANAGED 2ND OUT OF 700+.
				57	
MON 8TH	110	TRAVELLED	" "		ARRIVED HOME AT 11PM AFTER SETTING OFF AT 8 AM.
TUES 9TH	111	8 xc + FELL	3 ROAD	11	HAD A DAY IN KENDAL. RAN ON THE SCARS.
WED 10TH	111½	3 xc	10 ROAD	13	RAN EASY.
THUR 11TH	112	3 xc	9 FELL + xc	12	WALLA 9 AT NIGHT.
FRI 12TH	110	3 xc	FARTLEK 10 xc	13	RAN AROUND LAKE 20 400 SECTIONS
SAT 13TH	111½	10 FELL		10	RAN TO WASDALE VIA STY HEAD TO WATCH WASDALE RACE
SUN 14TH	111	12 FELL + xc		12	USUAL 12 COURSE. GRANGE WALLA ETC. 1-32-00.
				71	
MON 15TH	110	3 xc	10 xc FARTLEK	13	RAN WELL. LAKE COURSE. 65 MINS.
TUES 16TH	110½	3 xc	10 xc FARTLEK	13	FELT GOOD, DIDN'T STRAIN. SAME AS LAST NIGHT
WED 17TH	110½	10 FELL + xc		10	TRAINED IN MORNING AND THEN TRAVELLED DOWN TO BALA.
THUR 18TH	111	5 xc		5	EASY RUNNING TODAY. RAN AT SHELL ISLAND.
FRI 19TH	111		5 xc	5	EASY RUN AGAIN AT BROADHELART. FEEL GOOD.
SAT 20TH	111		SNOWDON RACE 9 FELL	R 9	RAN HARD BUT WELL. WON EASY AND BROKE BOTZ: RECORD.
SUN 21ST	112		5 xc.	5	ACUTELY STIFF. STRUGGLED TO RUN AT ALL.
				60	
MON 22ND	112	3 xc	5 xc	8	VERY STIFF AGAIN. BARELY ABLE TO RUN.
TUES 23RD	112	3 xc	8 xc + FELL	11	RATHER BETTER TODAY. DECIDED TO RECOVER FULLY.
WED 24TH	112	3 xc	8 xc + FELL	11	RAN BETTER BUT LEGS VERY TIRED AND STIFF.
THUR 25TH	111½	3 xc	9 FELL + xc	12	RAN YEWTHWAITE COMB COURSE 1 05. STIFF LEGS.
FRI 26TH	111½	3 xc	9 FELL + xc	12	SAME COURSE AS LAST NIGHT. WET AS USUAL. BAD SUMMER.
SAT 27TH	112	10 ROAD	DID 5 MILE ALSO 300 TEAM AT NIGHT	10	RAN F.C.R. AROUND LAKE 56 MINS LEGS PARTICULARLY H/STRINGS STIFF
SUN 28TH	112	12 FELL + xc		12	CUT LONG RUN DOWN. TIRED AND STIFF HAMSTRINGS.
				76	

Plate 25. A page from Kenny Stuart's training diary (July 1985)

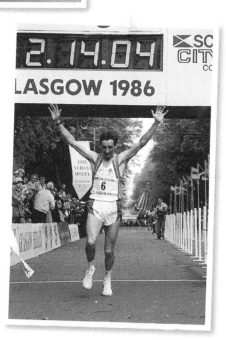

Plate 26. Kenny Stuart winning the 1986 Glasgow Marathon

Plate 27. John Wild working on a 16 Sqn Tornado at Nellis AFB near Las Vegas in 1987

Plate 28. Anne Wild winning the 1989 RAF Germany cross country championships

Plate 29. Rosie Stuart on top of the podium at the 2005 Black Forest Games

Plate 30. Emma Stuart, selected for the 2005 World Mountain Running championships in Wellington, New Zealand

Plate 31. John Wild
training his son Jack for
the 2015 Stafford half
marathon

Plate 32. Kenny Stuart signs an autograph at Joss Naylor's
80th birthday celebration in 2016

the Blisco Dash, way down in mid-November. The situation before this race was that if Bob Whitfield won Blisco and Wild came third or lower then Whitfield would win the championships. This would hardly have been just, as Whitfield hadn't won a race all year, although he had come second on five occasions, and was only that close because Wild's nightmare 20th place at Wasdale counted for him once he had dropped out of Borrowdale. Both John Wild and Kenny Stuart were running this race for the first time. This showed when Wild led Stuart off the Blisco summit on the wrong line. The more experienced Whitfield took a better line, leaping into a lead as he charged down towards Blea Tarn. On the switchbacks on the Blea Tarn road Stuart and Wild both overtook him though. Stuart just outran Wild by 15 seconds, with Whitfield just 6 seconds behind Wild, and Malcolm Patterson next home. The race was memorable for Patterson because of what happened beforehand. Travelling up the night before in a friend's car, it broke down. Whilst his friend decided to take the car back home, Patterson spent the night in a service station and then hitched up to Langdale at dawn. 'So, I was a little the worse for wear and remember catching another hour's sleep outside the Dungeon Ghyll. I guess this took the weight of expectation off me, so I wasn't so nervous and maybe did better as a result. I was very pleased with my result, though was far enough off the pace not to see anything of the first real Wild versus Stuart battle.'

All of the first three finishers were inside Billy Bland's course record from 1981, with Stuart's new record being 36-54. John recalls, 'I was in agony the whole race as I'd twisted my ankle on a Blisco reccie the week beforehand (not the op ankle fortunately). I was worried I wouldn't even make the start.' On setting the Blisco record, Kenny had this to say, 'There was a little bit at the top where you can put a bit of effort in, but you can come off wrong. John Wild would probably have beaten me that day if he hadn't had trouble. Winning a series of late season races gave me confidence for the 1983 season.'

By Billy Bland running in to 6th place, it was enough to seal 3rd overall in the championships for him, ahead of Hugh Symonds, who was two places behind him in the Blisco race (in 8th, one behind Jack Maitland). Symonds was pretty harsh on himself in his diary, recording that there was, 'no determination from the start. Need to go from gun in short races. Oxygen debt inevitable, makes no difference. Tired on the hill. Better to get there early!'

Bland recalls that he was good at the downhill in this race. Referring to Wild and Stuart going off line, he comments that, 'the descent off there has also caught ever so many people out in the Langdale race. I could never, ever, see how they couldn't see their way there, it was simple to me. Mind, you only need one to go off in mist for them all to. But that race also has too much road in it for me.'

Wild's 29 points in second place gave him the overall title by five points, from Bob Whitfield. This was a pretty remarkable result after eight months and fifteen races, particularly as he couldn't run for one month of it. Wild acknowledges that he lost some momentum to Bob Whitfield because of the operation. However, the fact that all the 'Longs' were run by August, and that the last three championship races were all 'Shorts' may have helped Wild's cause somewhat, as he came back from the operation with limited long distance training completed. After coming second to John Wild in his first race since reinstatement at Burnsall, Kenny Stuart had proceeded to win the four remaining championship races. He managed to finish in 12th place in the championships off just these five results. Although this didn't include any 'Longs', which were all run by then, it did give a real glimpse of what he might do in the championship the next year, especially as he won the longish non-scoring Tour of Pendle as well.

In 1982 the championship for professional fell runners was sponsored by Skipton Building Society and administered by Northern Sports Promoters. The programme for their Presentation Dinner and Dance (at Melling Hall, in Lancashire) chose to use its review of the year (which is extracted in part here) to comment on Kenny's change of code, and get a few digs in as well:

The opening event at Rusland on May Day ... struck a note of 'Carry on Kenny' - as the defending Kenny Stuart of Threlkeld, Keswick, launched into the new season just as he had concluded the last one, in devastating form. Stuart won handily from last year's championship third placer – and hopefully improving – Graham Moffat of Sedbergh.

As a pipe opener, Stuart had looked the part when winning a close-season cross country race at Oxton in the Scottish Borders, and, also suggested his adaptability to longer distances, by breaking the record – when an unofficial 'guest' – in the arduous twenty-two mile 'Buttermere Round' road race, which is normally an athletic club member exercise.

This event preceded Rusland, and a week after the May Day meeting, Kenny was flanked by athletic club members again in another 'twenty-plus' mile event, this time over the Lakeland mountains at Duddon Valley. Advisable familiarity with orienteering intricacies was the loophole for detaching this particular event from AAA dictatorship and one which enabled Kenny to officially contest a mountain marathon.

A modest map and compass user, but a more than accomplished fell runner, he made good use of the latter attribute to employ the proverbial fox and hounds tactic, before implementing his victory kill, in the final sprint for home, some two and three quarters hours later.

Proven then at long runs besides the traditional 'straight up and down' variety, Kenny was finally caught in the political cross-fire which currently shams (and shames) our 'sport', and the resultant deprivation for him, was to spend the next three and a half months at the heart of what may well have been his best ever form-displaying summer ... in quarantine.

So much then for the muddled intent of the AAA! ... the

'Amateur Apartheid Association' as one well-meaning wag aptly described them . . .

Kenny Stuart, who was finally allowed out of the 'sin-bin', and after picking up the threads, won the Blue Riband of AAA competition the Ben Nevis Race and also broke the record in the 'amateurs' concluding championship race – the 'Blisco Dash' at Langdale, where he finished ahead of that code's overall champion, John Wild.

Ironically, Kenny also won the AAA governed race over the Grasmere Guides race course, which was originated 'to show the guides up for what they are worth'.

Kenny Stuart finished the year by winning the short Wansfell race on 27 December, expressing delight at the traditionally steep up-and-down course, much like the old pro races. He reflected that he had, 'recorded eight race wins and won my first Ben Nevis after a tough downhill tussle with Billy Bland. Billy gave me a lot of help in later races with suggestions for route choices, etc. and most of the top fell runners of the '80s I found to be both genuine and friendly.'

I wondered if Billy Bland might have felt that in offering others help he was setting up others to beat him. Bland pointed out, 'that finding your way round is part of it. I wasn't bothered, I was pleased to see others racing. If they could beat us, then they were better than you. That is how I saw it. If I wasn't the best then I wouldn't be bothered about not winning.'

John Wild had won the championship again and Kenny Stuart was establishing himself as a serious rival. The stage was set for them to go up against each other for a full season on the fells in 1983.

PART FOUR

Head to head

CHAPTER 12

Too frightened to go on

Everything that had happened up to then, including Kenny Stuart winning the pro championships three times and John Wild the amateur championships twice, was just a prelude to an amazing 1983 season. Both athletes were at the peak of their powers and went hammer and tongs at each other over a full, and demanding, fell season. There was great interest in whether John Wild could sustain his form of the last two years, and also whether Kenny Stuart could handle the long races that were an integral part of the championship season. It turned out that they both could, and the scene was set for an epic encounter between the two of them.

The real fell running action for the season commenced on 10 April, with the first race that was on the championship roster. That year the scoring was again based on fifteen races that were categorised as five 'Long', five 'Medium' and five 'Short', with athletes choosing their best ten events, with three 'Long', three 'Medium', three 'Short' and one other of their choice. (The particulars of each race are shown in a subhead just before the discussion of each one in the four chapters covering 1983.)

It was guaranteed to be a tough season, as these fifteen races came in just 24 weeks, with nine of them in consecutive weeks. You have only to look at the scoring for the current (2016) season to see how the athletes were being pushed to their limits in these championships. Now there are just four nominated races, one each in the 'Short' and 'Long' categories and two 'Medium'. Runners must complete three races, so can even 'duck' the long or the short if they so choose, if that distance isn't their forte. Yet, as we will see, in that 1983 season John Wild and Kenny Stuart set six course records between them in the fifteen championship races that year.

John and Kenny had very different approaches to the 1983 fell championship season. John carried on with his cross country racing in the early part of the year. In early February he came 3rd in the RAF cross country championships (behind Steve Jones and Roger Hackney), then 7th at a very muddy Inter-Services cross country on 28 February (where Jones and Hackney were first and second again), before securing 15th place in the English National cross country championships on 5 March at Stopsley (Luton). This was Wild's best result at the National, and coincidentally it was one of the few occasions where I will have been in the same race as him. I certainly won't have troubled him, being as I was somewhat further back in the field. I do see from my training diary that it may have been a short course, as I commented that there was, 'some doubt about the distance being 9 miles!'

Considering that he won the Inter-Counties title twice, it is surprising that Wild didn't get any higher than 15th place in his National Cross country appearances. When asked, he could only respond, 'I can't for the life of me understand why I never really ran well in the National. I seemed to have a block. Whether or not, I have often thought, we were racing cross country from October, and come March maybe I got a bit stale.'

Meanwhile, Kenny Stuart chose to do three fell races, just getting himself focussed. Two were in February and one in March. First, on 6 February at Benson Knott, Kenny beat Hugh Symonds by 20 seconds, then he nipped up to Scotland to win the Carnethy 5 on 19 February (from Hugh Symonds again). Then on 20 March Stuart won the low-key Black Combe race from his brother Duncan, in a new course record – knocking 98 seconds off the time that Jon Broxap had set the previous year. Kenny felt he needed races because he, 'hadn't raced during that winter, and Carnethy was quite a big race in those days. I just went up and gave myself a blow-out and to see what was going on. Black Combe was the same.'

Kenny adds that, 'most of the top fell runners of the 1980s I found to be both genuine and friendly. When the 1983 season started I came out very well conditioned, but found John Wild a tough opponent and we often had to run ourselves legless to record wins, but despite these awesome battles we were always the best of friends when the competition was over.' That last sentence encapsulates the attitude of these two fine athletes, who certainly gave not an inch in races, but enjoyed a marvellous friendship outside of racing.

In their individual ways John and Kenny had proved their early season fitness. John was confident of having a good season, having also trained really well over the winter. In his own words, he was 'looking forward to some good competition as I'd had it fairly easy for the last two seasons'. Whilst he was waiting for his reinstatement Kenny had been adding more training over longer distances. Most of his winter sessions at that time were done on the roads because he was working from 8am to 5pm, so couldn't get on the fells. He reckoned he didn't need too many steep fell sessions as he felt speed was more important. Kenny had also seen John race a few times, and he had been impressed. 'At Burnsall in 1982 he'd well beaten me and I knew that at that time I couldn't touch him.' John knew Kenny was going to be challenging him this year. He had the evidence from the Burnsall race in 1982, when Kenny had finished second to him, and the subsequent four 1982 championship races in which Stuart was unbeaten.

How did others feel the season might play out? Predictably, Billy Bland had a view. 'I knew from the year before that they [*Wild and Stuart*] could beat me quite easily, so I knew they were going to do it again. In my view they were not proper fellsmen, so if one of those two were to win the championship, then it would come down to maybe what the weather did on the long 'uns that were counters. On flagged courses, with top and back again, then they were very similar and unbeatable. But in mist anything can happen.' As if to echo Bland's thoughts, the championship season was to take a spectacular twist at its first event.

10 April: Kentmere, Medium, 12.3 miles, 3300 feet (of ascent)

The Kentmere race was held in appalling conditions, with gale force winds and snow that produced a whiteout on the tops. There were 375 starters, of whom a mere 187 completed the race. Kenny Stuart had a clear lead at the first checkpoint, but was inadequately dressed for the weather and decided to retire, as he recognised that he was losing heat rapidly. 'I dropped out of this race high up in a blizzard. The thing was I'd set off without much clothing and basically I was too frightened to go on. I was losing more heat than I could keep. I had a comfortable lead by the first checkpoint and given the chance feel I could have won, as I felt more or less in control. I knew most of the course at Kentmere because I had a look over it, up Nan Bield and through the Pass and round. I misjudged it completely to be honest. I had a windproof top on, and my chest had got so tight I wasn't breathing properly, so I thought no thanks. I was leading, with quite a good lead, so turned back and saw the next blokes coming through. I thought well they are going to go on and win it, but many of them turned back as well.'

The blizzard conditions may have freaked Kenny out, and many others, but half the field soldiered on to complete the course. The winners were Jon Broxap and Sean Livesey, who came in together, some six and a half minutes ahead of the next finisher, but 18 minutes slower than the winning time the year before. Hugh Symonds was one of those who retired because of the appalling conditions, and even now insists that, 'it is wise to drop out if it is that bad.'

Malcolm Patterson was deeply affected by this event. He recalls that he, 'was massively discouraged by the experience of the Kentmere race – ironically my first major race against Kenny – where I fell victim to the cold conditions and retired, along with Kenny and a good percentage of the field. It left a mental scar! I still thought I could be an orienteer at the highest level, so I concentrated on that for much of the 1983 season.'

No-one got any sympathy from Bill Smith though, as he commented in *Stud marks on the summits*, 'Competitors were warned of the conditions prior to the start, so there could be no excuse for those who had to turn back due to being inadequately dressed, while among other retirements were no doubt runners with solely athletic club backgrounds to whom such conditions were both strange and fearsome.'

John Wild wasn't even able to be there, as after the National cross country championships he had broken a bone in his foot – at work, helping organise a *Superstars* competition. He then wasn't able to train for six weeks, the worst injury he had ever had. He says he, 'cheered up a bit when I heard what happened at Kentmere!' The injury meant that John missed not just Kentmere, but also Blisco and the Three Peaks. John can laugh now, saying, 'that was a real ball-ache. I missed the first three races of the championships.' From then on he was always chasing Kenny in the championship, as he had to make sure he covered his ten events. Having missed the first three, he had only two to spare.

He described the slightly bizarre circumstances of how the injury happened. 'We had a *Superstars* competition at work. I had donated a trophy I won in Spain for cross country, so I agreed to be part of the organising team. I was goalie in the football shootout where the guy dribbles towards you and shoots. I dived one way and the ball hit my foot and broke a bone, one of the metatarsals. It was the most painful thing. I had to hobble home without a shoe on. I was going on a solid steel bike to try to keep fit. I missed the first three races. Kentmere has always been one of my favourite races, but I don't know how I would have fared as it was that bad.'

17 April: Blisco Dash, Short, 5 miles, 2133 feet

Just one week later Kenny won the Blisco Dash, from Bob Whitfield and Jon Broxap, with Wild obviously absent with his injury. The previous year Kenny Stuart had beaten John Wild at this race, although he was fortunate as Wild went slightly astray with his navigation. This time Stuart had a good lead by the summit and came down fast, as he was aware of Whitfield's descending ability. 'Bob actually passed me coming down the rough stuff, in the ghyll. I passed him near the bottom of the ghyll and went away on the road. He was a good descender was Bob.'

Coming in 6th at Blisco was an interesting runner, Dave Hall. Hall, who is now in his sixties, was born and lived in Hertfordshire, running for Verlea AC. He took up running at school and used to win races, which he enjoyed. He also joined the Scouts while at school, who were very active in hillwalking and they used to go up to the Lakes and Snowdonia a lot. I met him after a fell running friend from my athletic club bumped into him on a long bike ride and got talking about mutual interests, and she mentioned this writing project.

I arranged to meet Dave (in the tea bar at Van Hage's garden centre, near Amwell in Herts), and he explained that he had, 'done the odd fell race in the 1970s, and in 1982 decided to get a bit more serious on the fells.' The result was him gaining 78th place in the British Fell championships in that year.

'I started off on the fells and was still running for my club down here (Verlea AC), but in the end I joined Kendal AC as I was racing on the fells so much. At one point I plastered Hugh Symonds' place and lived there for a while.' At Wansfell at the end of 1982 Hugh Symonds had approached Hall, and asked if he wanted to join Kendal. 'I said maybe. Dark Peak, Horwich and Cumberland Fell Runners had all shown an interest by then. Hugh sold it to me really, and I definitely wanted to join a Lakeland club. At the time Keswick AC had a 'policy' that meant they liked you to live in the Keswick catchment area, so were out of the frame for me.'

In 1983 Hall was still mostly living down south, but working up in the Lakes a lot, as a plasterer. 'I used to do quite a lot with Billy Bland and Chris Bland. Chris was a slater and Billy a drystone-waller. We would often work on hotels up there, as they often liked to employ locals.' Billy Bland confirmed that he and Chris Bland, 'built the odd house, as well as extensions and stuff.' He says he never had to advertise in his life, and always had plenty of work to do.

Dave Hall reckons now that the Blisco race was quite probably his best fell racing achievement. 'That was the closest I ever got to Billy Bland [who was 5th, five seconds ahead]. I was catching him all the way down the road, towards the finish by the Old Dungeon Ghyll. Another 100 yards and I would have got him! Also I was with him at Coniston two years later and he hurdled the cattle grid and I had to step on it and he got away.'

24 April: Three Peaks, Long, 23.2 miles, 5276 feet

The third race in the championships, and the third weekend in a row that championship races were held, was the Three Peaks race, taking in Pen y Ghent, Whernside and Ingleborough. It was run at the end of one of the wettest April months on record, and the times were affected accordingly. Kenny Stuart moved into the lead going up the second peak (Whernside), stretching out to win by nearly four and a half minutes, proving he could now win the long races too. Hugh Symonds came in second, ahead of 20 year old Sean Livesey, who had won the shorter Junior race up Pen y Ghent the year before. Kenny commented, 'I knew I could get round as I'd looked over part of the course. Still, I didn't want to go it alone and went out with Hugh Symonds. The going was heavy and I was bothered with cramp and a bit scared I'd have to ease up. I'd have liked a better time but they told me after it was the heaviest going for years and the course was a mile longer, but then I wouldn't know as it was my first time there!'

Kenny also offered the thought that it was not a surprise to win the race. I challenged him to justify that statement, as it was his first, and only, go at the Three Peaks. He calmly replied, 'it was really wet, it was terrible. I was very fit at that time and it wasn't a surprise. I had started doing two-hour training runs on the fells on a Sunday ready for the 1983 season. It was more of a cross country style race than a traditional Lakes fell race. I was slightly worried about getting cramp, which I did get on Ingleborough, but I got through that. It was about 2 hours 50 minutes of running because of the wet.'

From his position in 9th Malcolm Patterson concluded that Kenny was in a class of his own that day. Patterson remembers it as another disappointing race for him. 'I had heard so much about this race, and dreamed of doing it long before I took up fell running. I lost touch with the leaders before even reaching Ribblehead. I had not got enough speed endurance. It was too much of the "cross-country style" and too many flat bits in between the hill climbs!'

7 May: Ben Lomond, Medium, 9 miles, 3192 feet

Two weeks later and it was up to Ben Lomond, with Kenny and John both toeing the line. John potentially had a problem looming as his championship chances had been jeopardised by missing the first three of the fifteen championship races. He needed to complete ten of the last twelve races to be in with a chance of winning the title for a third straight time.

Kenny used his climbing skill to take it out on the ascent, with John chasing hard to stop a gap opening. They changed places several times on a swift descent, but John prevailed. He collapsed after finishing, having knocked one second off the course record. That new record came from two athletes pushing themselves to the limit to beat each other. On this point John thought that 'it was a cracking race - good competition and good for the sport.' Knowing of his injury, Kenny hadn't expected him to even be there, and commented after the race that he, 'hadn't seen the course but it is marked and straightforward. It was a gruelling race. When John gets yards on you, that's that.' They showed their social side too, Kenny agreeing the weekend to be, 'good race wise and drink wise.'

Looking back, Kenny remembers, 'just having a damned

hard race with John Wild. He had come back from injury and I thought I might have a chance and he was running hammer and tongs all the way. I tried to break him on the way up and he wasn't gonna have it. There was a good bash after in the Rowardennan Hotel. The usual carry on, yeh.'

Jack Maitland confirmed that there was a certain amount of post-race drinking at the time amongst the athletes. 'The culture around fell racing at the time was to have a few beers. I was part of that too. There were very few people who didn't drink a bit.' He also reflected on his own performance, having checked back in his own training diary. 'I thought I had done well. I have written "fantastic run plus result. One bad patch on the climb, 4th at top. One of my better descents. Shows it can be done." I also underlined – *drink water beforehand*.' Maitland had run 107 km that week, so had tapered a bit.

John had broken the Ben Lomond course record for the third year in a row. That is pretty remarkable given that it was very wet and slippery underfoot, and that it was his first race after the injury that had kept him from training for weeks. He notes, 'looking back in my diary now I was quite surprised to win this. I hadn't had much of a build-up.' That remark requires a little unpacking though, as John is being a bit coy about his getting back into training after injury.

The injury happened in a *Superstars* competition and has already been described in detail. It was very painful and John couldn't walk properly, let alone run. 'I think I missed over three weeks without being able to run,' he says. 'However, I tried to keep aerobically fit by going out at lunchtimes on an old RAF bike. It must have done some good! I missed out on some races although the weather did me a favour at Kentmere, with Kenny dropping out. It would have been a hard job to come back to him if he'd recorded a 'Long' and 'Medium' win before I'd even started.'

John Wild admits that he never consistently recorded his workouts in training diaries, and the ones he had written he thought he had lost. But towards the end of our discussions he turned up to meet me with a loose leaf set of diary pages. He chuckled, saying that he found these in his storage - which is a 'temporary' steel container that has been in their garden for ten years. Part of the folder was a diary which he started again when his training resumed after the 1983 injury issue. Unfortunately it only started two weeks before the Ben Lomond race, so doesn't show the full build-up. However, these pages do show how well he had got back into things. In the first of these weeks he did 77 miles, with six double session days. The week of the actual race he did 80 miles in total, including one set of six 1000m reps in times that started at 2-52 and finished on 2-47. John looked at this and explained that, 'training was designed to be consistent throughout reps, but gradually getting faster reps over time. But I am surprised to find 100 mile weeks in my diary in fell running days!'

He also expanded on his training philosophy, which was illustrated by some pages from March to July 1981, when he was just coming on to the fells seriously. 'This training was a carry-over from cross country training, which I adjusted for the fells later. I was often racing and then doing effort sessions the next day. It was full on training, no days off, multiple double days in each week, sometimes even three-session days.'

After going through these diary pages with me, John added that he, 'got a bit emotional when I found these diaries, and it rekindled a lot of memories, all the effort I put in. I have really enjoyed our meetings too, going over this fabulous time.'

Wild had always liked the Ben Lomond race. 'This has always been a good weekend for me with good camping, good racing and a good beer up,' he added. In the race this time, 'Kenny pulled away going up but I got up level at the turn-round. We ran about two miles together before I managed a break with Kenny sort of half hanging on.'

John relived that race with me and then couldn't resist a risqué story about an occurrence after the race. 'How the hell I managed to beat him I do not know. I had hardly done any training for a month. It was good fun that weekend,' he laughs.

'We stayed in a tent and I think Kenny and his brother Duncan were staying in the hotel. Duncan got fed up with these Scottish girls not dancing with him. So he put a sausage in his flies, then said, "do you wanna dance, no, well what do think of this then". The prize I got that year was a stereo system and my mum had that in her house.'

John added: 'Kenny and I were head to head, when I got over the injury. Ben Lomond absolutely shattered me. I ran below my best that day. My experience as an athlete helped me beat him there, not fitness. I was a better descender than him, but he could go uphill better than me. 'Medium' length races suited me – this one, Fairfield and Kentmere for instance.'

Kenny did not regard himself as an outstanding descender on rough ground, although he felt he could hold his own against anyone on steep grass slopes. He believes that the very best descenders (Billy Bland, Ian Holmes) are born with naturally quick reflexes, agility and confidence. Kenny does believe, however, that this particular skill can be improved through experience gained descending in races and on long easy runs over rough ground. He feels that the most significant factor is probably confidence, and this can grow with experience and practice.

John Wild believed he was a good descender and seemed to have an eye for the ground, never falling. At one point he smiled as we talked about this, 'even Kenny Stuart was quoted as saying I took risks at Burnsall that he wouldn't take!'

Julian Goater, who often ran with John Wild in the RAF matches, made a telling statement in his own running book (*The art of running faster*). 'Try running down a hill and you'll soon realise you need even more strength in your quads than you do to run uphill. One of my RAF team-mates, John Wild, turned to fell running and, after a year or two during which he became British champion, his quads developed so much he needed a complete new set of trousers.'

Alan Warner obviously knew John Wild's abilities well, having both coached and team managed him. 'Descending skills, well that was John. At cross country he was merciless. He would hang on to the back of whoever he was with but then down the hill he would be away. Remember, he rarely had big hills nearby to train on, and he had to do a lot of travelling to race on the fells. Of all the guys I worked with, John was one of the top ones. He was a great athlete, and was dedicated and loyal.'

CHAPTER 13

Nothing to do with fitness

There was no let up, with further championship races the following two weekends. Having come back at a 9-mile 'Medium' category race, John Wild now faced a 14-mile race with 5000 feet of ascent – the Northern Counties race at Buttermere.

14 May: Northern Counties, Long, 14 miles, 5000 feet

It was to be one of Kenny's favourite race venues, as he loved its steep climbs. He had felt ill the week before, and surprised himself by winning by three minutes from Billy Bland, who had actually taken Kenny on a course reccie a short while beforehand. There were four or five together going past Newlands Church and Kenny made a break up Causey Pike. Jon Broxap was third, just in front of John Wild. That gave Keswick AC the first three places, and their dominance at the time is shown by them taking both first and second team spots. John acknowledges that he wasn't really ready for this race. Ben Lomond, the week before, had been his first fell race since November, and the effect was still in his legs. It was also not really his kind of course. He was not one of the best climbers and he lost the leaders going up Causey Pike. Having lost sight of Kenny he ran much of the way with Bob Ashworth before moving away towards the end. It was fine weather, but Sean Livesey managed to make an error coming off Whiteless Pike to find himself in Buttermere and not in his previous second place. His retirement gave John a valuable extra championship point.

John shrugs and says, 'I had an off day there really. There was no way in the world I was going to keep up with Jon Broxap. That tells a story, doesn't it. Jon was a good athlete, but he shouldn't have beaten me on a 14-miler.'

Kenny summed up his racing with this quote about the race and his break on Causey Pike, 'this must be my favourite long race. It is steep and I enjoyed the climbs. I was a bit surprised to win as I had flu the week before, but I felt all right on the day. There was a group of us together going past Newlands Church and I tried to get away going up Causey Pike. I thought if I kill myself here I'll kill a few others too and really put an effort in. I just felt good, it went like a dream.'

Kenny added one more comment that illustrates that there was significant support and encouragement for him from the traditional amateur fell racers, even as he commenced to run them into the ground, 'To be fair Billy Bland had shown me round some of the course, enough to get me round most of it. Billy offered. I went up there and met him and we went round the back end of it. At that time it started and finished at Honister Quarry, coming straight down from High Spy.'

22 May: Fairfield, Medium, 9 miles, 2999 feet

The Fairfield race followed just a week later, with John Wild feeling he was still getting over the Northern Counties. Before the season started John had sat down and made a list of who he thought was going to win what and he had Kenny down for this with himself second. Again it was nip and tuck, with Kenny and John taking it to each other. Kenny reckoned it was definitely one of the hardest races of the season. He really had a go at winning, thinking he could get him on the final run in. But John put a burst in down the last downhill stretch, and was just stronger that day.

A comment from John gives a real feel for their rivalry. 'Kenny was hanging on that day. I tried so hard to break him. We were neck and neck and it was only on the last downhill section that

I managed to break away and then my legs were like lead on the track in to the finish. I remember we crossed the finish line and he said, "you effing bastard!". A tough little race is the Fairfield.'

Having tried to run hard on that last stretch when racing there myself I can well imagine what they were going through as they raced it out after over an hour of cut and thrust. The long descent off Low Pike has your leg muscles throbbing, and THEN you ask them to produce more on what is not an easy finish. John explained that it was his kind of course. 'I like these 'Medium' races and try to base most of my training round them. They're more like cross-country.'

When I mentioned John predicting, to himself, that it was Kenny's race to win, Kenny laughed and responded, 'Noooo! I think it was John's type of race, but I was running very well at the time, and there were only seconds in it. It was just that he was slightly faster at the finish.'

Jack Maitland was 3rd, but significantly nearly three minutes behind, completing the same 1-2-3 as the previous 'Medium' category race (Ben Lomond, two weeks beforehand). In Maitland's view he had a great descent, overtaking two runners on the last downhill. His diary notes: 'One bad patch on the climb, probably set off too fast trying to keep with those guys, blowing up a bit and rallying. Was 7th at the top, pulled up from 7th to 3rd with consistently aggressive descending.' Reading this last phrase causes him to laugh heartily, as does the next diary entry. 'Probably have to lose some weight to match John and Kenny on ascents. Hill sessions may also help!'

So, after the first six races in the season there was an unexpected look to the championship table. The scoring was 32 points for a first place, 29 points for second, 28 for third and so on down to one point for 30th. Jon Broxap had run all six races and was on top with 167 points. Kenny Stuart had run five and was second with 154 points (from three wins and two seconds), with Symonds, Whitfield, Livesey and Short next after all doing four races. John Wild was in 7th place with 92 points, having won two and come 4th in the other. Jack Maitland and Billy Bland were next, also having done three races each. But there was plenty of the season left, with another possible nine races to be fought over.

4 June: Welsh 1000m, Long, 19.9 miles, 8005 feet

There was now a two-week break before moving down to Wales for the Welsh 1000m race, the third of the 'Long' category races. It was a class field, with Hugh Symonds in contention and Billy Bland making a rare excursion to Wales, in response to stick he was getting for not running long races outside the Lakes. Hugh Symonds loved this race, largely because of the fact that it finished at the top of Snowdon.

Early on, going over the Carneddau, Mike Short established a lead by dint of choosing a different route to the main contenders. John Wild knew the course, having run it twice, giving him a slight advantage over Kenny Stuart and Billy Bland. However, he was worried at Mike Short getting a gap, which was a couple of minutes at its most. Kenny was not sure what to do. It was his first time in Wales and he had no idea where the course went. His plan was to stick with whoever was in front and then try to make a break on the climb up Snowdon as it's on a path all the way. John was hanging on to the pace, starting to get cramp and secretly hoping Billy would win to take the points off Kenny.

By Ogwen, Short had been reeled in by Stuart, Wild and Bland, and from the A5 road onwards it was just those three, but it still wasn't clear how it would end. Over the last tough grind to the summit of Crib-y-ddysgl there was nothing to choose between Kenny and John, with Billy being dropped three-quarters of the way up. Stuart thought it was his. Amazingly, after almost three and a half hours of running Wild didn't clinch victory until the final run-in alongside the railway line near the summit of Snowdon. Twenty miles and it came down to a sprint finish. Kenny generously acknowledged that, 'in the end it was nothing to do with fitness, John was just harder. I really fancied my chances against him going up to finish on the top of Snowdon. I ran it twice and never won it though.'

John was somewhat surprised about how it panned out, as he notes that they were, 'together until Ugain and then hit the railway and I sprinted up there. We were both surprised that when we had got to Pen-y-Pass Billy Bland just fell off the pace. We had expected a hard time from him.'

It was almost halfway through the season, with seven championship races done, and Kenny and John had won three each (with neither finishing at Kentmere), although in a sense John was still playing catch-up. Having won the 'Long' Welsh 1000s race, John needed to do the same in the remaining 'Longs' (Wasdale and Borrowdale) to knock out the 4th place he had achieved at the Northern Counties. Kenny had come second to John in the two 'Mediums', so he needed to beat him in the remaining two in the second half of the season (John's preferred distance, remember).

18 June: Buckden Pike, Short, 3.7 miles, 1594 feet

Another fortnight and it was off to Yorkshire for the Buckden Pike race. John Wild couldn't believe his luck. It was more like cross-country and he thought it none too tough a course. He thought he'd been handed the points on a proverbial plate. At the time he was back training really well and feeling very fit, but he had a bit of a cold on the day.

Wild comments that 'there just didn't seem to be any fight in anyone.' Kenny was very disappointed with his run. He thinks he may have been getting a bit stale. He felt pretty good at the start, but there was nothing there once the race started. 'John was exceptionally good that day although I wouldn't call this a true fell race, not a championship course, not even an 'A' category.' This is a view John concurs with, but he still reckons everybody else had an off day. He made a break early on and nobody went with him, and he went on to set a new course record. John also remembers the Morris Dancing from the pub.

Kenny added a comment that in retrospect may have been crucial to later performances. 'I had a slight virus, which didn't go down very well. It bugged me for quite a while did that virus. I went over to Italy to run a race near Verona and I wasn't anywhere near right and I was 16th. When I got home I thought I could run better than that. I know these athletes are good lads, but I am better than that.'

John Wild recalls an unusual experience during the race that day at Buckden Pike. 'I think it was where I had to turn a sheep over that was on its back. When that happens it can't get back over, and the crows peck its eyes out - I learnt that from Joss Naylor. I flipped this sheep over, but it was already dead!' I told Joss the sheep story from John Wild, and he laughed and said, 'Aye, it happens. My son Paul had one once and it took five weeks of patience, for him to get the sheep to stand up properly again.' Joss added that this sheep is still alive and is as good a Herdwick as you can get.

Further down the field (in 17th that day) Dave Hall remembers it as a very hot day, 'which was no good for me. That course is too runnable as well.' Despite that, Jack Maitland found the descent very steep and slippery, commenting in his diary on his performance. 'Much better than last year, but need to do better. Lose weight, more speed work and more rest.' He admits that his training was volume based really. He also ran a half marathon on the day after Buckden Pike, in 73 minutes.

Strangely, John Wild chose to run in the non-championship Blake Fell race the week after Buckden Pike (on 25 June). Blake Fell was a seven-mile Category 'B' race. Wild duly won from Hugh Symonds and Jon Broxap. Hugh Symonds remembers this race particularly well. 'My wife Pauline went into labour at breakfast time. I wanted to race. I took Pauline to hospital in Kendal and said I would stay with her. The midwife told me it was not going to happen for hours and insisted it would be best to go. So I phoned the hospital from Lamplugh and was informed that it was still not happening. So I did the race, which

I led for a lot of the way. I think I got quite a lead on John Wild, and he beat me on the run-in, which was very frustrating. If I had won that race I think our second son Joe's middle name would have been Blake. I don't think I ever beat John Wild, and I am pretty sure I never beat Kenny Stuart.'

I asked John to explain the circumstances behind him choosing to run this race. 'We went up there for a week with a trailer tent staying by a pub, and I was planning on doing a race on the Saturday [*Blake Fell*]. I got a call to say that Joss Naylor was doing the *Lakes, Meres and Waters* run [*This joins up twenty-seven water bodies in Cumbria and the trip is about 105 miles, including several high passes to get from valley to valley*] and he wanted some runners to go with him. I said I would do a couple of hours starting out at some ludicrous time in the morning like 5-30am, which ended up as four hours as he was such good company. I ran much further with Joss than I intended to, I was enjoying it so much. Joss was trying for a record. I got a couple of hours of sleep after that and went to the race. In the race I let Hugh get far too big a lead early on, but clawed it back.' It was reported thus, 'Naylor completed the round in 1983, taking a 'mere' 19 hours 20 minutes 14 seconds. He was paced on the Ennerdale to Wastwater section by club mate John Wild, who left him at Wasdale to nip off and win the Blake Fell race.'

As Joss recalls, 'John was with me that morning. He just turned up, and it was great to see him. I also had a lot of help that day from apprentices at Sellafield. We came out of Ennerdale and we got lost in thick mist. I said to John "we are wrong here". When we got down to the lake I asked him how far he could go. He said "as far as Devoke Water", as he wanted to go to the race. It got really hot later in the day, when the race was on, and Pete Hall got heat exhaustion and they had to take him in to hospital.'

John then revealed that there was an unfulfilled plan for that trip. 'In that same week Kenny was interested in doing one of my kind of speed sessions. Before the planned day I was out on the fells with the dog for three hours or so running over rocks and that. Then I got down to a sheep track and I twisted my ankle. It was the same ankle as I had the operation on which nearly cost me the championships. So I never got to train with Kenny, which is quite sad. Kenny was really upset about us not being able to train together that time. He wanted to know how I trained. I was quite happy to show him. It might have been 3-minute efforts or 5-minute ones, or mile and a halfs, or whatever.'

9 July: Wasdale, Long, 21.1 miles, 9022 feet

Now came another twist. Both John and Kenny decided not to run Wasdale, and by doing so gave themselves four weeks between championship races. John reasoned that Wasdale wasn't the race for him with so many other championship races around that time. Kenny was still going through a bad patch and wasn't too keen, even though he thought he could give Billy Bland a race over that course, but in retrospect wasn't sure if he could have beaten him on a hot day as it was. Wasdale was arguably the toughest of the races on the roster for that year, being over 21 miles and with over 9000 feet of ascent. Kenny says that not running Wasdale was not because of his viral situation. 'To run a race like Wasdale, the weeks were just too close together, so I didn't do that one. I never actually got to run Wasdale in the end. It just didn't fit in.' John just candidly says, 'it was too tough for me.'

On the day the temperature was up in the 80s, and 59 competitors retired, mostly suffering from heat exhaustion. Billy Bland claimed it was just a training run for him, carrying a sponge to dunk in every stream to cool himself off. With his local knowledge he absolutely knew how to find the streams which he also might take a quick drink from. He finished in 3 hours 49 minutes 50 seconds. Tony Richardson, who was second, was estimated to be still at the Scafell Pike checkpoint at that time. Hugh Symonds had run with Billy as far as Seatallan but dropped back as he started suffering in the heat, and finished 8th.

When asked, Hugh Symonds explained that it was more about what he had done a week ago. 'The week before I was first at Skiddaw, I suspect in one of the fastest times still, 63-09. Kenny Stuart has the fastest of course (which is 62-18). I went really fast downhill, but that did me no good at all. Sometimes looking back I think I over-raced. To race Skiddaw six days before Wasdale is not clever. You really hammer your legs running off Skiddaw. I now give advice to my boys about over-training, and certainly warn them about the dangers of over-racing.'

Billy Bland's stream drinking comment prompted me to ask Kenny and John for their views on hydration. Kenny said he always tried to prepare his body for the specific stresses of competition and this meant dietary aspects as well. For example, he experimented by getting up early to do a 20 mile run and only taking two cups of tea prior to the run in order to simulate the conditions of a long race early in the day with limited food and liquid intake. In the previously noted interview Kenny had commented that whilst he would always advise runners to guard against the dangers of dehydration, he doubts whether the body of a top fell racer under the severe stress of competition would be able to utilise any food or liquid that might be taken on board during a competition. He also pointed to the reports on the dangers of excessive intake of water in hot conditions (hyponatremia).

John commented that, 'it amuses me to see joggers out for a half-hour run carrying water as it's not necessary. On the fells, as with other runners, you tended to take water when required, mostly from fell streams. I do remember though, carrying a plastic bag with a powdered sports drink called Accolade in it and then dunking this in a fell stream to drink, hoping there wasn't a dead sheep upstream. I also remember Anne giving me liquids when possible at crossing points.'

Kenny's comment about hyponatremia prompted me to ask Hannah Sheridan, from The University of Birmingham *High*

Performance Centre to summarise current thinking on the topic. 'Over-hydration and hyponatremia is not very common and the most likely situations for it to occur in is in recreational endurance sports people, like a 4-5 hour marathon runner. They often don't understand hydration guidelines and 'panic' drink. They also have much more opportunity to drink as they are running at a much slower pace for longer. In sweating we lose water AND electrolytes so by rehydrating with just water you don't replace salts and this is when hyponatremia may occur. In top athletes, dehydration is much more of an issue as there is limited time to drink and they are going so fast that it is not convenient to take fluid on board.'

Moving on to the first weekend in July, Wild and Stuart both ran an international race in Italy. The first official British fell running teams were selected for an Italian International Mountain championship at San Giovanni, near Verona. The English team of John Wild, Kenny Stuart, Jon Broxap and Sean Livesey finished second to Italy. Wild finished 6th behind five very strong Italians. Kenny remembers, 'I had a stinking bad race. It was in the middle of a really bad patch in the middle of that season.' As we know now, Kenny had experienced some kind of virus for a while. But he went out to Italy and thought everything was OK. 'I set off in the race and just had nothing at all, absolutely nothing. John came 6th and I was about 16th. It was one of those days when you are struggling to put one leg in front of the other, it was surreal really.'

Kenny expanded, 'I had flexible holidays and had no problem with going to foreign races. I told my grandparents that I was going to Italy in a month to represent England. My grandmother said "that is ridiculous, it such an awfully long way to go". It was a drawn out carry on to get there. That year it was so damn hot, we were coming off a pretty cold summer. No-one was acclimatised really.'

After competing against European countries and, after finishing a dispiriting 16th in Italy, Kenny came to realise the depth of mountain running talent away from home soil. 'I felt that more frequent competition with the Italians was my only chance of beating them, as merely increasing the frequency or intensity of my own training would probably end in injury or illness. Also, my training was always geared to the climb and I never practised descending; the hill reps and fartlek sessions in my training schedule enabled me (I believe) to withstand intense pace changes during races which proved invaluable later at international level against the Europeans on their type of home terrain.'

John Wild points out that it, 'was essentially an uphill race. We ran the course the day before. Danny Hughes was team manager and was with us as we were running through the cherry groves and I took all my clothes off and ran in front of him, mooning.' Danny took a photo of the bare arse disappearing (which sadly couldn't be used in this book).

It was a ground-breaking event though. Discussions at the event were initiated by the FRA that led to thoughts of a possible future World Championships in fell/mountain running (which were inaugurated in 1985).

CHAPTER 14

Drinks had been taken

The two protagonists came back together for the next championship race, another of the 'Mediums', which Kenny reckoned was his sort of course – runnable most of its nine miles. Interestingly, John had been up in the Lakes five or six days beforehand and looked the course over. He liked what he saw and he also felt it was his type of course, with plenty of grassy running.

16 July: Kinniside, Medium, 9 miles, 3000 feet

Kenny got away early on, going up Blakely Raise. John had put it down as a possible win on paper, but Kenny was going really well that day. According to John, 'I'd be walking up a steep slope and look up and see him still running. At times like that you just have to try and concentrate, get the breathing going and ignore it when it starts to hurt.' In fact Kenny thinks he ran it all the way. He got away twice in the race, having gone a bit off course at one point.

Talking about it again recently, John was quite excited. 'Yeh. What I can remember is the smell of aniseed. They did hound trailing on the same hills. Kenny was a terrific climber, no doubt about that. He had got a stone of weight on me, mind. Legs like tree trunks and a stone lighter! He was brilliant all-rounder, but what I am saying is that I don't know anyone who could climb like him. Something like Melantee I had no hope against him, I don't know why I bothered to drive up there!'

It was a good quality field, with Jon Broxap finishing 3rd,

Sean Livesey 4th, Alan McGee 5th, and Billy Bland 6th. Kenny's 1-04-40 winning time was counted as a new course record even though it was a few seconds slower than Alan McGee's time from 1978, because he covered a greater distance with its slightly modified start and finish. Kenny's view was that, 'on grassy descents like these I feel I can hold my own with anyone, whereas John is marginally faster over rough downhills. They said at the end it was a record as its now slightly longer. It is a comparable time to Alan McGee's, anyway.'

It was a really hot day and John went out like a bull in a china shop, as he often did. Kenny recalls that he, 'went with him and thought well I am not sure about this but got the feeling John wasn't running at his best. As John always did, he hung in for grim death even when I was pushing it. It was only when I got on the last climb on the back of Winder up a really steep slope, which I should have walked but I ran it, that I started to break him and went on and saw it through. I was surprised as I thought it might be his course.'

John Wild recalls that it was too hot on that day and he couldn't handle it. 'It was brutal. I had trained hard that week, maybe overdoing it. Anne and I had been up there with the trailer tent.'

30 July: Melantee, Short, 3.5 miles, 1500 feet

Another two weeks on and it was back up to Scotland for the Short Melantee race, another race with a course record held by Alan McGee. Conditions were good, with some light drizzle but the course was considered to have been drier than in the past. Kenny felt it was a particularly good run for him, as he felt really good from the start. It is a steep hill and he walked some of it, although he didn't think you'd gain much by running. He noted, 'I'd never been over it and I was impressed, but no-one was going to beat me coming down there. I took the bull by the horns, as it was my type of race. Typical guides race style of tough course, straight up and down and quite rough. I ran as much as I could and coming down I just hammered it. John admitted he had nothing that day.' Kenny led from the start, beating John into second by a massive 1 minute 18 seconds.

For John it was probably a mistake to go up for the Melantee race, as he injured his ankle again. It was only on the Thursday beforehand that he decided to run the Borrowdale race, which came a week later. John hadn't seen the course before either, and all the way he was hanging on hoping somehow he'd magically beat Kenny. 'It knackered my legs for Borrowdale. Kenny also did the Half Nevis AND still won Borrowdale. Unbelievable. But Kenny and I pushed each other hard, and it was a hot day. I drank gallons of juice afterwards.' Hugh Symonds wore heel spikes that day. 'I very rarely did that, but it was good for that course, which was a lot of grass and no road.'

Discussing this prompted John Wild to mention Reebok making him a special pair of spikes. 'You know I designed a fell running shoe, don't you, that they put into production.' John knew Chris Brasher and John Disley (the founders of the London Marathon), who had connections at Reebok. 'I said look I don't fancy heavy studs, so they had this pimpled rubber on the back of their steeplechase shoes, and I asked if they could design a shoe where this is the whole sole. They said "what for?". I told them, and how they should be and they came up with these shoes. I still have a pair at home. This pimpled rubber swept up the toe, up the heel and around the side. They called them the Wild Country. But they got in to copyright problems in the States because Wild Country was also an SUV tyre. So, they had to change the name, and I think they called it Wild Runner. They made me a pair with heel spikes in. In later years I used to do training weekends with Reebok at Merthyr Mawr on the sand dunes. I went along as a coach or as an athlete. This would have been in about 1985.'

The day after Melantee, Dave Cartridge, Hugh Symonds, Kenny Stuart and Jon Broxap did the longer Half Nevis race. Coming in from 2nd to 5th respectively, they were given a masterclass in fell running by Colin Donnelly. He broke Billy

Bland's course record for this six-mile race, taking a big lead before the turn and increasing it on the descent. The improvement to the path may have helped, but it was still undoubtedly an outstanding piece of aggressive running. Kenny's recovery powers were legendary. 'I did it and John couldn't manage it. He couldn't get out of the car! [*laughs*]. It is a three-race weekend. Cow Hill is on the Monday, or something, but we drove home instead of doing that. I was fourth in the Half Nevis. On the way to the start line I went to his car and said to John "are you going to have a go" and he said "I am too ill". He had a van or minibus, which he slept in.'

Kenny remembers that, 'the atmosphere at races during this period was very friendly and the intense rivalry of competition soon gave way to friendly socialising afterwards. My alcohol consumption during the week leading up to a race was very low or non-existent, but after big races, especially those with an overnight stay, the atmosphere and craic often led to some unforgettable encounters and sorry return journeys – enough said, but John Wild was never far from the joyous throng!'

6 Aug: Borrowdale, Long, 16.8 miles, 6562 feet

Another week on and it was the last 'Long' of the championships, at Borrowdale, which should have been Billy Bland's to win as he knew the course so well. John Wild was hoping that if he couldn't win then Billy would and do him a favour, but Billy just couldn't climb that day. He'd dropped off the lead by Esk Hause, but caught up again going down the Corridor Route. By the time Kenny, John and Sean Livesey got to Styhead they'd left Billy again. He turned round and said it was no good and Kenny noted, 'Billy doesn't say that unless he means it.' Billy says somehow he, 'just did not fire that day, partly because it was such a hot day'.

Sean Livesey was going really well, but fell back from the leaders going up Dale Head. Then Kenny started moving better and reached the top with a good lead. Kenny wanted it badly.

He thought it was his hardest race ever and he pushed himself beyond the limit, perhaps. He concludes, 'Sean surprised us, but going up Dale Head I really put my head down and first Sean went then John, slightly. I felt bad. Then I started knotting up with cramp on the way down and even had to stop for a couple of seconds.' John comments, 'It was only in the last section that I just couldn't hold him. Again it was a hot day. No excuses, I was going well, but he was better on the day. I could see him all the way down the descent. It wasn't a sprint finish, it was a gradual pull away. We had great fun that night though, at the Borrowdale Hotel.'

Kenny obviously enjoyed winning this one, and his comments show both his commitment and the resulting painful after effects. 'It was another very hot day. It was to and fro with Billy until we got down the Corridor Route ready to go up Gable, and Billy dropped off the lead as it was too hot for him. John was still there as he always would be, and he was there until we got to Dale Head. I struck off and started to run up the track as hard as I could and he stuck like glue for a while and then started to just drop. When I got to the top I started descending and halfway down I got tremendous cramp in my calf muscles. I was standing and watching him coming and I thought "well he is not going any faster than I am so I might as well carry on". We were both laid out after that. I was really tired, the skin had peeled off the back of my heels on both feet. So I put some sticking plaster on and went to the dance that night and did some big stuff! To be quite honest I taped them up every day and trained with it after that for a while. There was like an eighth of an inch of skin. The whole pad was off, but it eventually healed. It wasn't particularly sore, strangely. Actually it wasn't that unusual to happen to us.'

Once again, it says something for the sport and its rivalries that Billy Bland had shown Kenny over the course prior to the event. He helped Kenny get to know the ropes a lot, as had John. As Kenny says, 'we've had some hard races and knocked ourselves up against each other and still gone out and had a few beers after.' It appears that this was one of those occasions, as Kenny notes, 'it was a good night out. That's what I like about fell running, the social side. Sometimes it is too good!'

20 Aug: Burnsall, Short, 1.5 miles, 899 feet

The championship show then moved on to the Burnsall Classic. Both Kenny and John liked the event, and had run well at this short race (last year it being Kenny's first amateur race). Despite his heavy racing schedule, John surprised the organisers somewhat by choosing to race the relatively low-key Downham Village fell race (in Lancashire) in the intervening week. He had challengers in Dave Cartridge and Sean Livesey, but came away with a new record on this 5.5 mile category 'A' race. He reckoned that it might be possible to reduce that time by a further couple of minutes, but this race is no longer held.

John had always liked Burnsall. He'd had a couple of good races there before and was looking forward to claiming top points and his hat-trick. It was a cracking race, which Kenny knew that if he was going to win he had to do it going up and John knew it was a question of hanging on all the way to the cairn. Kenny was first to the top in 8 minutes 45.6 seconds (which seems an amazing level of accuracy for recording a summit time), but on the descent John flew down taking risks that Kenny said he wasn't prepared to take, including leapfrogging the wall.

Once John got in front there was no stopping him and he really let go on the way down. 'I didn't look round. I got rid of that habit in my track days!' he says. Kenny had given it his best shot, 'I ploughed it to the top giving it all, but John hung on. Once he snatched 15-20 yards that was it. I had gone out hard with the intension of breaking John. Although it was a roundabout sort of ascent compared to the traditional guides race straight up and down job, I posted about the fastest time that was ever done to the summit. It was really fast. I went up like billio. John was two yards behind all the blooming way. I couldn't shake him. He just dug in with his head down and then he set off down that rough stuff and I have never seen anyone fly over it like he did. He vaulted the wall as though it wasn't there. It was incredible, fantastic to watch.'

John's time of 12-48 knocked two seconds off Ricky Wilde's 1977 record. It was a great time, considered better than Fred Reeves's old professional record, which was run on a course that went straight up and down, rather than in a loop.

Mark McGlincy felt that this may have been the best race he ever saw. 'John wasn't first at the top, and he was either class or reckless (whichever way you look at it) on the descent.' John Wild just says, 'I remember Kenny was trying really hard. I thought I might be a better descender than him. So I managed to nip in front of him at the cairn and took Ricky Wilde's record. Leapfrogging the walls? Yeh!'

Giving his take on this classic race Dave Hall commented that he was, 'pleased with 11th place. I was not a great descender. My philosophy was to get as high a positon as possible on the ascent and try not to lose too much on the descent. I remember seeing John Wild looking at the wall in advance of this race. The side you take off from is about three foot high, but the side you land on is nearer ten foot. Apparently he hurdled it and all the others put one foot on top and jumped off.'

Hugh Symonds came 8th in the race, having gone off too fast. The day after though he won the Sedbergh Hills race in a new record of 2-01-37, which was later beaten by Robin Bergstrand and Keith Anderson.

In 1983 *Compass Sport* magazine included an interview with Kenny and John that was conducted after the Borrowdale and Burnsall races. It was set up by Anne Wild and published under her maiden name (Horrocks), so it was not obvious she was related to John Wild. The interview was headlined 'Best of Pals'.

It was introduced by these words. 'The championship has been conducted in an exemplary fashion – hammer and tongs on the fell with no quarter given (you should have seen Wild descending the fell at Burnsall – one of the all-time great moments of fell racing!) but with the best of friendly spirits out of the races.'

'Wild and Stuart both greatly admire each other's athletic prowess but also enjoy each other's company, particularly over a few pints after a race. Anne Horrocks, conscious that post-season comments could be mixed with "delight or disappoint-ment", interviewed fell running's two stars of 1983 together at Borrowdale and Burnsall before the season ended.' [*These were races twelve and thirteen in the sequence of fifteen*]

For me the most interesting thing the interview revealed was John Wild's typical Summer and Winter training that year, which can be compared to Kenny Stuart's training reported in the same interview, and the other. (Bear in mind that any one training week is just a snapshot of that person's training, which may vary greatly over time, and from month to month.)

In responding to the question about Summer training John Wild noted:

Average 70 miles per week.
Mornings: week days - short steady, Sat/Sun – steady.
Afternoons: Speed 4 x 1600m, steady 10 miles, speed 6 x 800m, steady 7-10 miles, speed 6 x 1000m, 12 miles, 15 miles. Speed sessions can vary with track sessions sometimes thrown in.

For Winter John listed:

Average 70-80 miles per week.
Mornings: short steady.
Afternoons: 3 x 1.5 miles, steady 10 miles, speed 10 x 400m hill, steady 10 miles, 6 x 800m/6 x 1000m, steady 10-15 miles, steady 15 miles. Some weeks both winter and summer may have increased training or mileage to prepare specifically for one race e.g. National cross country, or through injury as May 1983 when I reached 90+ miles. Other different speed sessions are occasion-ally thrown in to relieve boredom.

Kenny's Summer training was a similar mileage, with a different balance:

> *Mornings:* 3 miles cross country each week day; Sat - 3 miles cross country or road; Sun - 15 miles fell and cross country 2-2.5 hrs.
> *Afternoons:* 9 miles fell or 10 miles road, Grass reps 7 miles (5 x 1mile), 12 or 15 miles fell and cc, Grass reps 7 miles (8 x ½ mile), 9 miles fell or 10 miles road, 5 miles (2 x 2 fell) in 20 mins each or 40-50 mins hard. Only intensive running done on Tuesday pm and Thursday pm and Saturday morning sessions. On week days done during lunch hour.

Kenny's Winter mileage was similar, being noted as:

> Total 80-90 miles per week.
> *Mornings:* 3 miles cross country, Sat – work or 9 miles cross country (70 mins) with various intervals and hills, Sun – 15 miles fell and cross country 2-2.5 hrs.
> *Afternoons:* 10 miles road in 65 mins, road intervals 7 miles (5 x 1 mile), 12 miles road, road intervals 7 miles (8 x ½ mile), 10 miles road in 65 mins, 5 miles intensive fell. All night sessions during week done in darkness on unlit roads with road intervals timed with a torch.

Two of the main differences were John's greater emphasis on speedwork in the summer, and Kenny's higher average mileage in winter. Neither were doing excessively high mileage, and had appropriately varied workouts, that in both cases suited their differing personal circumstances.

3 Sept: Ben Nevis, Medium, 8.7 miles, 4419 feet

The penultimate championship race of the year was at Ben Nevis. There were strong winds and no-one seemed to want to take the race on initially, but soon a large group got away as there was a significant injection of pace by Sean Livesey. About halfway up (around Red Burn) only Kenny Stuart and John Wild were with him, with Dave Cartridge, Hugh Symonds and Jack Maitland some hundred yards behind. On the steep climb above the burn Jack Maitland made a move on the leaders, and took the summit prize.

John recalls that day well. 'It was certainly rubbish weather with tough conditions. I never did see the top of the Ben on a race day! I got the record but was a bit fortunate really. The mist was down to the Red Burn and on the way up there were four of us bashing away.'

Coming away Maitland led Stuart, with Wild and Livesey about 15 seconds behind. Down by the Red Burn there was a cloying mist, and somehow John Wild came out of it in the lead, as he recalls, 'Jack Maitland and Kenny got away from Sean and myself by six or seven seconds, but they must have taken the wrong line on the descent because we came out of the mist in front.' Kenny remembers that they, 'went astray slightly coming down which was a pity because I feel I could have held my own with John back down the road. When we got back to the Red Burn we thought we were in front and in fact Jack Maitland went over the line still thinking I'd won and he'd come second.'

John takes up the story again, 'Once on the tourist track I relaxed a bit, because even though it is a rough path there are still sections where a runner like me can open up.' John raced to a win, bettering Dave Cannon's record from 1976 by 1 minute 20 seconds. John adds, 'I was inside a highly respected record but it was courtesy of Jack Maitland who had really pushed it going up. Even Kenny took a back seat on the climb that day.'

Despite the conditions the first three all beat the previous record. John thinks it could have been even better. 'If we'd been together then it's certain there would have been an even faster time.' This record should be saluted for what it is. John Wild's time is just 1 second slower than Kenny's all-time fastest time for the Ben, which Kenny set in 1984 and reckons was his best and toughest race.

From his view in around 10th place for most of the race Dave Hall recalls, 'I was with Dave Cartridge as they passed us as they were going down and we went up. A group of four were well away. That was probably the only race I got beaten on the road - by my long-time rival Pete Barron. I had left everything on the ascent.' Hall also has a theory on why the Ben Nevis time has not been beaten since 1984. 'Later they re-routed the path to stop it getting more eroded. The race carried on the old line on what was now either no path or a worse path. The weather does also pay a huge role in times there, as there can be snow on the tops.' It is clear from the comments from the participants that several top athletes all pushing themselves, and each other, to the limit was a major cause for these fast times. In recent years that hasn't often been the case, as there are arguably fewer top flight fell runners running these races now.

A feel for the après-race atmosphere at these events can be gleaned from Dave Woodhead's report in *Compass Sport* which noted that, 'after the prizegiving a good time was had by all at the Imperial Hotel, Fort William. John Wild was in very festive mood with Kenny Stuart in fine voice, but it was hard to pick between Brent 'Bagpipes' Brindle and Hugh 'Phonebox' Symonds as to who was the celebrity of the night!'

In trying to piece together the evening's events with me, John Wild admits that they were quite raucous. Presentations followed the race in the evening, but the pubs were open all day and many were getting drunk. 'Hugh took all his clothes off and ran out of this telephone box. His wife wasn't there but she would have been so embarrassed.'

Hugh Symonds's post-race antics may have been naivety, and may partly have been because he had not run particularly well. 'It was my first ever Ben, I think. It is a race that I would be amazed if anyone has ever won when doing it the first time [*Wild had already done it in 1981, Stuart didn't win till his second attempt*]. If they did then they have my respect.' Symonds then went on to elaborate on the shenanigans that he both witnessed and was part of.

Hugh added that, 'The Ben Nevis race is organised in a very officious manner. At the presentation the whole committee sit on stage, maybe a dozen men and women. When John Wild won the hall was packed. John wore, I seem to remember, a velvet suit, and marched up on to the stage in a kind of military fashion and he asked for the microphone. He took the microphone off the chairman and said "Good evening ladies and gentlemen, I would like to thank the race committee for organising this race and the award ceremony. But the day hasn't ended. Everyone knows that everyone goes to the Imperial Hotel after the event to see the night through. There will be another competition tonight and that is for the man with the hairiest arse." The committee were not sure where to look. Everyone was laughing. We went to the hotel for beers, and were standing around talking and then people began to get motivated by this hairy arse business. I think one or two clothes were coming off. For some reason, maybe I had had a few pints, I stripped off to just my running shoes, and just thought I would just do a short sprint outside. Then there was this flashing police light, nothing to do with all this as it happened. I saw it and thought they would see me anyway. So I got into this telephone kiosk and ducked. When the police disappeared I sprinted like hell back and I can't remember whether they hid my clothes or what, but I did get dressed pretty quickly.'

Through the mists of time (and the haze of alcohol?) John Wild remembers it slightly differently, but accepts what we might call the bare details. 'My limited memory of events is that I won several awards that night and had to keep going up on stage, where indeed all the committee were. I had the winners medal, a race record award, the team award [*actually Keswick won the team award*] and even a prize for the first serviceman. The last time I went up, I did get the microphone and stated that I'd also won another award, as the man with the hairiest arse - and then I bared my bum on stage.'

Kenny's explanation of what happened was that the committee 'would come to the hall for the presentation and there was a bash after, where the runners weren't invited. It was a committee job. But this year they allowed the runners to come. Everything went fine until someone (from Lancashire I think he was) went to the table and bared his backside to the kilted gentlemen and that was it - everybody out. That finished that. "Drinks had been taken", as they say.'

Having shown Jack Maitland the race memories expressed by John Wild, he agreed that he had thought he was second to Kenny. Jack ruefully commented in his diary at the time, 'must try to reccie thoroughly before next year'. He was also injured that week. He recalls, 'I was very rarely injured in my career. I do remember that one, a knee injury. It made the entire week a struggle to be OK to run at Ben Nevis. I just did 64 km that week. As I was able to run it was a successful experiment to have an easy week. In the week I had struggled to run at all, having to abort a run on the Wednesday. It was too painful to run on the Monday, after just two minutes I stopped. I was walking and jogging most of the week. I was doing a job beating on an estate at the time.' As to the shenanigans after the event Maitland just said, 'there were some unclothed antics, including an underpants relay! Hugh Symonds tried to hide from the police in a phone box. It was not the smartest place to hide.'

The plot thickened somewhat when Dave Hall recounted his memories of the evening to me. Although not entirely corroborating the other stories, he did confirm the hairy arse part. Dave thinks it was John's idea to do a streak relay round Fort William too. 'Once it had started a police car did turn up. Hugh Symonds was sweating at this point because he was a maths teacher at Sedbergh School at the time. He went in to the phonebox and we gave him a load of clothes. He then had this V-necked sweater that he put on the wrong way round, saying when asked that it was that way round because he had a cold chest. The relay started in the car park, involved a lap round the car park and went to the end of town and back. It was meant to be the first three teams from the race, plus a guest team. Billy Bland wouldn't streak, so Keswick were disqualified. I think Horwich took their place, because Brent Brindle was part of it. Brent scarpered round the car park with the police chasing him and Hugh went in to the phonebox. Someone else was out there but the police didn't do anything about anyone. It was really naked, not just underpants. It was a reaction to the stuffy committee and it was to break the ice. I think the runners were an inconvenience to the Ben Nevis race committee.'

Dermot McGonigle, from Ireland's Newcastle AC, ran the race and was at the 'party' afterwards, and he recalls, 'I still have vivid memories of that day. With Hugh attempting to get his kit back on in a telephone box outside the hotel as a Highland Constabulary panda car spoiled our plans to run a starkers race up and down the High St. I seem to recall that in the next issue of *The Fellrunner* it was suggested that PB actually stood for phone box! It is fair to say that the weekend made a big impression on me and convinced me to give the sport a right good go!'

Whilst not suggesting this type of activity was prevalent at fell races, Dave Hall did expand on the unique atmosphere at the Ben Nevis races. 'There was sometimes rice fights at the Chinese the night before. They would say you were banned for a year, which was no problem as we wouldn't be there again for a year! There was also a song which John would start. It was a bit like *Old Macdonald had a farm* except it was something like *If I could I would like to be*. Wild would be doing pilot impressions (think hands for goggles) with people turning torches up to the roof like searchlights. Then they would go through other jobs. But he used to start it.'

CHAPTER 15

One of us had to come second

There were three full weeks after the Ben Nevis race before the concluding championship race, which was at Thieveley Pike, with the title depending on the result. John Wild had needed to win the last three races of the championship to take the title again. The tension was palpable, as John had won the last two races and there was just this one to go, which was reckoned to be his type of race. But he needed the rest that the three weeks provided. Meanwhile, Kenny Stuart must have been thinking that it could all be slipping away from him, which would have been devastating after the huge commitment he had made in each and every race he had competed in during the year.

Kenny agrees that you might have thought it was slipping from his reach. 'In a way, yes it was. But one thing I may not have mentioned is the fact that I didn't feel any pressure going into that last race. I had resigned myself to the fact that if I had run second to John in the championships it was a helluva thing in my first year. So, I was pretty relaxed about it all. John was expected to win, and I thought that to be an advantage for me. I could only run like hell and see what happens. I had won that race the season before, but John was still getting over an injury at that time.'

Talking about The Ben Nevis race and its after effects, John notes, 'the worst thing about the Ben Nevis race is not the race but the drive back with stiff legs.' Kenny Stuart had a slightly shorter journey back from the Ben. He went to the race with his brother and stayed in a guest house. 'We went in an old Ford

Escort. We both had cars but my brother drove. I drove up in a Mini once. The thing is the time to travel to Fort William is not much less now because of the increased road traffic. It was always a helluva journey.'

John's wife Anne corroborated these views, saying, 'I remember John being quite tired after the weekend's activities (and not just the race!) and it was an especially hard trip back from Fort William in the old minivan. I knew that John was pleased with the Ben Nevis race, both the victory and the race record, although he did give credit to Kenny and Jack [*Maitland*] for their ascents.'

It interested me to see what training these two dedicated athletes fitted in to those three weeks before the vital final championship race. John recalled at the time that he found it hard to get back in to training. 'In fact in the seven days after [*the Ben*] I only trained on four. I followed the usual routine with speed work on the Wednesday before Thieveley and then an easy couple of days.'

Looking back on it now John adds that without the benefit of a diary record for those weeks he can't actually remember the specific training prior to Thieveley. 'It would not have been any different to most other weeks. I would have done speed work sessions such as 3min/1min efforts in Happy Valley and perhaps even a few efforts on the canal bank. I would also have tapered down towards the end of the week.'

Kenny showed me his detailed dairy entries for those three weeks and I noted 82 and 84 mile weeks in weeks one and two, and suggested to him that he may have stepped up his training in an aim to refine his fitness even further by doing what I unsubtly called 'even more training'. He swiftly dismissed this idea, saying, 'there was no need to, because I was running well anyway. I didn't need to do any more - that amount was normal for me, for the time. I knew what I was doing.'

Nevertheless, he did reveal that two years later (in 1985), when he set the still extant record for the Snowdon race, he was doing less mileage. This was because he had improved and didn't need a huge mileage. 'The extra years of continuity had got me there. I had found out how I ticked, how to prepare, how to rest, and to get to a race and be ready for it by then. I felt that it was the peak of my fell running. I was confident of beating just about anybody.'

Back to 1983, and Kenny's diary reveals that in the two 80+ mile training weeks he did a minimum of eight miles a day, trained twice every day but one – the Sunday before the Thieveley race, when he ran just once, 15 miles of fell and cross country. A pretty tough training regime.

Kenny did explain that the morning runs were usually three miles, 'just on the river bank. Down the road, cross the A66 just to get myself out. It would be seven and a half minute mile pace, just easy cheesy. Just a loosener, a warm-up really. This was September, so there was still daylight enough to run in the evenings after work. The daylight hours wouldn't have affected anything in that training period. It was when the clocks went back that it all changed.'

With the training done, how did the two protagonists go into that last race? I asked both Kenny and John to look back and try to summarise their physical and mental states.

John simply says now that he, 'certainly approached the race with a degree of confidence, but not overly so. I always had a great respect for Kenny and especially his climbing abilities, so I never expected an easy race!'

Anne Wild expands, 'John got back into his normal training routine as soon as possible and I don't recall him having any injuries or niggles in the lead up to Thieveley. I also don't remember him being overly nervous either and it was never in his nature to be over confident. As it happens, he's still the same and the glass is always half empty rather than half full!'

As for Kenny, he now says he went into the race having eased up properly. He was obviously fit and prepared for it physically. 'More than that, mentally I was probably ready to accept defeat. It was quite a relaxed situation. When I woke up in the morning I knew I felt good and I just decided that the only way to beat John Wild in a race like that was to take it by the scruff of the neck. Mind you, I did that at Burnsall previously and he ripped me apart coming down. He was tremendous that day, vaulting the walls like the steeplechaser he was.'

Kenny adds that the fact that it was a course that would suit John at his best took the pressure off him as well. 'If it had been a really steep up and down course where people would have been saying, "you will beat John on this", I might have felt a lot more pressure. But I didn't.'

Kenny may not have felt any pressure, but he did admit to me that he had two rituals that he performed before every race at the time. As we wound down one of our conversations about this period he somewhat sheepishly admitted that he always put his left sock on first, and also always had to put on his left shoe before the right one.

Going in to the race John Wild had 277 points and Kenny Stuart had 279 points. Up for grabs were 32 points for the winner, 29 for second, 28 for third, 27 for fourth, and so on. So, if John won he would have 309 points, and whatever position Kenny finished it would be John's title. If anyone else won John had to finish at least three places above Kenny to win overall. Any result with Kenny in front of John would give Kenny the title. It couldn't be more finely balanced, and there was all to play for - for both athletes.

24 Sept: Thieveley Pike, Short, 4.3 miles, 1312 feet

The current race website gives a description of the course:

> From a boggy field beside the Ram Inn, Cliviger, the race follows the Mary Towneley Loop to Scout Farm where a sharp left takes you up a mercifully short, ridiculously steep climb to the moor, which levels off towards a ruin. After crossing a couple of fields it's back onto rough moorland for the climb to the Pike, steep at first then it eases as you follow the fence to the trig point. A fast grassy descent precedes

a shorter, technical drop to the fell gate. Then you battle through a young plantation before a steep 'sting in the tail' brings you back to the ruin. A second grassy descent leads to the bridleway for the last push to the finish in the field where you started.

Comments from Kenny and John bring this description to life. Kenny notes that, 'for a course like that you get there early enough and you reccie as much as you need to. There is a stream to jump, then through a railway bridge, and as soon as you are through that there is a bank, it is not fell, it is just a massive grass bank. You can see it in the famous Neil Shuttleworth photo. You can see that I am well bent over as it is so steep.'

John adds that, 'one thing I do remember about the day though is that during the warm up I'd done a reccie of the finish area, and in the final run in to the line we had to cross a stream/ brook. I picked the place I was going to cross and treated it like a steeplechase barrier. If it was a close finish, I didn't want to be hesitating where I crossed the stream.'

So, to the race itself. Early on Wild tracked Stuart, and through the wood he closed to two or three yards on him, but he lost a bit going up the last climb and Stuart stretched 30 or 40 yards clear. By the summit the race order was decided, as the first seven there remained in those positions, and all seven finished inside the course record.

John Wild pushed Kenny Stuart all the way, meaning that Stuart's time took a massive 1 minute 45 seconds off the record. Wild recalls that, 'he really went for it, and I didn't have a hope in hell of catching him on the ascent. I was hoping I would catch him on the descent, but it didn't happen. He was through the railway arch before I was even in sight. Once he was five yards away there was no way I was going to catch him. It is conceivable that I could have won, it was my sort of distance, but again he was better on the day. As it turned out, it didn't really matter where I crossed the bloody stream!'

Kenny Stuart admits that he had decided to set off and to take as much out of himself, and the others of course, as possible. His view was that, 'every race that season had been hard, so I thought I might as well kill myself on this one too. At the finish I was 20 seconds clear and I must admit I felt exceptional that day.'

Looking back now he adds, 'just after that photo [*mentioned above*] I straightened up and began to run like hell and just took off, and John was still walking. That was the time to hit him. I never looked back because you know with John he would be pushing and pushing behind you. Unlike these cyclists who try to make a break in races and keep looking back to see if anybody is chasing them, I just went and then realised I had got a lead and I thought he might still get us coming down, but I was too far in front by then. It was good day for me.'

There was massive interest in the race, and a report in *The Fellrunner* summarised the race thus:

The weather remained fine though overcast and misty on top. The going was remarkably dry underfoot with the exception of the notorious area around the railway bridge. The going doubtless contributed to the amazing new record performance put up by Kenny Stuart, greatly helped by John Wild's pressure in this his last chance to retain his championship title. Kenny carved no less than 1-45 from the record. Most people expected either Stuart or Wild to win but no-one could be certain which and most would have been happy with either outcome. It is nice to see a new title holder on the one hand but Wild's performance this year has earned him the greatest respect, coming from behind after a later start due to injury.

The standard behind the Stuart-Wild tussle up front was amazing, with the first seven finishing inside the course record. It finished: 1 Kenny Stuart 22-57, 2 John Wild 23-17, 3 Sean Livesey 23-46, 4 Jack Maitland 23-52, 5 Dave Cartridge 23-54, 6 Hugh Symonds 24-05, 7 Malcolm Patterson 24-11. The race report noted that, 'fine performances by youngsters Livesey, Maitland and Cartridge bode well for the future.'

Jack Maitland's preparation for the Thieveley Pike race was hardly conventional. The week beforehand he did a double at The Two Breweries race and the Moffat Chase – two 18-milers in a row. For Thieveley he now says that he should have worn studs or even heel spikes rather than PBs, as it was so slippy on the descent. His diary notes, 'a slightly disappointing run. Hoped to be third, but vast improvement on last year both in position and time. I was inside the old record. Always looking for improvement. More speed work and cross country in the winter.'

Maitland had caught a train to Todmorden, stayed in the Youth Hostel and cycled to the race in the morning. That was the year he moved to Leeds, and he thinks his move was possibly the day before Thieveley Pike. He reflects now, 'I was doing the racing and having fun. I wasn't expecting anything. Fell running wasn't the thing I was hoping to do well in. I was doing my best, I am not making excuses. Those guys [*Wild and Stuart*] were way better than me.'

Malcolm Patterson came 7th and says even now that it was a bit surreal for him to do this race. 'I had missed all of the epic Wild-Stuart battles until this last one – the decider. A bit like Jack, those guys were in a different class to me that day and even though I raced, I felt I was just a bystander. It felt a bit like turning the TV on late, and only watching Coe and Ovett battling down the home straight. In retrospect, I bitterly regret missing so much of the 1983 season.'

Kenny Stuart still has great memories from the race. 'I just felt very much at home because it was a sheepdog trials sort of race, very much in the vein that I had been running in local shows for ages. It sat with me very comfortably actually. I was in an environment that I was very aware of and very happy with. My dad was down with me, and the rest of the family weren't there. One recollection I do have that I was quite surprised and taken by, was that after the race Graham Moffat (who had driven down from Sedbergh to watch), who I raced in guides races for years, came over to congratulate me and that was a very touching thing to happen.'

John just says now that he can't remember too much about the race, 'apart from trying like hell to hang on to Kenny on the climb. He had a phenomenal power/weight ratio and with me a stone heavier, it was always a hard job to stay in touch on a hill, although I did manage it on occasions like Burnsall. I also remember talking with Kenny and other lads afterwards, and of course cracking the bottle of champagne.'

Although giving it his all, as he always did, he then put it in perspective. 'I can't say I recall being devastated by the loss of the race or the championship hat-trick; it was just one of those things. At least I didn't run badly as in some of my track races or the National cross-country. After all, it was only sport and didn't register so high in the great scheme of things. I'm actually just as proud of the fact that I was a competent Tornado engineer as I am of any of my running exploits.'

In *Feet in the Clouds*, Richard Askwith reported that John Wild's wife Anne brought along the bottle of champagne 'to celebrate when he won'. In discussing the occasion with me, John Wild adamantly retorted that it was not like that at all. 'The champagne story was not true. Askwith did not get it from me. We took the champagne for whoever won.'

Anne Wild adds her take on the situation. 'Yes, I did take champagne to the event but it was definitely left in the car until *after* the race, so writing that I'd said it was for John when he won the race was both untrue and unfair.'

She also gave her thoughts on John and Kenny's rivalry, and of John's fell running efforts. 'I remember John being philosophical about being second to Kenny in the race and thus losing the championship, and I also recall him both warmly and genuinely congratulating Kenny on his victory. I also remember conversations afterwards where John was actively encouraging Kenny to do some serious cross country and road running (he'd been going on all season how good an athlete he thought Kenny was!). John wasn't especially upset or depressed in the days after the race and he'd already resolved that that was that for the fells and he would concentrate his training on running a marathon. I'd certainly seen him in worse moods after poor track or cross country races. I think I felt more upset for John, especially as he'd had such rotten luck with injury at the start of the season. It had been a great three-year adventure for the two of us, one Labrador and a fluorescent green minivan, but it was perhaps time to move on.'

Kenny responded to the comment about his cross country exploits, before giving an insight in to how it went post-race, both at the venue and back home. 'I had not done any serious cross country really. John always said that with the ability I had I would have been able to run cross country for England, which I did eventually - I got an ECCU vest on the back of running 5th in the Inter-Counties. Later it became a GB trial and I just fell short, coming 15th at Gateshead.'

Was there a 'do' after the race? As Kenny recalls, 'I think we just had a drink and a coffee and a sandwich maybe and just set off to drive home as normal. There was no big deal about it. There were no mobile phones then so you would arrive back home and people would say "how did you come on"? Nowadays you'd be ringing someone at home straight after the event. On arriving home, I think I came in and got changed and went out for a drink with my mate down the village. The conversation probably went something like this:

> *Have you been running today?*
> Aye, yeh.
> *How did you come on?*
> Oh, I won.
> *Ah right, OK. What do you want to drink?*
> [That would be it. Full stop.]

After the race the two of them reflected on the season (as reported in *The Fellrunner*), and looked forward to what might come next.

John: I was disappointed, not with missing the championship hat-trick, but simply just losing that year. It seemed a lot of hard work lost on one race and after a season like that it was a shame one of us had to come second. I haven't made any plans for next year yet though I suppose I have to do a marathon sometime and I would like to do a good one. As for the fells, I'll just have to see. We really enjoy the fells, there's a nice lot of people and we've had some great weekends. Any chance Kenny and I get to have a beer we take it! I don't think there's anyone around next year who can touch Kenny, though I think Sean Livesey could come through the year after. He's only 20 and had a terrific season. The only other dangers I can see are if a good cross-country runner tries a few races because I believe a good runner with background should always beat an out-and-out fell runner. I've enjoyed this season. I think I can sit back and say I couldn't have done any more.

Kenny: I'll run the fells next year and go for the championship again in a roundabout sort of way. I won't make a conscious decision to win it, I'll just go and enjoy my racing. As for an international vest at road or cross-country, well, it is not really an ambition, more a sort of hope. When I'm sick of hurting myself on the fells I might have a go. I've only ever run two road races, both 10's and I found them different. Of the two I think I find road the hardest but then I've trained to hurt myself on the fells. As for John, I think he'd make a good marathon runner. Whatever he goes in for he dedicates himself to. At 30 he must have his best years ahead as a marathoner if he goes with it now.

The end of season table showed Kenny first with 311 points, John second with 306, followed by Jon Broxap (274), Hugh Symonds (257), Sean Livesey (247), Billy Bland (219) and Jack Maitland (190). Of the championship races Kenny and John had a one-two in 10 of them (with Wild winning six and Stuart four of those). Of the others, Kenny won Blisco and the Three Peaks when John didn't run, and at the Northern Counties John could only come 4th to Kenny's victory. The two that neither ran

in were Kentmere and Wasdale, which were won by Broxap/
Livesey and Billy Bland respectively.

Mark McGlincy made an interesting point about the pecking
order for that season. 'Kenny Stuart was rarely beaten by anyone
except Wild and Bland. Jon Broxap is another runner that
season who was putting in good performances. He was a very
good runner allround. To me he is someone who doesn't get the
recognition he deserves, although he did run for England.'

Dave Hall competed in seven of the 15 championships races,
and came 12th overall in the championships. Reflecting now he
explains, 'I couldn't come to terms with the long races in those
days. I was good at 'Medium' and 'Short'. I think the fifteen
races really found the best fell runner. What was unique about
Kenny and John was that they could win Burnsall, say, one
weekend then potentially win Ennerdale the following weekend.
Today's system [of only four races] would do me fine. Billy
Bland struggled with the short races. If you took out the mile of
road at Ben Nevis I think he would have been unbeatable there.'

Dave Hall expanded on his theme. 'Both Kenny and John
were very blinkered. Justifiably they were also very confident
in themselves. To have two people around at the same time
is a bit like it was with Ovett and Coe. Also Kenny and John
were so good at every aspect, going up, coming down, 'Short',
'Medium', and 'Long'. It was unique really. I don't think there
has been anyone else like that. You had people like Colin
Valentine and Andy Styan who were really good descenders,
and people like Billy Bland really good over the rough stuff.
But did anyone win any races that Kenny and John were in in
that year?' In fact, either Stuart or Wild won all thirteen of the
championship races they entered.

Having spilled the beans on some of the post-race antics of
the time, Dave Hall then gave another side of one of their char-
acters. 'John Wild was known to let off the odd fire extinguisher
or two [just the once according to John]. Kenny was very unas-
suming though. I was climbing at Shepherds Crag a while ago,
and ended in the café there with a girl I was climbing with. We

were just chatting away and she said she lived in Threlkeld. I asked her if Kenny Stuart still lived there. She said her kids went to school with his kids. She then asked me how I know him. I said, "I used to do a lot of fell running with him". She didn't even know about that aspect of his life.'

Although the championship races were done, the fell season wasn't over yet. Kenny Stuart ran 15 miles on the fells the day after Thieveley Pike race. He often did the Butter Crags race in October, and sometimes used to race late in the season. Then he would be looking for active rest for a while.

Kenny explained that these 15-milers that regularly appeared in his training on Sundays were usually done on his own. 'I didn't train with club mates a lot. That way I could decide exactly what sort of pace I felt I needed to be at. I sometimes used to go down to the club to do the Keswick 5-mile road circuit round town. I always recall banging around on maybe a Thursday night and doing two laps for 10 miles, thinking that it was uncomfortable as I was running too fast as it was like a competition for some club mates - they were flogging themselves. I could handle it, but it was not for me.'

John adds that just a few weeks after Thievely Pike race he was, 'back on duty as RAF Captain in the first cross-country race of the season at Oxford. Life went on!'

On 9 October Kenny returned to the Butter Crag race and won in very wet and misty conditions. It was so bad that race organiser, Pete Bland, was blowing a whistle at the summit to ensure everyone found it. It was a good field, with Sean Livesey second, and Jack Maitland third – the day after coming second in the Cumbria Lakes Marathon in 2-23, on a windy day. This marathon went from Cockermouth to Keswick on the back road, which is quite hilly, and then back on the flat side of Bassenthwaite. Maitland takes up the story. 'I sat behind Dave Thomas, who was quite a big guy, for over 10 miles in to the wind and tried to take him out on the way back. He was stronger in the end.'

According to Maitland the Butter Crag course was, 'very

slippy and a treacherous descent. I picked the wrong shoes. I was pissed off with myself as I didn't do a track session that week. But I was pleased with that marathon time, and feel it was a surprisingly good result on the Sunday considering. I had recovered from the marathon well but was sluggish at the start. I had done a 20-minute run on the Sunday morning, which I would often do.'

Reflecting on his marathon efforts, Maitland pointed out, 'I did three marathons in 1983, so I know exactly what fitness I had. All were between 2-23-27 and 2-24-22. That was just how I was and is why I did the Cumbria Lakes Marathon, and then raced the day after. Remember that orienteering had five- and six- day events sometimes, or maybe an individual event Saturday and relay on the Sunday.'

A week later, on 16 October, was the 20 mile Three Towers race. Strong tail winds pushed Martin Bishop to a new course record, beating that previously set by Dave Lewis. John Wild came 5th after what he describes as a 'heavy night' at the FRA dinner the previous evening. Dave Hall recalls that this allowed him to beat John Wild for the first, and only, time. Hall adds, 'I never beat Kenny or Billy. The nearest I got to Kenny was in the queue in the bar after. Kenny was one of the few I couldn't match on the road.'

John Wild summed up both the deciding race, and the season. 'It was winner takes all. A whole season down to those few seconds.' Two exceptional athletes from very different backgrounds had put themselves on the line all season, resulting in Kenny Stuart gaining his first fell running championship title, and in John Wild being denied his hat-trick of titles in the process.

PART FIVE

Changes

CHAPTER 16

Following white flags in snow

Talking after their epic season-long battle on the fells in 1983, John Wild suggested that he might move to the marathon, and Kenny Stuart thought he would go for a second championship win on the fells. In looking forward to the 1984 fell season Hugh Symonds acknowledged these plans, as he commented (in *The Fellrunner* magazine):

'Kenny Stuart will be defending his title but 1983 runner-up John Wild has expressed doubt about going for a fourth summer on the fells. Others likely to be making a bid this season are the rising young Sean Livesey and international orienteer Jack Maitland.'

Being reminded of that, Jack Maitland commented, 'I think I still saw myself as being an orienteer at that time, probably the last year that was the case. Later on I decided to give up orienteering as I didn't get in to the British Senior team in 1985 for the World Championships in Australia. Being young the two years to the next World Championships was an eon to wait. So I then temporarily retired from orienteering, intending to come back. But I did well in fell running in 1985, particularly in Europe, and then I won the British championships in 1986. So I never went back.'

John Wild commented, 'I'd decided sometime before the 1983 season to run a marathon. But the thought of a possible hat-trick, and competing with Kenny was also a deciding factor to carry on with the fells in 1983. I perhaps even put that marathon off in 1983 because I was so enjoying the fells.'

John confirmed that he had actually started training for the London Marathon in October 1983, but was still running cross country for the RAF. 'I was still the cross country captain then. To be honest I thought coming off the fells I had got enough strength anyway. I was running 20+ miles in training. It was one of the best cross country seasons I had as well.'

Although now a champion fell runner, Kenny Stuart still liked cross country racing, and was Keswick AC's club captain to boot. 'I won the county championships (possibly at Egremont), beating some good runners, and quite fancied my chances at the Inter-Counties, hoping for a top twenty spot. I went there convinced I would do really well. We set off and I wasn't 100%, but I was astonished at the standard and the speed of it. I ended up 78th going backwards, being pushed by some fell runners I would always beat. Mike Bishop was one of the top cross country guys at the time.' At this point Kenny showed me his very neat racing record book, with details of his whole competitive career – which confirms that Colin Moore won the Inter-Counties that year, with Eamonn Martin second and Mike Bishop third. Eventually Kenny got his Inter-Counties position down to fifth in 1988 at Derby, and only 30 to 40 seconds behind the winner, Carl Thackeray. That year he was also tenth in the National Cross Country, which was won by Dave Lewis.

Pauline Stuart also ran at those Inter-Counties, noting in the Keswick club newsletter:

Boob of the year must go to the County Cross Country selectors who presented me, Gill and Daphne with knee length, size 40" chest county t-shirts for our run at Leeds in the Inter-Counties. Try tucking those in your knickers!

In early February John Wild had what was for him an average result in the RAF cross country championships, coming eighth, and on 24 February he was only 18th in the Inter-Services, his equal worst position. However, he did have excellent results elsewhere. He won the Midland Counties cross country championships at Corby, with the *Evening Telegraph* reporting that, 'Marathon men, one would-be and one well established, enjoyed the sticky underfoot conditions in Thoroughsale Wood to give Tipton Harriers a one-two ... Sergeant John Wild outsprinting Andy Holden after the pair had been locked together for practically the entire eight miles. Wild used the race as part of his-build-up to the London Marathon and – a double Inter-Counties champion – also filled one of the blanks in a considerable roll of personal honours.'

Wild was also part of the winning Tipton team at the National 12-stage relay, running 26-37 on the seventh leg, over approximately five miles. I had assumed road training was now more important for him, and that he was on high mileage in his marathon build-up. On putting this view to John, he explained how it panned out. 'I was obviously training hard on the roads, but often with RAF races I ran what the manager called a "Captain's Race" in the RAF championships. I ran enough to justify selection and to support the other runners. I think I was ill for the Inter-Services which was still apparent when I missed the National Cross Country championships. Andy Holden was second in the Midland Counties and made the England team for the New York World Cross Country championships (which was possibly another reason why I got picked).'

Wild also won a hard, and loaded, cross country league race for Tipton around the time too that also proved instrumental in him getting selected for England's World Cross Team for New York without running the National. 'I was leading the race, running very strongly with Richard Partridge (of Birchfield) in second. Partridge's coach was shouting from the sidelines for Richard to "sit on him", to which Ian Stewart was heard to comment "sit on him - he'll need to lie on him". Richard also made the World Cross England team that year.'

Wild seemed to be facing a conflict with juggling the different strands of his running career at this time. He was obviously in serious training for a planned marathon debut, but couldn't seem to decide on where his cross country priorities lay. A *Daily Telegraph* report on his Midland Counties cross country win noted that he was looking forward to running in the National Cross Country Championships at Newark the next month to help his club. But, in the next sentence he was quoted as saying, 'I am not interested in qualifying for the world championships in New York because I am preparing myself to run in the London Marathon.' He may have said he was not interested but he did get picked, as noted, and did travel as reserve, which just added to his commitments at the time.

A preview of the National in the press the next week gave some background to the strength of the Tipton team at the time and of John Wild's training regime. He is quoted as saying, 'I've been putting in a few extra types of sessions just recently and it seems to be paying off. I've been slack over the last few years but the extra work this winter has given me more strength and more confidence.' Wild had been speed training with Julian Goater, stationed at RAF Stafford, which he felt played a big part in the improvement. 'We've done four or five sessions together since the New Year and it certainly helps to have someone so quick to train with,' he added.

Meanwhile, Kenny Stuart opened his 1984 fell season with a win in the Category 'C' Benson Knott fell race on 5 February. It was down near Kendal and was just a training race for him. Stuart dominated the race, winning by a minute and a half. He followed that with a trip to Scotland to win the Carnethy 5 fell race on 18 February, winning by over a minute from Colin Donnelly, showing some brilliant early season form. Kenny has very few memories of the race. 'Coming off the top you came down a massive scree run, which I think has been changed now. I was coming down thinking "hell, I feel fit". I ran well.'

On 11 March John Wild, running for Tipton, won the Milford 21 fell/country race, by two and a half minutes from Paul Davies-Hale. He had heard of the Milford 21 back in the mid-1970s, when he gave an RAF colleague a lift to it one year. When Wild moved to the Stafford area in 1979 he used to train on Cannock Chase and the Milford 21 became a target. 'I'd won it before 1984 and quite honestly on that day Davies-Hale had got me beat until he got cramp up the last nasty vicious climb about 1k from the finish.'

On 8 April Wild ran brilliantly to become the inaugural winner of the Stafford half marathon, while at the same time admitting that road running was not one of his favourite forms of running. He had recently taken the decision to 'hit the road' and train for the London Marathon, and the half marathon was part of his build up.

He won Stafford in 65-04, a clear minute ahead of his nearest challenger Max Coleby (Gateshead AC) in 66-16. At the time Wild was a serving flight systems electronics instructor at RAF Cosford and a member of Tipton Harriers. 'Having made the decision to run my first London Marathon [*in the spring of 1984*], I had been training really hard. I had even kicked my favourite forms of running, cross country and fell racing, into touch.'

Talking at the time he noted, 'coincidentally, I had one of the best winter seasons I ever had. I was really flying, but I remember being very nervous prior to the race. I knew going into the race that I had done the training but it was still like a crisis of confidence.' Looking back now he adds, 'I used to run my 21-mile Sunday morning run in two hours and I have recently done it on the bike using the Garmin, and measured it at 20.86 - it was very hilly too and some of the hills even had me gasping on the bike.'

The race started and finished at the County Showground and headed for the town centre, which meant a long downhill stretch to start with, but a steep climb to the finish. 'I didn't really take the lead until Radford Bank. One of the Gateshead boys [*Coleby*] was quite a seasoned distance runner, and he figured strongly, so I was nervous I guess. It was a good field and of course the first mile we did in about 4 minutes 20 seconds as it was downhill. As soon as I took the lead I went away. I pushed it up the hill and I felt really good. I had plenty of miles in the legs from my training on the fells and I had the strength over the last few miles to win it, which was brilliant.' Could he have run faster in the Stafford half marathon? 'I think I could have. We didn't have watches that told you your pace and that. The last mile was also quite a severe uphill. The first mile had been downhill. Also I was on my own after about 6-7 miles.'

Wild then did the Coniston 14 (road race) just six days later in a relatively faster time, winning the race. 'The prize was a huge slate clock. It wouldn't fit in our cottage. I spoke to the director of the company and I said "it is a lovely prize but would you consider exchanging it". He said "what have you got in mind", thinking I was going to ask for money. I said I want to build a slate fireplace, and he said fine. I gave him the details and then a huge Volvo artic turned up with a load of blocks and slate tiles, much more than I needed. These blocks had been sawn on the end and I went up to Billy Bland and I said "how do I get rid of the smoothness". He said "you have to dink'em lad". He took me to his yard and got a bolster chisel and went dink, dink, dink and all the smoothness had gone. I went home tried it. Dink, nothing. I got tendonitis in the wrist doing it. I got a beautiful fireplace though, partly thanks to Billy.'

'I was ill for the National, but as I said, I got picked for the World Cross without running the National, which had never happened, so I must have impressed someone. I was only reserve, so travelled to New York, but didn't run.' Wild remembers it as a superb trip once he'd got over the disappointment of not actually being needed to run. He shared a room with the late Andy Holden who showed him some great places to go in New York. Once he knew all the team were OK he went out for a 2½ hour run before the race. For reasons best known to himself he put his plastic ID card down the front of his shorts. 'It cut into the end of my knob and caused an infection (try telling that to your wife after an away trip!). There was no cord on the card so I couldn't hang it round my neck and as I didn't want to carry it in my hand I just shoved it down the shorts.'

Wild continued, 'I had a great night on the beer with several athletes including Steve Jones, who'd had a great race. On the last day, Andy Holden took me to a bar that stated that if you bought the house special meal, you could have all the beer you could drink. I had no choice - Andy just ordered two specials! About two hours later, a waitress said "Hey, ain't you guys ever leaving", to which Andy replied "No - we haven't had all the beer we can drink yet". I hardly remember going to the airport and embarking, but Andy was still drinking on the plane. He certainly had some capacity!'

Wild never got to make his London Marathon debut in May 1984, as he had a hamstring injury just three weeks prior to the big day. He emphasised that his training had been going really well. 'I was doing a standard 4 x 1½ mile session on a survey wheel measured section of road around the Cosford RAF camp. I used to knock these out in 6m 30s to 6m 40s pace with ½ mile jog recovery between each. I'd done a two mile warm up with strides, and I'd done the first effort. I was about a mile into the next rep when my hamstring went. It felt as if I'd been shot. The milkman gave me a lift back to the camp gates in his float and I hobbled to the medical centre where ice was put on it. However, it didn't recover and I watched the London Marathon from my bed, feeling really, really sick. All that effort wasted.'

He did, however, complete the London Marathon the following year - in 2 hours 22 minutes. 'Effectively, I never really recovered after that hamstring injury and my running life was never the same. All the hard work didn't come to much.'

The fell championship races for the year started on 24 March, at the short Blackstone Edge race. It was very poor visibility and two of the leaders accidentally took a short cut, for which they were disqualified. Kenny Stuart reached the top of Blackstone Edge first. The race report noted it had been, '1,000 feet of climbing in a mile and a half through a snowstorm and with the ground slippery from a cover of fresh snow.' Stuart ran a further half mile of boggy Pennine Way path, and on reaching the turn marshal for the descent he spotted two runners ahead. It was Jack Maitland and Mike Bishop, who had got lost in the mist, cut down too early and thus arrived at the finish first. A measure of his performance that day is the fact that Kenny was just two seconds outside the course record despite the conditions.

Kenny recalls it now as a strange race. 'It came on a blizzard half way up the ascent, as I was trying to break Mike Bishop, from Staffordshire Moorlands AC, because he had won or was second in the Inter-Counties that year. I was working really hard, and I broke him reasonably easily and went on to the first and second summits, came back down the same descent and saw two blokes in front of me. Jack and Mike hadn't gone to the second checkpoint, as they had missed it in the blizzard. I was declared the winner and they were disqualified.'

Jack Maitland's thoughts, which were recorded in his training diary, were as follows. 'I was first back after a brilliant run.' Reading this out to me he laughs at the situation. 'Holding off Mike Bishop, was a good mark. Both disqualified for missing a gate, after losing white flags against the snow. Would certainly have been second to Kenny. Pissed off.'

It was a bizarre day altogether, as far as Malcolm Patterson is concerned. 'I was gifted second place when there was no way I would have been higher than fourth. I do still laugh about trying to follow white flags in a snowstorm.'

The next day Maitland won the Edale Skyline race by one second from Pete Irwin, who was a well-known mountain marathon runner. Maitland grinned as he noted, 'Irwin famously couldn't read a map. He reputedly had one map of the Lake District which he took to every event!'

It may have been something to do with the date, but on the first day of April there were problems with 'disappearing' checkpoint punches at the Black Combe fell race that year. Eventually, Kenny Stuart prevailed from Jon Broxap as he continued his march through the championship races. Malcolm Patterson's preparation for this race was to stay out until 3 am at a stag night and then be driven the three hours up from Sheffield. 'I seem to remember going to register and then coming back to the car, lying down on the back seat and staying there until about two minutes before the off. So I was pleasantly surprised to feel good from the start and I was happy to settle for 5th.' He also mischievously suggested who the culprit that 'stole' the punches was, but my lips are sealed.

Two weeks later, on 15 April, the championship series moved on to the Blisco Dash. Kenny Stuart lowered the course record for the second year running, taking his third successive championships victory. He was running that well that people had starting speculating as to whether he could have a perfect score for the championship races, with a caveat that the longer races that were to come would likely be his sternest test. I asked Kenny if he ever considered that he might be capable of getting a full house in the championships races that he ran. 'No, I never really thought that way. It was a matter of going out running races as they came, you know. I never planned a season in that way. I planned a race at a time. So many things can go wrong. If you get misty days, bad days, injuries, you can't plan around that.'

Despite Kenny Stuart being in rollicking form he had to run at his hardest to see off Jack Maitland (a Leeds University student at the time), coming home in 36 minutes 28 seconds at Blisco. Maitland hadn't done a race the day before that time as he was up in Scotland doing some mapping. In his diary he recorded it as, 'not a very good climb. My calves tied up. Made a mess of top, must reccie. Pleased to be so close to Kenny. Looking forward to a race with Kenny when I am with him on the descent. Definitely aim to come second in championships now, but may have problem getting enough long races in.' As it turned out he did struggle to get 'Longs' in, only racing at Sedbergh out of the five championships ones, which resulted in him finishing 5th overall in the championships. Maitland did come back to Blisco though in 1987 to narrowly beat Malcolm Patterson and set a new course best of 36 minutes 1 second, which was the record for ages.

Malcolm Patterson claims to remember little about the 1984 race, apart from the fact that he was, 'annoyed, rather petulantly, that it was Jack and not me that was up there challenging Kenny! I suppose it was some sort of karma that saw Jack beat me again in 1987. It was just my luck to be in great form that day, to find a great route, to break a Kenny Stuart record ... only to be outsprinted. But all credit to Jack, he just wasn't going to let me win!'

On 5 May at the Category 'A' 9-mile Coniston fell race Kenny had to work hard to hold off Hugh Symonds and Jack Maitland. With brilliant weather, it resulted in a new course record for him of 1-06-13. Symonds recollects how he came close to beating Stuart that day. 'I was ahead of him on the descent off Coniston Old Man. I was pulling away thinking I could win. There was nothing in my mind which said I can't beat him. I got ahead but on the run-in he had greater leg speed, and he beat me, by 15 seconds.' Deep down it seemed that Symonds just couldn't get the better of Stuart. He even admitted to me that, 'when Kenny wasn't at a race, that would be when I used to think I could win the race.' Illustrating the point, Symonds had won the Three Peaks race six days beforehand, when Kenny had not raced there. It was Symonds's first Three Peaks win, with a record for that longer version of the course.

A week later, on 12 May, it was the 14-mile 'Long' Northern Counties race, from Buttermere. Despite not always taking the best lines early on Kenny Stuart destroyed a quality field to set a new record, beating Jon Broxap by over five minutes. The races were coming thick and fast now, and eight days on Kenny Stuart won the Fairfield fell race from Hugh Symonds.

Malcolm Patterson loved the Fairfield route, claiming it was a race that suited him, though he never won it. On this occasion he was pleased enough with the result, coming third. 'I just remember at some point about halfway up the climb feeling strong, but looking up to see Kenny, with Hugh in vain pursuit, pulling away from me and realising that, short of a miracle, I was never going to be able to match him in a fell race (or in a singing competition).'

After seven championship races Kenny Stuart had a perfect 224 points (7 x 32 points, having won every championships race) and was already leading second-placed Symonds by 35 points.

Kenny Stuart won again at the short Saddleworth race on 3 June, although he could not beat Ricky Wilde's course record from 1978. He just didn't feel he was in record breaking form on the day. Jon Broxap and Hugh Symonds must have been getting fed up with chasing Stuart, coming 3rd and 4th here, with previous multiple winner Andy Darby coming in second, but 26 seconds behind Stuart.

The eighth championships race of the year was at Ennerdale on 9 June. Kenny Stuart was less certain of the route choices on this course, so allowed Bob Ashworth to lead early on with a small pack behind him. Soon though Kenny, Hugh Symonds and Billy Bland began to break away going by Black Beck Tarn. Kenny pulled away somewhat over Pillar, but Symonds brought Jon Broxap, Billy Bland and Bob Whitfield back to him over Haycock. Kenny was able to pull away again to win from Symonds by nearly two minutes, with Broxap and company five minutes or so down at the end of this 23-miler. Kenny recalls that even early on as he was coming off Great Bourne he, 'was in that sort of disinterested mode again, I think. By the time I got to Innominate Tarn Billy and one other were way in front and I got back to them climbing Pillar. I got on his back and one of them said "Christ almighty you have made up some ground there in good time", so I was going well. I was getting better and better as I was fitter and more confident. With John Wild not being there it helped my confidence too. So I would say I was a better runner then than in 1983 actually.'

John Wild's only Services track championships race that year was on 19 June, when he came fifth in the RAF 10,000m track championships, in 32-28.4. Even the steeplechase had been dropped for his concentrated effort on the roads. John is not sure about that last point as he notes. 'I have a feeling I ran the 'chase in the Inter-Services though, as the RAF hierarchy stopped me and some others going to Sweden. I had said I didn't want to run the 'chase and because of this we weren't allowed the foreign trip, although we went the next year. But I swallowed my pride and didn't have a paddy over it.'

'My training was going well though, with a great routine. I used to run sessions like four times a mile and a half measured out around RAF Cosford. Two mile warm up and then the mile and a halfs, with half mile recovery.'

Two weeks later the fell championships were off to the Eildon Two Hills race (on 23 June). Kenny Stuart was first, and knocked 1 minute 8 seconds off Allan McGee's time from 1977, in beating Maitland, Symonds and Broxap. This is one of the course records that Kenny still holds. Maitland's forward focus can be seen from his diary comment at the time. 'I went well after a cautious start. Knowing course more fully would have helped. Now working towards World Mountain Cup/championships in September in Italy.' So, Maitland was thinking more about his own fell running potential then.

CHAPTER 17

Ripe for a fast time

Kenny Stuart was running so well now that he started thinking about going for some course records. The Glossop fell race, on 1 July, was included in the 1984 fell championships, but several championships contenders chose to miss it. Kenny was one of them, as he wanted instead to have a crack at the Skiddaw record that same day. Hugh Symonds scored good championship points, winning the Glossop race by over a minute.

Kenny turned in an exceptional performance on Skiddaw. He set off determinedly and was never really challenged. He beat Dave Cannon's 11-year-old record of 62 minutes 30 seconds, coming home exactly a minute clear of the field in 62 minutes 18 seconds. A contemporary report declared this to be, 'class running at its best and had he been pressed I'm certain that breaking the magic hour for the Skiddaw course would have been a possibility.' Over thirty years later Kenny's record still stands. He thinks he ran very well that day, but he doesn't think the hour was on. Being pushed he feels he could have run better but not by more than two minutes.

Pauline Stuart recalled that, 'Danny Hughes was really into international running at this time and he arranged for Ken and I to go to Lenzerheide in Switzerland. It was an uphill race and I came second. Ken also came second but he didn't run well.' Kenny said he just didn't feel right on that occasion. 'When you are at home and you have that power you just know you have got it. Eventually I went out to other races in other years and had it, and did myself justice.'

Kenny wrote an extended piece for his club newsletter, which shows the extent athletes were willing to go to in order to get good international competition, and also his appreciation of the environment both here and abroad:

Information passed on via Danny Hughes from the organiser looked promising, so looking through the FRA Calendar and finding no championship race on that weekend I decided to take the invitation up. Also invited was Jack Maitland of Aberdeen, but teaching in Leeds and Pauline Haworth who decided to go along and pay her own fare. On the Thursday, the day before travelling to London, I decided to put in an easy 12-mile undulating fell cross country type run – the only hot day of the summer and had a struggle to complete the course with little left in reserve. This didn't do my confidence any good at all but I passed it off as a mild virus, hoping a few easy days training before the Sunday race would bring me back on 'fettle'.

Pauline and I caught the 7am train from Oxenholme on Friday 5 July and with Jack flew from Heathrow to Zurich airport. After getting the tube into Zurich City, a further 1.5 hour train journey followed to bring us, via long, flat, narrow valleys to a large town called Chur. We were met here by 'Parpon' the race organiser and after driving up the mountains to Lenzerheide at 4500 feet above sea level we settled down in our accommodation, a superb guest house/hotel with private bathrooms and even a 'mini-bar' fridge in the rooms.

On Saturday we took in magnificent views of the mountains rising straight above the town before having a look over the 11km course. Apart from still feeling tired and stale I personally felt disappointed on seeing the route, which although felt steep enough was actually a road race which went up 2000 feet to finish at the Hotel 'Alp Lavoz' – the last mile incidentally comprising the only 'fell' of the race.

Saturday night saw us attending a function for some of the invited runners. This included Mike Short, and we had a good meal followed by an antiquated film show. A few pints of lager went down before bed and even though it blew and rained heavily on the hotel windows I slept well. Race day dawned very cool and misty – more like the Lakes than Switzerland! As the race began at 10am we didn't have to wait long before the suffering started.

Waiting jammed up on the line trying to get pole position with 100 other hopefuls, including 40-50 ladies, turned out to be nerve racking but once the former Swiss champion, Moser, fired the pistol nerves were soon forgotten. The start was all 'legs and elbows' and very fast, no doubt due to the first 1km being downhill on road, and soon a group of about ten hit the first slight climb on a gravel track. Hanging right in the middle of the group I waited for the first steep climb and tried to break the leaders up only to take the Italian Vallicella in tow and he seemed in no mood to settle for second. The steep winding tarmac seemed to run forever and on one of these twists in the road he stole ten yards which soon increased to twenty. Even though I felt legless I hoped he might fade on the last and only mile of fell, but on he went stronger than ever and eventually won by 40 seconds. The view from the finish area at 6500 feet was spectacular and with every finisher getting a little cowbell the noise was almost deafening. Jack officially finished in 6th position and after a slow start Pauline came through strongly to finish 5th lady. Shorty incidentally had an atrocious run by his own admission and struggled somewhere in the 20s.

After another good meal in part of the summit hotel Pauline and I left Shorty and Jack to walk back down the mountain and followed a path that twisted through woods and fields. Wild flowers grew among these hay meadows in abundance and this at 5000 feet, higher than the Ben!

Prizegiving started with a brass band and many speeches and with the sun now blazing down the major awards were presented only to be told shortly that the computer had 'shredded' the results and the main prizegiving had to be cancelled. The hospitality of the Swiss people, particularly Parpon, more than made up for this slip though, and on leaving the country the one thing that impressed was the high degree of cleanliness everywhere and the clear, almost non-polluted atmosphere, even in the large city of Zurich. So if anyone is into tarmac fell races get your rubber slicks tuned up!

Back in the UK, Wasdale (on 14 July) was not a championship race but still had a very good field. Billy Bland won from a 'very frustrated' Hugh Symonds, who had tried his hardest to stick with him on a very hot day.

It was the ninth Snowdon race on 21 July, and although not a championship race it was by now attracting around 400 athletes, including several leading Italians. Kenny Stuart had an eye on a win there but he was beaten by Pezzoli and Bonzi. The latter was even shorter and lighter than Stuart, but broke away from the other two to set a new course record of 1-03-46. Kenny in 3rd, Mike Bishop in 4th and Jeff Norman in 5th won a free trip to the Trofeo Vanoni race at Morbegno in Italy that October. Pauline Stuart set a new record in the ladies race of 1-24-03, but perhaps surprisingly says it was not really her sort of race, too much like a road race. Kenny just says he, 'didn't have a very good run. It was a really red hot day and I wasn't feeling brilliant. The consolation was beating Mike Bishop. It is not a race to have a bad day on.'

Seeking to get the facts right about his preparations, and drinking, Kenny Stuart pointed out that, 'most of the time the night before a race we weren't drinking. I recall going down to Snowdon and some of the Italians were drinking 6-7 pints the night before and still beating me. I would only have a pint and a half say beforehand if any.'

Kenny Stuart had chosen to miss the Moel Siabod championship race on 28 July, as he was preparing for Borrowdale a week later. In his absence Jon Broxap took a close victory, ahead of Dave Cartridge and Jack Maitland, whose diary noted that he had, 'a terrible climb. Coming down I hit the road and my calves went. One of my most pathetic weeks for ages. Stiff from Snowdon the week before, where I had come 6th in race won by Bonzi. Lost a vital position to Jeff Norman on the descent. Fourth Brit but it gave me very stiff calves.'

Kenny Stuart's perfect championship season came crashing down at the Borrowdale race on 4 August. Although he had not been racing well of late, it was always going to be Billy Bland that he had to worry about on his local course, on which he had already won on five occasions. Over 300 runners set off and climbed into a heavy mist early on. Onto Broad Crag Billy Bland began to drop all his main challengers - Livesey, Stuart and Broxap. By Great Gable Bland had a four minute lead. Stuart was in second, and though running well was unable to close the gap crossing to Honister, but did gain a minute or so climbing Dale Head. On the long descent to the finish Bland extended his lead to nearly ten minutes on Stuart, with Ken Taylor a further seven minutes behind in 3rd. This masterly performance from Billy did not stop Stuart from claiming the championship, with two races still to be run. Kenny chuckles, remembering it was a cloudy day. 'Billy took me through a route I had never been shown before. When I came out of Grey Knotts he disappeared into the mist. By the time I got my map out and realised where I was and got down to Honister, they said he was five minutes ahead.'

Billy Bland tells it similarly, through his eyes. 'Laal Sean was with me early on and Kenny. I got a gap on the stones over Broad Crag in a bit of mist, so they couldn't see me. I would give Kenny a race over wet stones any day. Sean told me later that he was the nearest to me down to Corridor. Kenny came up to him and they came down the Corridor together and then up Gable and according to Sean, Kenny said "we'll get him up here", which would have been a fair comment really as Kenny was such a good climber, although Sean wasn't quite so good. But they didn't! They couldn't catch me, and I won quite convincingly actually, in a good time I think. Kenny never came to that race again!'

On the very next day (5 August) was the Latrigg race, and many of those running Borrowdale on the Saturday had doubled up. Incredibly, after his mauling at the hands of Bland over 17 miles the day beforehand, Stuart came back to win and to set a new record to boot on this short three miler. He was running Latrigg for the first time, yet took 17 seconds off Hugh Symonds' record from the previous year. Explaining his recovery, Kenny notes now that, 'because of the fact that I hadn't really pushed myself the day before because of the conditions I didn't feel any issues the next day at all. The fells are rather different from the road. If you have done a half marathon on the Saturday and try to do a 'Short' fell race on the Sunday you probably wouldn't have able to do it. Fells didn't knock it out of your legs the same.'

Stuart seemed to float up the 1203 feet of climbing and raced down the greasy descent to win by some 45 seconds from Rod Pilbeam, with Jack Maitland third. Billy Bland was down in 9th place, nearly 2 minutes behind Stuart. After the race Stuart commented, 'it's an event with a bit of tradition [*it started in 1973, having been a professional race from 1891-1965*] and really enjoyable to take part in. There are not many races where so many folk turn out on the fell to watch.' Maitland had been in Sweden during the week running in the World Student Orienteering championships, doing the relay on the Friday, and travelling back on the Saturday. He reflected that he, 'must get more training in for World fell championships.'

The next championship race was on 19 August, the Sedbergh Hills race over 14 miles. Kenny Stuart missed it as he was training for the Ben Nevis race two weeks later. Sedbergh Hills was expected to be a race between Stuart's two closest challengers, Jon Broxap and Hugh Symonds, whose local course it was. Broxap and Symonds led out until halfway, when Symonds began to fall away. In the end he slipped to 6th place, with Jack Maitland having moved through on the second half to take the runner-up slot, albeit 1 minute 47 seconds behind Broxap. Jack Maitland warmed-up for the Ben by winning Burnsall on 25 August.

So, to the Ben for a championship race on 1 September. Kenny Stuart had his eye on the course record that had been set by John Wild the year before, 1-25-35. The cloud cover was patchy but down to the Red Burn at times. From the start in Town Park it was taken at a fierce pace, possibly due to the prize for first to the summit. Hugh Symonds took the prize, just ahead of Kenny Stuart, who attacked the descent with a vengeance. Despite his best effort he only just clipped Wild's record, by a mere one second. Jack Maitland had been first to the summit the year before but lost out in the mist-shrouded shenanigans coming down. This time a more cautious ascent allowed him to come through for second place, thirty two seconds behind Stuart, and a minute ahead of Symonds, who had run his fastest Ben Nevis time. Kenny said that John graciously remarked to him at a later date that, 'I deserved that extra second because in 1983 when he set that record, myself and Jack Maitland got lost in the mist.' Who knows what time would have been run, and by whom, if those three main protagonists had been racing each other out towards the end of the race on that day.

Kenny seems quite surprised how the race actually panned out. 'It was a misty sort of day and was quite slippery. Hugh was with me at the top and I think I let him go and he got the summit prize. Hugh was no problem, with due respect I can beat him coming down. I could see I had got so far in front of the others I thought I am going to win it easy. I got half way down the path from Red Burn and I could hear this steamroller coming - and it was Jack Maitland. He was all over the place. He just went past like a bloody steam train and I thought "I have to stick with him". I held him till we got to Achintee and then just dropped him on the road. But he was going at it that day.'

Maitland's diary entry gives a clue to the fast time. 'I was third at the top, but first from Kenny at Achintee (which is quite near the end). I caught him on the descent and he latched on to me to the roads. They had re-made the path - and got rid of a lot of rocks. It was ripe for a fast time. I nearly won, but lacked the speed on the road to finish. Disappointed in my climb, I felt I needed more rest.' Maitland never did win the Ben, saying that Hugh Symonds was his *bête noir*. 'He beat me when I thought I should have won the Ben. I also finished second behind him at the Three Peaks.'

Dave Hall remembers that there was more 'relaxing' after the race again this year. 'Kenny was a bit of a Jack the Lad actually. He is also a pretty good singer, I don't know if anyone has mentioned that. We always used to go to the Imperial Hotel. So it started off with us trying to get as many as possible in each compartment of a triangular revolving door and still get it to move. It moved on to me and Jack M mooning each other. Then Kenny got up on stage and was about to do one there. Someone said if you do that you will be banned from next year's race, so he started singing fox hunting songs. It was brilliant.'

Coming in 9th, Malcolm Patterson reckons he was older and wiser in 1984 than in 1982, and raced better. 'But I was still nowhere near the leaders and only three places higher and two minutes faster. I think I just have to accept that the Ben was too tough a race for me. I never raced it again.'

At the conclusion of the championships Kenny Stuart had 317 points (winning 10 of the 11 races he entered, being just 2nd to Billy at Borrowdale). Jon Broxap was 2nd with 286, and Hugh Symonds 3rd with 280. Pauline Stuart went one better and won 10 out of 10 of her championship counters, sealing her win at the Ben Nevis race.

Two weeks on and it was the Three Shires race, which although not a championship race always attracts a good field. I was also there to take on the 13 tough miles and 4000 feet of ascent, reasonably fit after a spring 2-43 marathon. It took me about that amount of time to finish the race. I suffered badly on the third main ascent. I was going up beside the wall on the steep side of Birk Knott when suddenly I collapsed to the ground and couldn't go on. I gave myself a stiff talking to and struggled upwards. A friendly face, and a sugar rush from a proffered Mars bar, revived me enough to shuffle down the fell and complete the race. If I had had a better day I might have beaten Kenny Stuart as he jogged in 26th. As the race organiser noted, 'It was nice to see Kenny enjoying a day out and not worrying too much about his image.' Kenny explains, 'Pauline and I just ran together. I just decided to have a training run. I recall that Mike Short's ambition when he was running well was that he would like to come back in later years when he was past it and just go and do all these races for a bit of fun. I thought I might try that, and just had a run round.'

At the front end Bob Whitfield, Mark Rigby and Billy Bland had broken away by the Three Shires Stone, with two summits still to go. They finished in that order, all within 37 seconds. Further down the field I can claim a moral victory over Olympian Chris Brasher, as he DNF'd, but he was there later to hand out the prizes, some of which he had donated.

There had been plans afoot for a World Cup of mountain racing in 1984, but they fell through. When this happened the Italians, who were one of the nations who were keenest on the World Cup idea, held an invitational international mountain race at Zogno, on 30 September. The organisers played to the strengths of their runners in setting up the course, which was just 9.5km long and only just met the requirement to have 250 feet of climb per mile. The course was also on tracks all the way, and rocky and firm mostly. England, Scotland and Wales sent teams, to run against the hosts, plus Austria, Switzerland and San Marino.

The England team was chosen by the FRA committee on the basis of performances in the season's shorter championship races. The race favourite was reckoned by many to be the Italian Fausto Bonzi, who at the time held the course record for the Snowdon race. He lived locally, at over 3000 feet, and was expected to do well. Malcolm Patterson took the field out early on, until Kenny Stuart put his foot down and gained a slight lead, leading at the turn by 10 seconds. He returned down to the finish in complete command, and beat Bonzi by 34 seconds. The Italians showed their dominance though by finishing 10 runners in the first 12 places, with just Scotland's Colin Donnelly splitting them in 8th place. Further English runners packed well, with Malcolm Patterson finishing 13th, Hugh Symonds 15th, Dave Cartridge 16th and Jon Broxap 17th.

Seeing himself reported as taking the field out early on, Patterson chuckles and expands. 'Yes indeed, nervous energy made me start too fast! I remember struggling on the second half of the climb as a result, not a usual occurrence for me! I then had a reasonably good descent, helped by cutting quite a few of the zig-zags much to the consternation of the marshals, though I think most of the Brits did the same. I did get really bad and deep blisters which took weeks to heal and had me walking like a ballerina. I was (secretly) very annoyed that Colin beat me that day by having a faster descent, a pattern that was to repeat itself in several key races over the years.'

Malcolm Patterson remembers also that the headline in next day's local paper was 'veni vidi vici'! Patterson also recalls that, 'Hugh Symonds was on the trip, and I remember him performing on the dance floor in the evening watched by a crowd of young Italian men. The fact that the club was called The Question Mark should have warned us heteros it was a gay club! The place was also prosecuted for running a prostitution ring in 2009. Kenny I recall sang hunting songs throughout the trip. Only during the race did he stop singing.'

John Wild had pretty much stopped running on the fells, so it was a surprise when he made an appearance at the Three Towers fell race on 14 October. His endurance was obviously very good, as he won this 20-mile fell race in 1-56-22, from Dave Cartridge. I asked John why he had gone back on the fells for this particular race. He replied, 'I'd loved the Three Towers from previous encounters, I think I'd won it three years before. You got bussed from Ramsbottom, ran the race and then had pie and peas in the cricket club afterwards. It's a decent tough race.'

It was a much better race for Malcolm Patterson than in 1982 (when he had navigational issues), coming 7th this time. 'I felt more in touch with John. Perhaps due to the nature of the course, Dave Cartridge beat me quite easily in the end, even though I was normally better than him on the fells. I do still have the stink of the maggot farm in my nostrils though – we used to have to run right past it on the final climb to Holcombe Tower.'

On 28 October teams representing England and Wales ran in the Trofeo Vanoni mountain relay race in Italy. This was something of a return match for the Italian presence at the Snowdon race in July, the first three English runners from there getting the trip to Italy. The race consists of three legs of 7250m. The Italians won with a final time of 1-30-47, with the England team second in 1-33-00, just 14 seconds ahead of the next Italian team. Bonzi had the fastest leg time of 29-14, with Kenny Stuart 2nd in 29-21, Mike Bishop 4th and Jeff Norman 24th fastest.

The season continued for Kenny Stuart when he ran in the second Dunnerdale fell race on 10 November. Kenny sat in with Black Combe's Graham Huddlestone, then moved away in the second half to win by a minute and set a new course record of 38-04. 'It was just another race. That was where Pauline won a pair of Brasher Boots. Probably worth £150 odd now, and this was only a little race. Chris Brasher had some input to it I think.'

The Keswick AC Club fell championships were closely fought every year, and at this time the title often went to hard-racing Billy Bland, who was having a great season again this year. At this time for the club championships there were fifteen Lakes-based races, with the athlete's best ten to score (with 22 points for first, 19 for second, 18 for third, and so on). Billy Bland won with 196pts from 10 races, with Kenny 2nd with 195 from only nine, winning them all except Borrowdale (where he was 2nd to Billy), but beating Billy in Lakes races at Coniston, the Northern Counties (at Buttermere), Ennerdale, Skiddaw, Latrigg, and Butter Crag (and Ben Nevis to boot).

Kenny Stuart had won the 1984 fell championship and was planning to have another crack the next year, whilst John Wild was heading for pastures new.

CHAPTER 18

Never an easy run with him

John Wild was posted to RAF St Athan (South Wales) in March 1985, but it didn't go particularly well, as Wild notes. 'I got given some duff jobs, just filling in really. It took three months to get a married quarter for Anne to move down. It was just a crap job, so I bunged in an application to go to Germany with the RAF. It was a shame that the only time I was at the same station as the main players was when I went to down to St Athan. I was coming to the end of my career then, but trained with Steve Jones a bit. There was never an easy run with him, he trained so hard.'

Wild also stopped being captain of the RAF team in 1985. 'I think Alan Warner decided that after Steve Jones had set the world marathon record perhaps he should have it. I was RAF team captain for 10 years, which was an honour itself.' Alan Warner recalls that it was actually Mark Flint that took over the captaincy, and not Steve Jones. At this time every one of the RAF team was an international. They had English, Scottish, Wales and Ireland internationals to choose from, and there were some quality runners who didn't make the RAF team.

Kenny Stuart won the county cross country championships, before going on to the Inter-Counties, on 19 January. Mike McLeod won with Kenny coming in 24th. The Keswick AC newsletter sadly reported that, 'unfortunately Kenny was not able to lead home a full Cumbria team due to a mix up over bus times, resulting in over half the team being left at home.'

Before the 1985 British Fell championship season started some of the contenders had a run at the Benson Knott fell race on 3 February. Kenny Stuart won without too much trouble, with Mark Aspinall second and Hugh Symonds third. Two weeks later was the Carnethy 5 on 16 February. Kenny Stuart showed his intentions for the season by setting a new course record of 48-08, well clear of Jack Maitland, who had several mates in Edinburgh and liked to race this one, and Hugh Symonds, who says he, 'didn't feel strong.'

The first championship race of the season was the Edale Skyline on 24 March. The weather was none too kind, with a snow squall in the later stages. Kenny Stuart had a virus, and started the race but pulled out at Lord's Seat. At the time Kenny thought it was mild flu, but later decided it was a heavy cold virus. He says it wasn't the start of his later viral problems, and that he recovered well after it. As to the race he recalls that, 'it was on my mind that I would start the race and I would be all right, but suffer afterwards. I thought, well at least I'd get the points and the race in. But unfortunately, I was too weak to get anywhere. I felt really groggy, you know what it is like, humdinging groggy. You just want to go to sleep.' Pauline was ill too and didn't bother turning up for the race.

Bob Ashworth proved to have the best knowledge and/or navigational skill and won from Billy Bland and Colin Donnelly, with Hugh Symonds (who acknowledges that he was lost at one point) and Jack Maitland close behind.

Further down the field was Malcolm Patterson, who wasn't really focusing on fell races in 1985, and even though this was local and his club's race, his heart wasn't really in it. He explains that he did get back into it though, 'when the orienteering season didn't go as well as I was hoping, I then switched back to the fells, running for England in my first World Trophy in 1986 and then having perhaps my best ever season on the fells in 1987.'

The Kentmere Horseshoe on 14 April saw Kenny Stuart return to the fray in fine form, winning by two and a half minutes. His closest challenger was Jack Maitland, obviously in good shape after recent victories in the Reebok Mountain Trial and the Pendle race. Whilst no match for Stuart, Maitland did come second, holding off Billy Bland by 15 seconds. A week later and there was a Keswick AC clean sweep at the 'Short' Blisco Dash, by Kenny Stuart, Billy Bland and Colin Valentine.

Jack Maitland wasn't competing at Blisco, but the next week he attempted a tough treble – to run the Mow Cop Killer Mile on the Wednesday, a 2000m steeplechase on the Saturday and the Three Peaks race on the Sunday. All went well at Mow Cop, as he set a new record of 6-31 for a race that has a gradient of 1 in 4 in places. There was a prize for the first runner to get under 6-30. Maitland was close, recalling, 'I won in 6-30 point something. There is a great photo of me finishing. Two years later Roger Hackney turned up and took the time under 6-30 for the prize.' Unsurprisingly, in his third race within five days, Maitland found Hugh Symonds too strong for him at the Three Peaks, coming in second just a minute behind, after leading for much of the way.

Hugh Symonds remembers this race vividly. 'We got to the bottom of Whernside and Jack starts running away from me. It was one of those moments when I thought "I can't go with that, I will die". So I let Jack go. I thought, "OK, second today is fine, I won it the year before". Going up Swine's Tail, is it called, on Ingleborough, it gets really steep by a fence. People were saying, "Jack is finished, you can get him". I thought great, I feel really good and strong. More than one person said you can get him. At the top you pass runners going the other way and you can see them. I looked Jack in the eye and I thought I can beat you Jack. It was about a mile from the finish when I passed him. I wrote in my diary: "first, just!".'

In the London Marathon that year, at the end of April, John Wild finally ran his first marathon, finishing 85th in 2-22-54. It was also my best marathon, as I finished less than twelve minutes behind John. As noted at the top of the chapter John had been suffering some problems some weeks before when he moved to St Athan, which were very de-motivating. He recalls,

'I arrived at St Athan and the general office had got no notice of my posting and so there was no post to go to. It was rubbish.' Consequently, he got shipped from one job to another wherever there was a temporary vacancy. He was also travelling back home every weekend, running the M4, M5 and M6 gauntlet to get home on Friday and back to Wales on Sunday. 'Anne and I had decided to move into married quarters and she would move jobs within the Civil Service. However, there was over a three-month waiting list. So, you can see, conditions were not conducive to good running. I don't remember much about the race other than that we stayed with Don Woodruff's son at Putney the night before and I travelled to the start by tube. I did suffer on the last five miles though.'

I wondered if Alan Warner had any insights on why Wild's marathon running didn't work out. 'No, because I was out of the picture then. I can't say what he did right, or wrong.' John Wild now says that he, 'never really recovered after that and running life was never the same. All the hard work didn't come to much so I started getting ready for RAF life in Germany.'

Jack Maitland was noted for liking to race frequently, and one week later he started a sequence of tough races on the Saturday (4th May), then the next Sunday (12th), Thursday (16th) and Sunday (19th). Remarkably, he came second in them all. Even more incredibly, he was beaten by Kenny Stuart on ALL FOUR occasions. In the first race, over 9 miles at Coniston, the weather played its part to a considerable extent. With mist coming in low only 299 out of 365 starters actually finished. None of this seemed to affect Stuart and Maitland as Alan Bocking noted in his *Fellrunner* report, which entertainingly described, 'a battle royal in the mist with them both dipping under the course record set by Kenny last year. The mist and their speed of travel took them over three minutes clear of the rest. Jack certainly scented victory, his leaping of stiles would have done the Grand National proud, but in the end Kenny's sprint just managed to preserve his domestic invincibility.' Billy Bland led the rest home, with Hugh Symonds 8th.

Maitland recently reflected on the Coniston race. 'I really pushed Kenny and I was leading in to the field and he still managed to beat me. We certainly did push each other hard. I was amazed when that record was beaten, by Keith Anderson I think it was. I thought it would stand a while. I didn't feel we could have pushed any faster that day.'

Kenny still marvels at Jack Maitland's running that day and how hard he had pushed him. 'I beat him by one second. He was incredible that day. He was doing that vaulting walls thing, he passed me just as I came off the last summit of Coniston Old Man and I thought "that is it now, he is going like a steam train". He got about 50 yards on me and he stubbed his toe and he went down like a rock, bang. He took a while to get up, and he did it a couple of times. We got on the flat and I thought "this is my race" and he was vaulting stiles and I was climbing over them. I got in the field where the Coniston race finishes and he was all for it going down the field. I am quite a good finisher and I just pipped him.'

Looking back, Kenny acknowledges that he was quite interested in racing the Italians in the Reebok Challenge, and more or less trained through the Coniston race. He didn't really ease off, and found himself struggling halfway through. He had a real battle with Jack and beat him by one second on the finish line. He was happy with that, but felt that the way he had run that Jack might think he was in with a chance the next week.

The next weekend saw the start of the Reebok International Challenge, consisting of three races in a week, with the first race being also the Northern Counties Fell championship, held that year at Buttermere. Over nine and a half miles Kenny Stuart took over three minutes out of Jack Maitland, with early leader Mike Short 3rd and Hugh Symonds 4th. It had been a gorgeous day and there was a helicopter filming the race for a BBC documentary. Kenny recalls, 'Jack was up for it after last week and fancied his chances at the Northern Counties, but I had trained through Coniston. When I eased off for the Northern Counties I was miles in front. I took a different path on High Spy and

they were all shouting, but I came back down and ran in to
Newlands and I was fine, heading off up Causey. My record
from then still stands as the course has changed.'

Four days later, the second in the series was a special race over
the Grasmere (Guides Race) course. In this Kenny Stuart set
what was the fastest ever time in either the earlier professional
races or the early (and indeed later) amateur races. His 12-01
beat Fred Reeves's 1978 professional record by 21 seconds,
with Jack Maitland, with 12-33, in second also beating Kenny's
previous amateur record. *Cumbria* magazine carried a profile
of Stuart in 2010, reflecting back on this occasion:

> On that day Tommy Sedgwick was seated on the summit
> when Kenny arrived, and was, in his words, "gobsmacked.
> He ran uphill so fast and reached the top flag with so much
> time in hand he could have sat down and had a picnic and
> carried on and still won," says Tommy. "He was untouch-
> able that day."
>
> Kenny modestly put it down to "just one of those days
> when everything works out and all the hard work put in
> during training finally pays off".
>
> "Happy days," he says. "In my younger days I used to be
> told I had a bad habit of glancing over my shoulder too often
> and this cost me a race or two as I was overtaken. But I can
> safely look back now on some great days. My records for
> Snowdon, Ben Nevis and Skiddaw are still unbroken, as is the
> one for the Ennerdale Horseshoe race."

Mark McGlincy recalls something Pete Bland had told him.
'Pete was watching and he was coming down the field with
Kenny and he was shouting "come on Kenny", and so Kenny
is thinking there is someone behind him. But it was Pete egging
him on to get the best time. Pete reckons Kenny might have
gone under 12 minutes if he had known earlier.'

Everything was right that day, according to Kenny. He hadn't
trained hard since the Northern Counties, and had lowered his

mileage. 'I was on form, the ground was dry, it was a sunny day, and fast running. It was a good men's field. It was the fastest over the course, but Fred Reeves still holds the record for the Grasmere Guides Race.'

When told the McGlincy story about Pete Bland he commented, 'I didn't really know how fast the time was. I came down across the line but you have no idea really. I carried a watch but I never timed myself. I could easily have knocked another second off, but that is beside the point.'

The third race, another three days later, was the nine-mile Fairfield Horseshoe, which was also a counter in the British Fell championships. There was a strong Italian presence in this one, justifying the sponsor's 'international' tag at last. Once again Stuart was in imperious form, beating Maitland by three minutes, with Pezzoli of Italy third. With three firsts and seconds respectively, Stuart and Maitland were obviously first and second in the Overall Reebok Challenge. Showing that being able to race frequently and well was not unusual for this era, Sean Livesey was 3rd overall, and Hugh Symonds 4th, and they had both done Coniston the week before too, coming 6th and 8th respectively in a high standard field.

Reliving these performances in his front room recently, Kenny explained how the third race panned out. 'The Italians turned out for this, and it was a misty, stinging, cold day really. I recall running in a t-shirt under my vest that day. There was a very strong wind. I sort of won it as I wanted, really. I didn't feel as though I ran particularly well, but the Italians didn't like the situation, the cold and they weren't particularly competitive that day.'

Hugh Symonds had done all four races, coming 4th at Buttermere, 5th at Grasmere and 10th at Fairfield. He reflected, 'This was all thirty years ago now! I had fish and chips on the way home from Grasmere, and was very sick. I went to Fairfield feeling not strong at all. The day after that I was still very weak. If you over-race it eventually gets the better of you.'

Jack Maitland remembers the Fairfield race very clearly.

'It was misty and we got a bit lost on the climb. The Italians just followed us. Later on I was descending and I came across Pezzoli going the other way! He couldn't stay with Kenny on the descent so was coming back for the next person for help for route finding. On the last bit into the valley I got away and obviously hung on for grim death.'

Just another week on and the circus that is the fell championships moved to Wales for the 14th edition of the Welsh 1000m race. This 20-miler took place in dreadful conditions, resulting in slow times and many retirements. It didn't seem to affect Billy Bland though, who came out on top after 3 hours and 4 minutes, in a race he had not always done well in. Less than a minute behind was Bob Whitfield, with Kenny Stuart languishing a further three and a half minutes back. Hugh Symonds came in 5th and his diary records it as, 'survival. Some people were in a terrible state, many shivering at the finish on Snowdon.'

Billy Bland tells a lively tale of a magical saviour. 'With me and Bob Whitfield there was a cigarette paper between us. I thought Bob had it. We crossed the road with Kenny and it was absolutely pissing down. I remember saying to Bob "let's get shot of Kenny". It was misty down to a fairly low level and the path was running like a river. We turned a right angle and I don't know what Kenny did, but we lost him. It was horrendous though. They asked us when we got to Pen-y-Pass whether we wanted to go on. We said "aye". Me and Bob had a real tussle there. I had a Mars bar left and we were chugging up to just before Crib Goch and I had a drink of water and the bar. He went away about 100 yards, but I knew I needed sustenance. That Mars bar was my masterstroke. I got him on that last bit with the extra energy. We know a whole lot more about nutrition now, but I should have been nibbling away at something a lot more than we ever did, any of us.'

Kenny Stuart has bad memories of that day, having got mild hypothermia. 'I was having to get across this raging river which they had strung a rope across, Billy and Bob went and I thought it was no problem I would catch them on the way up. I got to the Pyg Track and started to run and run and they were so far ahead I misjudged it completely. I was in a mood and thought "I can't be bothered". When you are hypothermic you just don't want to bother.' Pauline Stuart added that the operators had cancelled the trains to the Snowdon summit (where the race finishes), because the conditions were so bad. 'So then you still had 5 miles to come down. Hugh Symonds was in a right state.'

At the finish they handed Billy Bland a cup of tea and before it got to his mouth he was shaking so much there was nothing left in it. He recalls that, 'our kit bags had come up on the train and there was a big mound like a haystack, and they asked me what my kit bag looked like and I couldn't remember.'

The fact that John Wild had a 'bad day at the office' when he ran the London Marathon is shown by his form soon after. In that May an RAF team was taken on tour to Sweden by team manager Ian Sweet. The plan was to race two half marathons and also get in a week of good training whilst there. The first race was the Malmo to Lund Lundloppet, which has 1500 entrants. John Wild was part of the RAF team and faced 1976 Olympic steeplechase winner Anders Garderud, whom he had raced several times previously. Wild came 3rd in 67-02, with the RAF team taking the top four slots and sweeping to the team award. The Goteburg Varet was six days later, and was a different matter. Swedish runners took the first three places, and Wild came a slightly disappointing 21st in 70-47, but his RAF team still took the team title.

Despite his success in 1983 and 1984, some people were even now still questioning Kenny Stuart's ability in the toughest of long races. His performance in the Ennerdale race on the first weekend in June rather dismissed that idea. It was reported that, 'Kenny Stuart, regarded by many as rather vulnerable in the longer tougher fell races, dispelled all doubts as to his ability in this department as he sped round the formidable Ennerdale course in a new record time and well clear of his regular shadow Jack Maitland.' It had been good weather, with a slight breeze and cloud keeping the worst of the sun off the runners.

Kenny Stuart finished in 3-20-57, over three minutes up on Maitland, who was another three minutes ahead of Billy Bland. Hugh Symonds was 7th, being typically hard on himself in his diary, saying that he was not determined enough. Joss Naylor remembers speaking to Kenny after the race and that, 'he said, "between me and you, I was buggered". He said, "I had a job getting over the beck". He had given everything. He gave his last ounce, did the lad.' The comments from Joss sum up the commitment Stuart was making to his racing. It also tickles me to hear him referring to Kenny as 'the lad'.

Kenny Stuart beat the Ennerdale record by seven seconds that day. Billy Bland challenged him early on but noted, 'Kenny used to run with his head screwed on backwards [*laughs*]. He wanted to know if you were following, like. So, he wasn't that confident.' But Billy did reckon that if he or Maitland had gone faster that day Kenny would have gone faster still and won. He admired Maitland, but felt he had an awful style. 'Stylewise, he neither looked like a good runner nor ran like one, but hell he was good. He had some engine.'

John Wild's view was that you ran to your strengths. He never did Ennerdale though because it often clashed with an RAF track event, which was his priority. He thinks that for Ennerdale he did Kenny a favour in a roundabout way. 'I gave him real good competition and I think that made him train a lot harder than he had done previously. Kenny obviously had talent, but maybe he didn't train hard enough as a pro. Then the years of long fell training put money in the bank, as they say.'

Kenny's response to questioning his ability to win 'Long' races was simple. 'The only way a fit person was not going to do well in the long races was not to have reccied them. So, Billy Bland and Joss Naylor and these lads, they knew it like the back of their hands. If I was doing well it wasn't ability or stamina that would stop me winning, it would be because I took a wrong line or something.'

On 16 June John Wild made a surprise appearance at a

low-key fell race in Wales, having now moved to run for Newport Harriers following his transfer to RAF St Athan. He now ran alongside Steve Jones for the club as well as the RAF. Wild was with Newport until June 1986, when he was posted to an RAF base in Germany.

Wild won the 15-mile Offa's Dyke race from John Boyes of Bournemouth AC, having broken away over the steep climb of Hergest Ridge. Meanwhile a week later the championships race at Eildon 2 Hills, in Scotland, had a smaller field than might have been expected. Hugh Symonds won, admittedly in Kenny Stuart's absence from Sean Livesey. Kenny says now that he didn't need a race just then, quietly pointing out that he still has the record for that race, which he had set in 1984.

CHAPTER 19

Like winning the FA Cup

A few weeks later came what I consider one of the greatest fell racing performances ever. On 20 July 1985 Kenny Stuart set a new record for the Snowdon race that has not been bettered since, against a top field that included some of the leading Italians. Fausto Bonzi held the record of 63-46 from the previous year's race, but Stuart took this apart with a startling time of 62-29.

Kenny Stuart has very clear memories of that day. 'I got three quarters of the way up and Robbie Bryson started to push hard and I went with him. I expected the Italians to follow suit and they didn't. I was really on a knife edge when we hit the summit. So I let him get there, about nine seconds ahead of me. I was more frightened of the Italians coming from behind than Robbie. I just felt I could beat him going down. He wasn't a brilliant descender, and I had the strength to do it. I caught him and the Italian challenge didn't materialise. It was a bit like the Butter Crags race [*earlier that year*], in that I felt really good on the day, conditions were good. It was warm but not too warm, with probably a slight wind behind you going up. Everything just fell into place.'

At the turn in the race, Bonzi was 30 seconds adrift of Bryson and Stuart. The television report on the 2015 Snowdon race (which was the 40th anniversary of the event) noted in the commentary that on this day in 1985 the first five runners at the summit took under 40 minutes for the ascent, and that no-one has done that since, which Kenny thinks is quite likely to remain the case.

Bryson lost his lead going down, and Bonzi closed on him. Stuart pulled clear to win by over a minute. Renowned as a fast descender, Jack Maitland thundered down in a time that was actually six seconds faster than Stuart, taking 2nd place for his troubles, with Bonzi 3rd - well beaten yet still only 10 seconds off his record time. Colin Donnelly also distinguished himself, coming down in a time that matched Maitland to take 4th place from Italian Pezzolli, with Bryson 6th. Hugh Symonds was 12th, commenting, 'Bryson may still have the fastest time to the summit. He was good. But the path here burns your feet on a hot day, possibly worse than Skiddaw.'

Symonds went on to point out, 'that there is no point in being first to the top in a race if you are not first to the bottom. That was very much my attitude.' Taking up this point, I wondered whether Symonds was actually better at going up or down. 'At first I was much better at ups. I thought if I am going to be any good I need to train for downs. I had a good training partner in Bob Whitfield from Kendal AC. He lived in Clapham (in the Yorkshire Dales) and we used to alternate our training between Sedbergh and his patch (and run around the Ingleborough area). Bob was a fantastic descender. I think training with him helped me learn to descend. I would also choose some of the steepest places in the Howgills and specifically practise running downhill fast. I would do rep sessions with downhill as well as uphill in them.'

Although he admits he was beaten by the better man on that day Jack Maitland is justifiably proud of how much he and Bryson contributed to the result that Kenny Stuart achieved. 'Robbie was a great Irish guy, a good climber but not so good as a descender. Although I was well beaten by Kenny, I would be interested to see all-time records for times down Snowdon. Mine was a pretty fast descent time.'

As part of the race build-up in 2010 Kenny Stuart was

interviewed, now 25 years on, about his memories of the day, and thoughts about the record's longevity. In part, he commented:

> I remember the conditions being very good. I do recall being pushed at least until three-quarters of the way up by the two Italian chaps, who were very good. Bonzi held the record actually. Then it was taken on by Robbie Bryson who pushed very hard to the summit. It was a memorable ascent because it was very fast and I knew it. I held back a little coming off the top as I didn't know if Robbie had taken it out too fast. I think he had taken it too fast for himself, but I recovered and went on to break the record, fortunately.
>
> I think every fell runner knows when they start a race, within the first half mile he knows how he is going to feel, and I felt good right from the start. The year before that, it was a very red hot day and the Italians set a blistering pace and I died a death at three quarters. I managed to come back and hold on to third position but I ran 65 minutes and it felt a lot slower than that.
>
> I am quite amazed it [*the record*] still stands, but is something I am reasonably proud of. I think it is time it was broken. The record might stand for a number of years. If athletes of a certain calibre, maybe Africans, came over *en masse* they might break it. But it will take some breaking.

The day after Snowdon the Tour of Tameside started. Ian Sweet, who was the RAF road running manager, entered an RAF team in the Tour. John Wild was part of that team, looking for a new challenge, which this six race series in seven days would surely provide. Wild recalls, 'we had two teams actually. I was coaching a young lad at the time who was going through a difficult time, and I said to him you can go in the second team if you'd like.'

They took a trailer tent, two Labradors and an old Morris

Minor van, and stayed in New Mills, doing the races and then going back to the campsite. 'Then we went to the pub and slept in till about 10 o'clock in the morning. Craig Metcalf was the athlete, and he finished second overall.'

Metcalf was a former Guides racer from Skipton, who raced against Kenny Stuart in his teens. At the time Metcalf was a bit down and lacking motivation, so Wild got him to come along and share the trailer tent for the week. 'There was no pressure and we just put him in the team - and he had a superb week. It was a great week and there was even a comment in one of the papers that me and Craig were "beer bagging" during the week i.e. trying to drink as many different beers as we could. That was what we did', chuckled Wild when recalling the event.

'It was a great week, we had such fun. I got a stitch in the first race, coming about 14th. I won the hill race the next day, but got a bad stomach. I was ill for a couple of days. I was drinking loads of Lucozade. When I started winning there were loads of Lucozade appearing in the changing rooms.'

After his bad start, Wild was remarkably consistent, winning four of the remaining races, and only failing to do so in the half marathon (the fourth race, where he was second). Metcalf was also very consistent, being 2nd in two races, 3rd in three, and 5th in one (again the half marathon). Fell runner Colin Donnelly had a nightmare 74th place on the first day, then buckled down with a 19th, 4th, 3rd and 2nd twice, to finish 8th overall. That 74th place just may have been due to his having run the Snowdon fell race the day before!

At this time I too was looking for new adventures, and I had entered the Tour of Tameside in 1983, and again in 1986. In that second year Belgian Eddy Hellebuyck won, but Wild pointed out that he had a serious fall from grace later. 'Hellebuyck got done for drugs in the end, it was a bit miffing really. He was injured in 1985 and came back in 1986 and beat pretty much all the records I had set.'

Someone else who was looking for new horizons in 1985 was

Dave Hall. 'I trained for my Bob Graham Round and it affected my abilities and focus. I could do the longer runs, but had lost it on the shorter ones.' Thinking of this era, Hall suddenly chuckled at a Billy Bland story from his Bob Graham training. 'I was up there training for my Bob Graham and called in on Billy. He said, "I am doing a leg of the Cumbria Way Relay, do you want to come with us?" I said, "yeh go on". Part of it was going round Derwentwater over to Keswick. Training was an element to Billy. He didn't train with many people, but if he did would find out something about you, or find your weaknesses. I was going really well that day. He was desperately trying to drop me on the fells. We got to Rosthwaite and his wife Anne was there to give us water and a Mars bar. I was about 5 metres behind him and she said "are you struggling?" I said "no, I am shutting these gates behind him." Billy just looked across and said, "you should be opening the bloody things as well." That is Billy.'

At the end of that week, on 27 July, it was the Melantee championship race, which Kenny Stuart didn't run. The British fell championships races held in Scotland seemed to be much less popular than the English and Welsh at this time. It was won by Billy Bland, who stayed on to win the Half Nevis race the next day. On 4 August Kenny Stuart won his local Latrigg race, a three-mile non-championships race.

The next championships race, the 'Short' Gategill race, was on Kenny Stuart's doorstep, starting as it does at the Horse and Farrier Inn in Threlkeld and finishing at the Salutation Inn, also in Threlkeld, after a three mile run up and down Gategill Fell, which is part of Blencathra. Kenny duly won from Billy Bland, to strengthen his title challenge. On the same day Jack Maitland was running the Sierre-Zinal race in Switzerland, and became only the second Briton to win this prestigious event, coming home ahead of a massive field of 1,169 other competitors. He had reccied the descent at the end of the race, but still managed several falls on his crazy descent. At the high point, which is 12 km from the finish, he was fifth and a minute off the lead, but he clawed it all back to take the win in the last couple of kilometres.

Maitland ran a series of three international races in that period, with Sierre-Zinal the third of them. When we discussed his performances he acknowledges it as being his best. 'I was naïve and just took my fitness to the event. I knew the only Brit who had won it was Jeff Norman and that he had gone to the Olympics and held the Three Peaks record, so knew it must be high standard. That was an inspiration to me. My descending ability helped that day. I was a couple of minutes off the pace at the top. The guys that were leading weren't really expecting me and I came out of nowhere and passed them. I had won a race the week before so knew I was very fit.'

He gave more detail of the race in an interview with Hugh Symonds in *The Fellrunner* at the time, which shows his level of preparation, confidence and indeed perseverance. 'I had a pre-race time plan for the major points of the race and I reckoned I could afford a slowish start. On the descent I had a bad fall, which eventually required six stitches in my leg. This knocked the stuffing out of me for about five minutes and I lost a place and the idea of winning faded. Then I caught the next man and regained fourth place. I heard the course marshals blowing whistles for the walkers to clear the course for the front runners, even though I couldn't see them. As I regained strength from the fall the time gap between the whistles got smaller and I eventually could see the leader, and I was back in the race, 30 seconds down and 4 km to go. As I caught the leaders I threw myself down the hill and, despite another fall, which winded me, I won by 17 seconds.'

Kenny Stuart had what may have seemed a routine championship race victory at Burnsall in 13-23 at the end of August. However, Kenny's diary entries reveal that he wasn't well that week, and yet still managed a 67-mile training week, even doing 15 miles the day after the race, despite the virus. Kenny explained that he wasn't that well after the race, but ran OK. 'I think it was more of a head cold. It was a short race so stamina didn't really come in to it.'

date	am	pm	comments
Mon 19th	3 miles cross country	7 miles reps on grass	Heavy, wet track. Feel rough
Tue 20th	3 miles road	10 miles fell and cross country	Wet and muddy
Wed 21st	5 miles cross country	8 miles road fartlek	Ground soaked
Thu 22nd	3 miles cross country	3 miles road	Easy day. Feel bad.
Fri 23rd	5 miles cross country		Ran easy. Mild virus. Achey
Sat 24th	2 miles road	3 miles (Burnsall race)	Won but sore chest. Ground wet
Sun 25th	15 miles fell and cross country		Floods – a very wet summer!

Kenny's diary is shown here, and in one of the photos, as an indication of the amount and range of training that he did. When I asked for Kenny's permission to reproduce extracts from his diary, he was more than happy. 'I think people are interested in what runners used to do in training. They have this awful idea that there was something magical going on that they don't know about. They can look at that and see it is just standard stuff.' I pointed out that it may be standard stuff but geared to what he was hoping to achieve. It was all thought through, and not just another load of miles each day. He expanded, 'I used to write out for myself the days I wanted to do things, mileage, speed etc. Obviously if it was really wet and you couldn't go on the grass to do repetitions then you would do fartlek. When I lived back o'Skiddaw I used to run in Keswick and come home later, or run from my dad's house. Summertime was brilliant though because you had Great Cockup, which was fantastic training ground.'

Kenny decided not to defend his Ben Nevis title on 7 September. 'It is a hard race and a lot of travelling. We had been told not to go and run something like Ben Nevis and knacker your legs prior to the International race which was two weeks later. The Ben is always a risky race, isn't it?'

The Ben race was still a very high quality, with Hugh Symonds beating Jack Maitland and Billy Bland, albeit two and a half minutes off the record. Maitland says, 'that was the year I thought I should have won the Ben after racing well in Europe, but I came up against Hugh who was in great form.'

In the previous year (1984) Hugh Symonds had been first to the summit at the Ben Nevis race, ahead of Kenny Stuart. Symonds recalls, 'I won a bottle of whisky for that, but so what. In 1985 I was first to the top again. The night beforehand we went to a bar and probably had a pint and Jack Maitland was there grinning like a Cheshire cat. He had just won the Sierre Zinal and was obviously really confident. I thought Jack would be hard to beat but I knew Kenny wasn't there. Coming down about half a mile from the top Jack overtook me and I said to myself don't let it happen. I just ran and tried not to think of accidents or of falling. I pulled away from him and I won and I seem to remember it was a slower time then the year before.' Symonds thinks changes to the path have probably made a difference, and that the course is not as fast as it was. He summarised his feelings with this diary entry. 'First. Wow, a real surprise! Determination. Just raced the best I could. No easing back. It was mental and physical strength combined.'

At the end of September, on the weekend of the 21st and 22nd, the first ever World Cup in Mountain Running was held in San Vigilio di Marebbe, Italy, consisting of ladies race, junior race and long and short races for senior men. England, Scotland and Wales were all represented, with the hosts the strong favourites. The home nations had varying levels of financial support, with some of the Welsh paying their own way. The weather was steaming, with some athletes suffering badly. The senior long race was held on the Sunday, with the other three the day beforehand, allowing some men to double up.

The short men's race was an 8.5km up and down event, which Kenny Stuart won, with England teammates Ray Owen 8th and Sean Livesey 9th. Scotland's Colin Donnelly was 11th, with Jack Maitland 16th and Jon Broxap 17th. The next day

Stuart, Maitland, and Donnelly were among those that ran the 'long' course, which was an uphill only 14.6 km. Running only in this race, Hugh Symonds came 15th and Billy Bland a disappointing third England scorer in 25th. Jack Maitland and Colin Donnelly (both running for Scotland, of course) fared slightly better, finishing 16th and 24th respectively. Kenny recalls, 'yeh, that [*short one*] is the race I trained for and the one I wanted to win really. Up and down, my type of race. I did the long one the following day, which was up only, and my legs were quite stiff and tired. But I ran quite well, actually. No-one else doubled up. I don't know why I got that opportunity.' Pauline chips in, 'you were better than the others! You were the first Englishman by a long way, in fifth place.'

On being reminded of this event, and his result, Billy Bland gave some background in explanation. 'At the Welsh 1000m race a couple of years earlier, Andy Styan (who was on the selection committee) gave me an envelope at breakfast in the Victoria Hotel to say I had been picked as reserve for an international race as I was 'out of form'. I told him what to do with it. I'd never been a reserve for owt in my life and was not starting now. They weren't happy! I was 38 when I agreed to go to that one in 1985. I looked at the course and it was just up a forest road, not even straight up. To be honest I didn't have the best attitude in the race, though I didn't purposefully run badly. That was as good as I was then, on that course. I reckon I might have gone well in these Sky races they have now at my best though.'

As we talked about this event Hugh Symonds told me that he had, 'interviewed Jack Maitland for *The Fellrunner* that year. When he was sitting there I noticed that I had on show the Three Peaks Trophy and the Ben Nevis Trophy. I thought he might think I was a bit cheeky! But I am not sure if I wouldn't swap both of those for winning Sierre-Zinal, which he has done of course.'

Pauline Stuart ran in that first World Cup race. London Marathon founders Chris Brasher and John Disley paid for her to go out. 'Unfortunately I was pregnant, but didn't know it. I came 9th, but felt dreadful. I was sick on the way, it was a long bus journey from the airport and I had to stop the bus, which was really embarrassing. I thought "this isn't like me", as I am rarely sick. On the morning of the race I was throwing up on the start line, but ran anyway and 9th wasn't bad really. I was sick again at night, and again on the way back. I thought actually, I wonder if I am pregnant. When I got back I had a pregnancy test and found I was seven weeks pregnant. With each child I have had morning sickness from 6-13 weeks. It just happened to coincide with that first big international trip.'

The first three British runners at Snowdon that year once again earned a trip to Italy to run in the Vanoni Trophy Relay Race on 27 October, in Marbegno. It was a single lap marked course with an average ascent/descent of 340 feet per mile over the four and a quarter mile loop. Kenny Stuart ran first and set the fastest time of the day, just one second off Bonzi's course record, according to the report. Colin Donnelly lost a few seconds going off course and handed over to Jack Maitland some 50 seconds behind the leader. Maitland suffered a stitch and slipped to third in the closing stages. Kenny actually thinks he set a record for the leg. 'I won a tray for that, but I think I had drawn with the best time. I beat Valicella in this relay timewise, as he ran a different stage to me.' Pauline chuckles as she recalls that, 'Colin almost missed the start, didn't he. He always seemed to be with his head in the clouds. The team management had to go and find him!'

Reflecting on these times, Pauline Stuart also noted that she, 'won a trip to this event by winning Snowdon, but I couldn't run as I was now 12 weeks pregnant. I went anyway because I had won the trip, but another girl ran instead. That was it really because I had started a family.'

Discussing these races, Kenny Stuart picked up another thing that cropped up that still rankled with him. 'Valicella won the World Cup in Keswick, I think it was the short race up Latrigg in 1986. People would say to me, "how do you think you would do against that bloke". I would say I fancied my chances against him. "Do you really think that?" Well I had beaten him twice in Italy. People forget, or don't know the facts.'

Warming to the subject he followed with, 'it is the same with this World Cup business. They say "well you won in 1985, but how would you do against this the competition there is nowadays". You just don't know how you'd do. I just went on the start line against whatever lads were there in 1985. You can't do any more than win it. Ron Hill used to tell a similar story about winning the National or a marathon. You just can't say, and it is irrelevant.'

Back on the domestic scene, Ambleside AC had revived the fortunes of the Langdale Horseshoe race, which had slumped in recent years. The 1985 championship race, on 12 October, attracted 439 starters. A stellar field included all the current top 10 except Hugh Symonds. Kenny Stuart was sharing the lead with Colin Donnelly on Blisco but went offline on the descent to come in fourth, and comments, 'I needed to get points to clinch the title. I led going up the back of Pike o'Blisco which was the last checkpoint, and came off the wrong way and had to do a slight detour and ended up happy enough with fourth, because I think that clinched the title.'

Donnelly had an even bigger disaster, as he was unaware there was one final control and he took the direct line to cross the line in first place. He then gamely retraced his steps to the control and finally came in 12th. Jack Maitland had his first ever British championships win, from Sean Livesey and Billy Bland, with Kenny Stuart fourth. Although pleased to win Maitland did point out that, 'quite a few went wrong, and Billy Bland had some kind of ankle problem on the descent.'

The day after Langdale Kenny Stuart restored his pride by winning the short Butter Crag race, lowering his own course record by fifteen seconds from the year before, beating Sean Livesey again. The first four from Langdale ran again, but Bland could only manage a close 4th and Maitland 6th, over a minute off Stuart's lightning pace. The new record for this version of the race was now 12-22.

When prompted, Mark McGlincy gave me his thoughts on the Grasmere Guides and Butter Crag records, which are effectively the same course. 'The reason the Grasmere Record is often taken as the Guides race time, to be honest with you, is because it has been the Grasmere Sports and that was there before the amateur race, which was Butter Crag. That was put on as a different event in October from 1979, using the same course. I was there that day in 1985 (running in the under-17s race) when Kenny ran 12-22, and it was really heavy underfoot. Still the top 10 were all under 14 minutes, it was absolute quality.'

Mark McGlincy thinks the Grasmere Sports was the premier short race. 'If you won that it was like winning the FA Cup or the World Cup. My take on the times issue at Grasmere is that in Fred [*Reeves*] and Tommy's [*Sedgwick*] day they raced one another and that was the holy grail, and thus they pushed one another to do it. Kenny was brought up in that mould too. But I think the reason the likes of Rob Jebb and Ian Holmes haven't got the times is that they run different races from a mile and a half up to 20 milers. They are chopping and changing and not going for that one race. The Ben is probably held in higher esteem than Grasmere to a lot of fell runners now, especially on the club running side.'

Kenny comments, 'looking back on the fell running seasons during the mid-80s I have to say that I found them very demanding, with too many races at a wide range of distances and over wildly differing terrain. The depth of talent around at the time helped top runners to eclipse many records during this period and both local people and the media were informed and enthusiastic about fell running as a sport. Race organisers were able to offer more generous prizes because of sponsorship of various sorts, but I can't see the diminution in this as a reason for today's "easing down" of the running boom on the fells.'

In his end of term report in *The Fellrunner* Kevan Shand commented, 'I must admit that at the beginning of the year I thought Kenny would walk it, but what a fight Billy put up right to the last race.' Adding up their ten counters, Kenny Stuart scored 311 points (out of 320), with Billy Bland second on 295 and Sean Livesey third on 271. Kenny recalls that, 'during the eighties my toughest opponent had to have been John Wild, and obviously over the rugged Lakeland Classics Billy Bland was still the man to beat.'

Kenny had in fact won eight of the ten counters needed, both defeats (in the Welsh 1000s and Langdale races) being the result of navigational errors. Kenny's navigational frailty was common knowledge. One fellow fell runner commented that Kenny had told him that when he has been out on training runs on the Dodds he has got lost on his own ground! Pauline Stuart had a fairly untroubled win in the ladies championships, winning every counting race.

Then, on 20 October John Wild made a surprise appearance at the Three Towers fell race, which he had done several times before. Dave Cartridge won, with Wild (running for Newport) fourth, one place ahead of Jack Maitland.

In the Keswick AC fell championships Billy Bland turned the tables on Kenny Stuart to win the club title for the tenth year in a row.

PART SIX

Moving on

CHAPTER 20

He'll run a good bit faster

After their head-to-head season in 1983, John Wild and Kenny Stuart's running paths had been gradually diverging in 1984 and 1985, as we have seen. There were a number of further changes in 1986 in both Wild's life and Stuart's running ambitions.

John Wild got the posting to Germany (to Laarbruch) that he had requested, and was still training hard. His wife Anne did a bit of running while they were out there. He recalls that, 'she used to come out on a bike for my 21-mile runs. She started off doing keep fit, then progressed to running with some friends and she got the bug. She was part of the team that won the RAF Germany ladies championships. She did a half marathon in 1-27, and 10 miles in 61 minutes. We still go to the gym together.'

John showed me a cutting from the *Laarbruch Listener*, which had a photo of Anne running in the German championships, captioned 'Laarbruch's Anne Wild during a gruelling uphill run.' The report noted that, 'the RAFG Ladies Cross Country championships were held at Bruggen on a warm sunny day. A field of 28 ladies ran over a 5 km course through woods and hills. After a fast start Anne Wild pulled away on the notorious "Hill 60" and retained the lead to win by 25 seconds.'

In 1986 Kenny Stuart finally decided to have a crack at a road marathon. He says that the move to marathon just evolved. 'I wasn't really sure what I was going to do. After 1985 I realised that I had probably gone as far as I could in potential and ability [*on the fells*]. I was just going to be sitting on top of a tree trying to maintain that position. I decided to have a change, and why not. See what is there.'

He entered the Glasgow Marathon, which was taking place on 21 September. Kenny was now coached by Dave Cannon (a former fell running champion from 1972 and 2-11-21 marathoner himself), who helped Kenny with his move to the roads. Kenny described how this relationship with Cannon developed. 'At one point I ran the Derwentwater 10 and Dave was making a comeback, I think. Andy Taylor won the race and I was second, with Dave third. I knew Dave from the fells. His auntie lived across the road and he sometimes came to visit. He lived in Appleby. The agreement, or craic if you like, was that I would go on the roads and he would advise me, rather than strictly coach me. I would run things past him once a week and he would say either "yea or nay", or give me advice on when to change things. It worked out very well.' There was no real change in the training, apart from not running on the fells any more.

In early 1986 John Wild came 6th in the RAF cross country championships and 13th in the Inter-Services, but had capped his track racing efforts and didn't run at the RAF or Services track championships again.

Kenny Stuart chose to do more cross country races in his marathon build-up, including the Gateshead cross country in December 1985, where he came seventh in a race won by Peter Tootell (Stretford AC). The Keswick club were very proud of Kenny's performances, and obviously enjoyed his raised profile in athletics that the country and road running gave him (and them). In their newsletter it was noted that, 'Kenny ended his first full cross country season with an outstanding run in the National championships at Newcastle on 1 March. After winning the county championships for the third year in a row he finished an excellent 15th in the Northern championships at St Helens, before his remarkable 28th place in the National.' Tim Hutchins won this latter race, with Geoff Turnbull winning the Northerns.

In his marathon build-up Kenny Stuart ran in a half marathon in The Hague on 5 April 1986, coming second in an excellent time of 62 minutes 55 seconds, behind Tavares (Portugal). This was a Club (and Cumbria) Record. He went through ten miles in under 48 minutes, faster than his personal best. A few weeks earlier he had set a Club and Course Record of 29-05 at the Dalston 10 km. He also gained an English Cross Country Union vest against Combined Services and Universities, finishing 5th in a race in Aylesbury.

Kenny ran the Great North Run on 8 June, coming 7th in 63-16, in a race won by Kenya's Mike Musyoki in 60-43, with Steve Jones 2nd in 60-59. Amongst the athletes Stuart beat were marathon greats Hugh Jones and Charlie Spedding, winners of the London Marathon in 1982 and 1984 respectively. At the Great North Run Kenny missed out on the prizes, as they were only for the first six.

The format for the fell running championships also changed in 1986. The British championships went down to just six races, with two each in England, Wales and Scotland. A nine race English championships was also instigated, watering down the whole championship focus in my view. That year neither John Wild nor Kenny Stuart were competing regularly on the fells. But the British championships were still very competitive.

The Glasgow Marathon race report noted how well his build-up had gone and how he confidently took on the marathon:

With five weeks to go he [Stuart] put in a full distance training run with [Dave] Cannon at around 6 minute mile pace. A week later he checked out racing fitness with a fast ten in the AAA championship run from Bradford to Leeds. He finished fifth in 48-13. Over the last weeks he tapered down.

The first few miles were taken easily enough to leave plenty of room for style with a 5-20 pace bringing a close pack to five miles in 26-45. The next five were completed a minute faster (25-40) and as they came across the Clyde for the first time the pack had already begun to break up. Stuart, Nash and Konieczny were leading. The damage had all come from a quick burst from the Pole who was on paper favourite with a time of 2-13-39 to his credit. Over the King George V bridge it was a sharp turn right and into the wind. Now Konieczny tried to use Stuart to shield him. Nash did the same and Stuart found himself bearing the brunt of the weather.

'Fair enough,' said Stuart, 'all part of the game', unless he could do something about it. He could, and he did. He went with them so long, for after all he had a plan to work to – a plan which said 'Go at fifteen' – but enough was enough. At fourteen miles he went instead, and suddenly there was a gap behind him.

The gap became ten yards and no one was coming after him. As ten yards became twenty he was out on his own loosing rein on the legs which had been waiting for so long. From then on it was 'easy', and 2-14-04 after the start, Stuart crossed the line at Glasgow Green to beat John Boyes '84 record over a slightly different course by fifty seconds.

In Glasgow, Kenny Stuart's marathon debut time was 2-14, and he not only won but also set a new course record. At the time the world marathon best was 2-07 – a tantalising seven minutes faster. An interview in *Marathon and Distance Runner* shortly after his debut marathon gives a feel for Kenny's relationship with coach Dave Cannon, together with possible future plans:

Cannon offered to advise the Kendal man in his new career – and that has been a definite bonus for Stuart. Cannon made sure that his protégé didn't launch himself into a competitive marathon too early. "I wanted to make sure that when Kenny made his debut it would be a good one and that hopefully he would gain confidence from it," Cannon says. "He could have run London last April but we decided it would be better to wait for Glasgow in the autumn. We felt it was just the right level of race for Kenny to get involved in for his first attempt at the distance."

After the race Cannon commented that, "he's a good athlete

and I'm sure he'll run a good bit faster in the future." Cannon had told him not to make his attack too early. Completing the second half of the race faster than the first, Stuart gradually increased his lead and the margin of victory at the end was bigger than any other in the history of the event.

Kenny said, "I'll have a bit of a rest then tackle the winter cross country season. My next aim is to gain selection for a British team in a major race." Cannon felt that he should next do the London the next May, there was a possibility that he would come into the reckoning for a place in the British squad for the IAAF World Cup race at Seoul in April. "If that situation arises we will have to give it a serious consideration," says Cannon. "The final decision would however be with Kenny."

Apparently the BBC team were worried how they would handle the traditional post-race interview if Konieczny won, as the Pole didn't speak any English and there "didn't appear to be anyone around who spoke Polish."

In discussing his future plans as stated above, Kenny commented, 'the reckoning was, if I remember correctly, that the two marathons were fairly close together and that I would have to choose between the London and the IAAF ones. I got the nod for Seoul, but decided to go for London. It was money or a GB vest. I reckoned I could do that sort of thing after I had got a little bit of money in London. One of my regrets actually, although I did represent GB on the roads (in a half marathon in The Hague), was that I missed a chance to go to a marathon championship.'

However, in 1987 Kenny Stuart started having breathing problems, which affected his London Marathon debut that year. He had won his fourth consecutive county championships at Egremont on 13 December 1986. Then Kenny was fifth at that year's Inter-Counties cross country. Carl Thackeray won in 38-50 and Kenny did 39-10. Being just 20 seconds behind in 5th, he felt it was a good run.

Kenny went over to The Hague half marathon again as part

of his build-up, and came third in 64-20 (compared to 62-55 the year before). He also got an ECCU vest to go to Le Mans on 18 January 1987 for a cross country race. It was on a snow-covered course, and very cold. He was 7th, and first Englishman to finish. John Wild also remembers Le Mans, where he also ran twice, the last time in December 1981.

Unfortunately, Stuart dropped out of the London that year. 'We were busy at work, it was a red hot spring and I was trying to do the training and catch up with my work, which was spent baking in the sun all day. I was sometimes bothered with pollen and stuff. It just didn't work out. I felt groggy when I went down to London, I knew I wasn't right. I got to 13 miles and just wasn't there at all. I was forced to pull out.'

After London he came back in June for the Great North Run, but could only manage 64-47 for 16th place, 'feeling OK but not brilliant', being just beaten by Wild's old training partner Ray Crabb. Stuart also ran the Rhyl 10km in 29-11, won the Redcar 10 mile race in 49-05, and won a local ten mile road race in Cockermouth in an impressive 48-51. Then he went over to Dublin to run a marathon at the end of October, coming fourth in 2-14-56, 30 seconds behind the winner. 'That was another race where I felt OK, but not that brilliant. The lads I was up against I should have been beating.'

At the end of the year Stuart was in heavy training, mainly to have a go at qualifying for the World cross country champion-ships. His stated build-up races were to be the Saltwell 10 and the Morpeth to Newcastle 14 (on New Year's Day). The World cross country trials were to be held at Gateshead on 30 Jan 1988, with the World Championships to be in New Zealand.

The early results in 1988 showed something of a turnaround, as Stuart came 6th in the Morpeth to Newcastle road race. He then came 15th in the Gateshead Cross Country Trials (thus missing out on the Worlds), and had his best ever National Cross Country position of tenth at Newark (a race won by Dave Clarke by 46 seconds against a class field). It was then back to the London Marathon, for a steady 14th place in 2-13-36, although he had breathing issues again. This was the year Henrik Jorgensen won, taking a $30,000 prize back to Denmark, and Stuart picked up $1,500 for his own effort. Apparently feeling strong, he passed a lot of runners in the last five miles or so, up to which point time had been more important than racing in his mind. Kenny was disappointed at 14th though. 'It was not really breathing issues, I just didn't click. I got dropped from the fast group and ran it mainly on my own, apart from a Chinese bloke. Again, it was reasonable but not brilliant.'

When we were discussing his road running earnings Kenny Stuart wryly stated that one writer did claim that when he was running marathons he made enough money to buy his own house, which was not true. 'Because I didn't', Kenny said adamantly. 'We have just paid the mortgage off about five years ago! What happened was I was able to buy another car when I got back, as I won $15,000. I was able to cash some in to put a £2,000 deposit down to start a mortgage off.' Pauline added that, 'you had to apply for the money because it went into a trust fund. The AAA trust fund went bust and a lot of people lost money. We were lucky as it happened not long after ours came out for the mortgage down payment and the car.'

John Wild's only experience of using a trust fund was for his winnings from the Tour of Tameside from 1985. 'I wanted to buy a new car and they gave me the cheque to do that from the fund.'

Three months after London Stuart ran the Great North Run again, coming 7th in 63-48 and then in October came seventh in the Berlin marathon in 2-13-37, behind Tanzanian Suleiman Nyambui's 2-11-45 winning time. The Berlin course already had a reputation as a fast course, and is now acknowledged to be one of the fastest marathon courses in the world, as numerous world bests have been set there. Kenny again felt he had a solid run but felt he could run faster. Kenny thought an autumn marathon would suit him. 'The organisers paid for my flight, but the prize money wasn't brilliant.'

Stuart had been fitting in even more training, since being

advised by Dave Cannon. In the latter part of the year Kenny won the Derwentwater 10 mile race in 50-09. Then he competed in the Brampton to Carlisle 10, which he won in 48-35. He was hoping for a sub-48 time, but had no challengers as he was over one minute ahead of the field, and the wind was slightly against on this linear course. Finally in December he won the County Cross Country championships again, at Cockermouth.

John Wild had no significant race results in 1987, and in 1988 came 9th in the RAF cross country championships and 14th in the Inter-Services event, even though he was now posted in Germany. Wild had always been happy to help others runners, advising Sean Livesey in his early fell running days, and helping Craig Metcalf to second in the Tour of Tameside in 1985. In 1988 a contingent of Brits went to a mountain race in the Matterhornlauf. The race starts in Zermatt and rises 950m in its 12km up on to the Matterhorn ridge. Wild came over from Germany, with Keith Miller who was on detachment with him in the RAF there. Wild had been advising him on his fell running and they shared a camp together for the trip. Miller's 10th place in the race had him thinking of taking to fell racing when he left the forces later that year, but he never made that transition.

Whilst in Laarbruch Wild used to organise an event called the Chain of Command Relay. Every squadron had to put in an Officer, a Senior NCO, a Corporal, a Junior Rank and a Woman. He recalls that it was, 'fantastic and became really popular. We had a kid's fun run before it, and I used to dress up in a clown's outfit to lead the kids round the fun run.'

In 1988 Kenny Stuart was granted Life Membership of Keswick AC, 'to show appreciation for his loyalty to his native club.'

The training paid off for Stuart when he went to America in January 1989 and ran the Houston Marathon. There was a detailed report on the race, by an unspecified author, in the Keswick AC club newsletter. It gives some further insight in to the problems that had been experienced by Kenny:

I'm sure I am speaking for the whole of Keswick, not just

the club, in congratulating Kenny on both an excellent 2nd place in Houston, and also on a fine 1988 season for which he is classified 3rd in the new AAA Star Ranking Scheme for road racers – ahead of such notables as Charlie Spedding and Dave Long, both Olympic marathon selections. He was delighted (and a little surprised) to knock another 2 mins off his PB in this race with a time of 2-11-36.

Past winters have been plagued with a virus, flu etc., but this one has been relatively trouble free and allowed Kenny to get some good quality training in – a mixture of mileage, speedwork and races. The county cross country at Cockermouth was won in casual style with over a minute to spare before the 2nd finisher materialised, and 3 weeks later Kenny was lined up with the established X-country stars for the televised IAC meeting at Durham on 31st.

Despite the very impressive field, I expected to see him fare a little better than his eventual 20th place. However, bearing in mind that the X-C boys are in mid-season and thus enter each race rested and ready to run, Kenny was maintaining quality training. So after 4 weeks of 100 miles each he wasn't expecting a brilliant run and was further hampered by a stitch from lap 4 (of 6) to the finish. Even so, "I was a bit disappointed, and asking myself how I could hope to run a good marathon in 2 weeks' time." And so to Texas accompanied by coach Dave Cannon.

Race day, and due to the early start, the weather was cold with a touch of fog. As time progressed, this lifted and the race was run in slightly humid but otherwise ideal conditions. Initially, the front runners raced as a large pack and passed through 10 miles in 49-53, with the half marathon reached in 65-05. Both of these were slower than Kenny's 1988 London marathon times. By 16 miles the pack was reduced to just 4 runners: Kaitany of Kenya; Kvernmo of Norway; Janicki of the USA and Kenny, who was feeling relatively unstressed and confident. The Kenyan, who had run 2-10 when finishing 3rd at Chicago last year, made a break at 17 miles and Kenny, aware of Kaitany's ability, was content to let him go. Kenny had a morale booster in passing 20 miles in 1-39-04, and was comfortably inside his PB.

The Houston Marathon is a city streets course and although generally flat it is "not the easiest of races", with two testing hills beyond the 20 mile mark. It was on the 2nd and more severe of these hills, at 24 miles, that Kenny attacked for 2nd place, with the tiring Janicki unable to produce an effective response. Kenny maintained his pace for the remaining 2.2 miles and finished 22 seconds ahead of the American, 92 seconds behind the winner, who had broken the course record and so picked up a considerable cash bonus.

The next big race on Kenny's agenda is London – let's hope the new form is as prominent there. Once again, congratulations Kenny, Good Running in 1989.

1	Richard Kaitany	KEN	2-10-04
2	Kenny Stuart	ENG	2-11-36
3	D Janicki	USA	2-11-58
4	A Zachariassen	DEN	2-14-23
5	G Kvernmo	NOR	2-14-48

I asked Kenny to reflect on the build-up and the race itself. 'The difference was that it was after Christmas at work, it was a particularly quiet time of year for us, so you were your own boss as to how much energy you expended. I had a full month averaging 100 miles a week in good weather. When we went out there the weather was also cooler than it normally was. I knew at 5 miles that I was going to run well. It was so easy and I was so relaxed. There was a massive contingent of Mexicans there, also a load of 28 minute 10km runners, but most of them fell away. At around 21 miles I lost contact with Kaitany. The only other bloke left was Janicki, the US marathon champion, whom I ran with for quite a while, before I got away from him. Dave Cannon acted as an intermediary to get me the race in Houston, he worked for the Electricity Board actually as a linesman, going up the poles.'

Kenny was now starting to make real money from his running, picking up a $15,000 prize for his second place in Houston. Stuart was paid to run the London Marathon after his time in Houston, achieving 2-12-53 in 15th place that year, earning $2,250 in prize money to go with some sponsorship from running shoe companies. Marathon paydays were starting to get very respectable now, with London at the forefront. Douglas Wakiihuri's prize money was $58,500 for his three-second win (in a time of 2-09-03) over Steve Moneghetti. The London Marathon had offered Steve Jones a deal worth $200,000 and Gelindo Bordin (the Italian, who was European champion) $150,000. They both turned it down because the Boston Marathon had made them better offers.

The Keswick AC club newsletter's enigmatic reporter noted: 'It seems Kenny was again trying to hide from the cameras although the more observant amongst us spotted his slight frame hiding in the leading bunch for the first half of the race – after which time I don't think we saw more than a fleeting glimpse. Nevertheless, yet again a first class performance for Ken to finish 2nd Englishman and either 3rd or 4th Brit past the line. A time of 2-12-53 and an overall position of 15th in possibly one of the best fields ever seen.' Marathon watchers will know that London fields have become even more stellar since that time.

Since 1983 Kenny Stuart had isolated occasions when what appeared to be minor illnesses affected his performances, mostly colds and viruses. Usually they resulted in poorer performances than expected, and even once pulling out of a race he had started (Edale, in 1985). Then in 1986 he had started having some breathing problems. Unfortunately later in 1989 things really started going very wrong for Stuart, health-wise, and he was showing signs of post-viral fatigue.

He had started chasing money races, and did his third marathon of 1989 at the end of September. Coming 4th in 2-15-14 in the Birmingham Centenary marathon gained him another $3,575. Kenny agrees it was possibly one too many. The three in front were Victor Kotov (a Russian, who won in 2-12), Tony Milovsorov (with 2-13), and Schutz (of Hungary), with Steve Brace one behind him in 5th.

In the winter of 1989/90 Kenny Stuart won the Cocker-mouth 10k in 30-58, had another cross country county win (making that now seven in a row) and was an excellent 8th in the Inter-Counties. He then ran the National Cross Country championship race at Leeds in February, coming 17th, and turned to the roads for the City of Bath half marathon on 18 March to come 4th in 66-41.

John Wild and I talked about his and Kenny's relative strengths and successes at cross country and at the marathon. John's view was that, 'Kenny left it too late to do really well over the country. I think he may have even left his marathon running too late. With hindsight he had become ill too by then, which was affecting his training, and was getting on a bit [he was then 29]. I think he got a bit bogged down with the hat-trick of fell running championships, as I did too. I should have done marathon running two years earlier [Wild started at 32]. I didn't want to be known as a great fell runner - that just wasn't the aim.' I re-joined with, 'well, you were'. But John insisted, 'I prefer people to think of me as a cross country runner.' I pointed out that Billy Bland said John was a better runner than him. 'I never wanted to be known as a fell runner. Well, Kenny Stuart was a better fell runner than me, Mike Short too for that matter. But I ran for England or Great Britain on the road, cross country, fell and track and I don't think anyone else has ever done that. That mattered to me. I love the fells though.'

On being shown those thoughts from John Wild, Kenny responded, 'Yeh. I think I did put a lot in to the three cham-pionship years on the fells. The whole thing could have shifted along a lot quicker, at an earlier age for me. I could have got reinstated earlier from the guides racing, I kept going for more years than I should have done. Really it was because I was years and years in the wilderness, not really winning a lot, and gradually just improving. Those years could have been shorter and I could have got into marathons by the age of 26 or something like that. I think John is exactly right.'

Back on the roads, Kenny Stuart had to drop out of the 1990 London Marathon and the effects of his lingering illness virtually stopped him running, with another DNF in the Moscow International Peace Marathon in August.

Kenny did run in the county cross country championships at Carlisle in December 1990, but was only able to come second, thus his consecutive run of wins ended at seven.

Kenny Stuart made a half-hearted comeback in 1991, but his post-viral fatigue meant that he couldn't perform as he would wish and it was a short-lived effort. The club newsletter editor was still clocking him, noting that he/she, ' ... witnessed Kenny Stuart's brief return to the fells, running freely without pressure of being expected to win and winning Gatesgill anyway.'

John Wild ran his last two RAF cross country championships races in 1990 and 1991, slipping to 25th and 42nd respectively. He had gone to Germany in 1986 and came back in 1991 to RAF Cranwell. He was thirty-eight then. John Wild had begun to suffer with his knees and stopped competitive running before he was forty. 'John raced for the RAF after his career had peaked,' commented Alan Warner. 'He loved the RAF. To him working with these guys, and the rapport with Steve Jones and others, was brilliant, so he wanted to keep it going as long as he could.'

John Wild never wanted to run as a vet. He liked running to keep fit and he still used to run a bit with international runner Mark Flint, but racing later on never appealed to him. He thinks he did a random steeplechase in about 1992, in an inter-station event. He became an officer in 1991 and took over as the RAF long and middle distance head, helping to select athletes for different races. 'Then I went on a photo engineering course in 1994 and I got side-lined by that and never really got involved in athletics after that. I wasn't really a born organiser actually. I had coached Mark Flint for a while. Once when I was coaching Mark Flint we both got picked for England at cross country at Amorbieta, and I won that year. Mark Flint went on to the roads as well and ran a good Great North Run one year. We were sometimes mistaken for brothers!'

Towards the end of his RAF career John Wild was the last commanding officer at Sealand, the oldest RAF station still going, and he had to close it down in 2006, as it was surplus to requirements. 'The most emotional thing,' he recalls, 'was all the memorabilia. It included a lovely silver rose vase engraved with a message: "thank you for the hospitality, Charles Lindbergh". He was on one of his round the world jaunts in 1928 and was diverted there due to poor weather.'

Just before he retired from the RAF John was asked to be starter at the RAF championships race. 'I was quite emotional. I had run there (at RAF Halton) since 1967, the ATC championships were there, and we had training weekends there, so I had some amazing memories.'

Alan Warner expanded on this occasion, as it nicely illustrated John's character. 'John was coming to the end of his RAF career, but one of the memories I will always have is him turning up to the RAF championships, as I did, being invited as guests. This was years after his career as a runner had finished. He was so thrilled that he was invited to start the race. He came over to me and was very emotional. He was so honoured to have run it so many times, run the Inter-Services so many times, and then be asked to start the race. He was leaving the Air Force a few months later. He would be about 55 years old. As well as being loyal, he is very emotional, and things like that just topped off his career.'

CHAPTER 21

Treat winners well on the continent

It is worth looking at the impact and influence of several other runners, particularly Jack Maitland, Hugh Symonds and Matt Patterson. They had varying degrees of success in the years from 1986 onwards, but as John Wild and Kenny Stuart's running career paths diverged they became pivotal players on the fell running scene.

Jack Maitland was more focussed on the fells than he had ever been before, winning the 1986 championship title with 123 points. Second was Colin Donnelly with 119, followed by Rod Pilbeam with 113, and Billy Bland still challenging with 111 points. Maitland came back from a trip to New Zealand on 5 March 1986. He raced Black Combe (coming first) on 23 March, the first British championships race Llanbedr-Blaenavon (first) on 29 March, and Coity fell race (first) on the next day too. Maitland still liked to race regularly.

Jack Maitland commented to me: 'I must have changed my attitude a bit to win the championships. I started by going down to Wales to reccie the Llanbedr-Blaenavon championships race, which others may not have done, as it hadn't been on the championships list before.'

Maitland still managed to fit in some European races, despite trying to win the championships in 1986. 'The first race in Europe was Sierre-Montana (coming 20th) on 27 July, then Val des Dix (8th) on 3 August and Sierre-Zinal (7th) on 10 August (it was the previous year that I'd won it).'

Jack Maitland also notes that, 'Mike Short blazed a trail for

the Mount Cameroun race, and Martin Stone organised a trip
there in 1988. I went with him and Helene Diamantides. Martin
was instrumental in getting me there then, and that led to the
return invite in 1989, when I won.'

In 1987 all five of Hugh Symonds' family had been cycle
camping near Vignemale on tricycles. Vignemale is the highest
peak in the French Pyrenees. 'I had researched that there was a
mountain race at the end of our tour near Courteney. I won that
and they invited me back in 1988 to do the Vignemale race.'

He recalls, 'I felt quite ropey, driving out there. It was in July,
the week after Wasdale [where Hugh had come sixth]. After
about an hour into the race I was lying about 10th. Despite
the altitude I began to feel better and by the top I was third, on
the rope section. I seemed to be going faster than others and
within half an hour of the top I was leading. I was running in
Walshes and descending faster than anyone else and went on
to win and broke the record. They really treat winners well on
the continent, with a lot of razzmatazz. Having not expected
to win it was wonderful.' In discussing his best races, he also
noted that, 'at Wasdale I was second twice which was hugely
frustrating. In one of these I was ahead of Billy Bland at the top
of Scafell but messed up the navigation in the mist. Ennerdale
victories were really satisfying, as were the Three Peaks ones
and the Ben, which was a surprise.'

In our conversation, Hugh and I drifted into talking about the
abstract topic of 'best ever fell runners'. I had already nailed my
flag to the mast by saying that the triumvirate of Joss Naylor,
Billy Bland and Kenny Stuart fitted the bill for me (for reasons
explained in detail in *It's a hill, get over it*'). Hugh admitted
that he once had just such a conversation when staying with
Gary Devine in the Pyrenees on a bike trip. He went on, 'Gary
asked me who I thought was the best ever fell runner. I said
Billy Bland or Kenny Stuart - two different things, chalk and
cheese. Gary Devine surprised me by coming back with Colin
Donnelly as he, "still holds records. He also won the Ben Nevis
race almost 10 years apart" [*1979-1986 actually*].'

In 1989 Hugh Symonds really tapered off performance-wise in races. He was frustrated, but clearly it was because he was totally focussed on his plan to cover all 303 of the 3000-foot mountains of Britain and Ireland in one continuous run coming in 1990. 'I was doing really long training runs and basically slowed down.' At this point he also reflected on his own plans for doing a Bob Graham Round (BGR). Many fell runners think the Bob Graham Round is a difficult thing to fit in during the summer if you are a competitive athlete. Hugh subscribes to this view, commenting, 'to be fair my years as a successful fell runner were only really between 1982 and 1988. I am so glad I had that period. I now think it was a bit short really, but that is just the way it went. There was no way I could consider doing a BGR in that window when I was at my best. But if you did the BGR one summer you would knock out several races. Doing the continuous mountains run I slowed down even more. If you go out running for six or seven hours or so for nearly 100 consecutive days you are not going to be fast any longer. I was actually talking to Steve Birkinshaw about this recently at the Sedbergh Hills race, after he had run all the 214 Wainwrights in just over six days. I think he found it interesting to talk to me, but was probably not very encouraged!'

When it came to reflecting on his achievements Hugh Symonds found it hard to choose a particular one. 'One would have to be that mountain effort - running from Ben Hope to Brandon in 97 days and then writing the book about it. That would have to be the highlight for me. When it comes to individual races they were all so different. I can't really decide. I would probably make it equal between the Ben, the Three Peaks and Vignemale.'

I wondered whether Hugh Symonds had ever considered writing about his fell running career, and later cycling adventures. Hugh responded that, 'he had never really thought of writing anything else. My inspiration came from people like Bruce Tulloh. I saw people doing huge runs and thought I wanted to do one of these. I wanted to do something like that, and write about it.' (You can read about it in his book *Running*

High: the first continuous traverse of the 303 mountains of Britain and Ireland.) 'I don't know if I ever wanted to write another book,' he chuckled.

In 1991 Hugh Symonds also tried to race again, but not very successfully. 'We were having a big building job done, and I also got plantar fasciitis for a year which was horrible. By the time I became a vet in 1993 I was back on an even keel. I won a couple of vet 40 races, one vet 50 and now one vet 60 race, which was the Wild Boar race two years ago.'

But Hugh admitted that in the end he really did want to do the Bob Graham Round. 'I would have really regretted it if I hadn't. I had half thought of doing it on the way down through the Lakes on the mountains of Britain and Ireland run. Wouldn't that have been cool? So, I knew I was slowing down on becoming a vet. I started running with Mark Higginbottom, and we said to each other "why not do the BGR". We supported each other with a couple of friends in some parts. I am so glad I did it (in 1995).'

Meanwhile, it was a kind of fade-out from elite performances in Malcolm Patterson's case, as he explained. 'After a great year in 1989 (apart from a very bad race at the Worlds which I shouldn't have run five weeks after having my appendix out), I did very little fellrunning in 1990 and then when I did come back in 1991 I had another bad race at the Worlds in Zermatt and this really dented my confidence. Basically I decided I wasn't going to get any better, so I gave up international running and went back to orienteering for a few years. I did return to serious fell running in the mid-1990s, but at a lower level, and I was British Vet champion in 1998.'

When asked what his greatest feat/race on the fells was, Patterson came back with a list and an interesting perspective. 'One of my childhood idols was the late Billy Bremner, captain of Leeds United FC who was 'ard as nails. His motto was "You get nowt for coming second". So it is ironic that whilst I was pleased with my race wins – such as Ben Lomond in 1987, or Dollar (in Scotland) in 1989, where I set a new course record – my best races were when I didn't win. So, second to John Wild at both Ben Lomond and Skiddaw in 1982, 2nd at Snowdon in 1989 to John Lenihan (he was later World champion in 1991), second at Blisco in 1987 when Jack Maitland and I both beat the record, 13th in that Zogno (Italy) International in 1984, 8th in the World Trophy in both 1987 and 1988.'

CHAPTER 22

Finished as firm friends

Many sportsmen have a real difficulty knowing when to retire from top level sport. In team games like football, it is often when you stop getting picked for the top teams. For running it isn't always that simple. It can get into your blood so much that you just can't stop. I know that in my own case I failed to acknowledge the tail off of my running and in fact had a 'fade out' that was longer than my actual 'career', by a ratio of about fifteen years to ten. In the end injury and health issues decided it for me.

Another parallel between Wild/Stuart and Ovett/Coe is that of having unsatisfactory career endings. Steve Ovett suffered respiratory problems at the Olympic Games in Los Angeles in 1984. His last significant win was in August 1986, when he won the 5000m at the Commonwealth Games in Edinburgh. He then failed to make the 1988 Olympic team, and retired from athletics in 1991.

In 1986 Seb Coe won the gold medal over 800m at the European Championships in Stuttgart. He was injured in May 1987, and was out for the entire season. The following year he was not selected for the British 1988 Olympic Games team, when he failed to qualify from the heats of the 1500m at the Trials. After a spell of altitude training he had picked up a chest infection. Coe had one final good season in 1989. Aged thirty-three, he won the 1500m AAA title, and won the silver medal at the World Cup over 1500m.

In this era of stories emerging at a later date, in December

2012 Scotland's *Herald* newspaper printed the reported view of a rival (in an unattributed article). It stated that:

> Sebastian Coe's final track race in Britain was fixed, according to a runner who says he accepted a payment of about $10,000 to lose the competition. Ex-British international athlete Ikem Billy says he was told by Andy Norman – who was then promotions director of the British Athletic Federation and who died in 2007 – to throw a race in September 1989 in order to allow Coe to win. Norman was Billy's agent at the time as well as the race promoter. Coe is not accused of being complicit in the fix or of knowing about Billy being paid to lose.
>
> According to Ikem Billy, the former European junior champion, less than an hour before he was due to step on to the track for the race, he was approached by Norman and ordered not to win the race. He says that on top of his race fee of about $5,000, he was offered $10,000 to lose. Athletics fees then were paid in US currency. Billy says the approach was witnessed by another runner who competed in a different race at the meeting. "I hold my hands up," Billy said. "I was paid to finish second. I admit that it was fixed. Andy paid me to finish second. He told me: 'Make sure you don't win'. Everyone was scared of Andy. He dominated the sport. He could do what he wanted.
>
> "That night, an hour before the race, he came up to me and he said, 'The people here have come to see Seb Coe win. They don't care about you'." Billy was that year's national champion at 800m and had been unbeaten by any other Briton over two laps. "Until that night," he said.
>
> "Andy knew Seb wasn't in shape and that I would kick his arse. I remember coming off the final bend, I was on his shoulder, looking round and thinking I could go flying past any time. Instead I just eased off."

Coe retired from competitive athletics in early 1990, after having to bow out at the Auckland Commonwealth Games with yet another chest infection. In the final of the Commonwealth Games 800m in Auckland, Ikem Billy placed fifth ahead of Coe in sixth, while Matt Yates took bronze.

John Wild stopped running as his knees were causing him such trouble. 'Since then I have had four arthroscopies on my right knee and three on the left. The surgeon said this is your last one. That was just before I retired in 2008.'

John had arthroscopies on both knees in the early 1990s. 'I attended a clinic at Oswestry in mid-2010 and was diagnosed with osteoarthritis and put on a stem cell therapy trial. The first stage was High Tibial Osteotomy, where a wedge of bone is removed from the tibia which when joined together, kinks the leg over to the left, thus creating a gap and stopping the bone to bone contact. It also created a gap for the stem cells to go in. The first operation in February 2011 didn't take, so I had another in August 2011 with a bone graft and bigger steel plate and screws. All is OK now and I can more or less do what I want, but do not run!'

There was a big RAF cross country reunion in June 2012 to celebrate their winning the Inter-Services championships 22 successive years from 1973-1994, which was attended by Steve Jones and had Dave Bedford as the main guest. Seeing a photo of this event, John reminisced about Bedford's influence on runners of the time.

'Dave Bedford revolutionised the way we used to train. It was all miles with him, doing 150-160 miles a week. I was doing about 80-90 a week, and it was all intense. According to my training diary at one time I ran over a hundred miles a week for over two years.' I asked John if that might have something to do with the state of his knees then. He retorted, 'builders, farmers and plumbers get bad knees, not runners! Now there are people I know getting heart problems, and it may be because in the 1960s we used to train through colds/flu, and not having a rest when we should have. I am getting an ECG every year now.'

In 2013 John and Anne Wild went up to Burnsall and stayed in the Red Lion for that year's race. 'We told the Burnsall committee about coming up and they invited us to lunch. There had been a centenary lunch before the race in 1982, which we attended, and the photograph is on the pub wall. It is a shame to see yourself all those years ago! We had a great weekend, and were made to feel very welcome. Anne and I walked the course the day of the race and I got lost! I didn't remember it.'

Life does have a habit of going full circle. Having never really shown an interest in following his father into running, John Wild's son Jack ran his first ever race in 2015, at the age of 21. John was amazed at the turnaround in interest, saying, 'he has just started running and asked me to set him a training programme – something that wouldn't have happened a year ago! He never developed an interest in running, but was pressured into getting to a minimum level of fitness in order to pass the Army 1.5 mile entrance run. He struggled initially with reaching the minimum standard of 11 minutes 30 seconds, but eventually reached that, and he can now run it at just over eight minutes.' Jack Wild, based in London with the Band of the Irish Guards, completed a 16-week training programme under his father's direction in preparation for a 2015 Half Marathon. Fittingly it was the race John won so convincingly in its inaugural year, the Stafford Half Marathon. Jack was given bib number 1984 (the year of his father's win), which he wore with honour to finish 98th in 1-25-17.

In 2016, with some more serious training behind him, and again guided by his father (who admits he wasn't easy on him), Jack Wild ran the race again and came 65th in 1-23-47, a minute and a half improvement. John says, 'he still lacks confidence, but I am impressed with his discipline.'

Kenny Stuart's career-ending illness has been detailed earlier. Commenting on the series of illnesses he experienced, Kenny says, 'a lot of these were just colds. I always seemed to get run down around February/March time. You had had a full winter training on the roads, in the dark, in the cold and wet, and you were at your lowest ebb. It caught up with you.' The medical tests he had were inconclusive, but he was told he probably had ME (Myalgic Encephalopathy) or Chronic Fatigue Syndrome.

Kenny Stuart has obviously reflected on all this over a long period of time and summed up his thoughts for me. 'I don't think we really know, and probably never will. It certainly was an immune deficiency problem, and that was recurring. During tests it was proven that I had a predisposition towards allergies (atopy). I had my tonsils out when I was a kid, and things like that. It runs in the family. My grandfather had bronchitis year in and year out when he worked in the quarries. My dad and grandfather both had their tonsils out. It was like a weak chest in some ways, I suppose, but not something to stop me running. All in all, the racing and the working, and the fact I was very stressed by family circumstances, mounted up. I suppose if I had laid off and say come back in six months' time and start afresh it might have worked for me. But I tried to plough on through for six months and my body wouldn't respond at all.'

'The conclusion they came to was that I had had a stomach virus. I had what was like post-viral fatigue, which they called ME. I was rotten for six months, I could barely drive. I would get halfway through a long journey and be absolutely knackered. This was after the marathon period. Dave Cannon had something similar, and was leading a similar life, training twice a day and working up a telegraph pole.'

Kenny Stuart suggested to me that never seeming to get injured may have had some influence, in that he trained extremely hard and never really gave himself rest and recovery time, which is often forced on athletes who have minor injuries and stop training temporarily for that reason.

Some people think Kenny overcooked it. Mark McGlincy's considered view now is that, 'he didn't need to train that hard as he was naturally talented. Fell legend Bill Teasdale told me once that he came across Kenny out one day walking with Pauline. Anyway he stopped and chatted, and he says to Kenny "you don't look so good." He says he looked green. Bill said to

him "what you doing all this mileage for, you don't need to."
That was when he was running on the roads. It is so easy to
think more is better. He might have done better on less, but you
just don't know. Everyone is individual.' Mark then mused that
he, 'would have liked to have seen him achieve more and gone
on a lot longer.'

Telling Kenny that story, he thought for a moment before
responding. 'It is possible. Training too much for the type of
work I was doing at the time maybe, the combination of everything.' Pauline's view was that Kenny's, 'training was quite
light in comparison to some people, in terms of mileage. It was
because you were doing a manual job.' Kenny expanded on the
training regime. 'In winter I had to go out at 5pm in the dark,
set off from here and go to Thirlmere and back, on the road. I
had to run the white line, you didn't have any lights, but traffic
wasn't as busy those days. You also couldn't choose the better
weather of that day like full time runners could. So you had to
go out in a snow storm or a cold east wind.'

After all his own physical difficulties over the years I was also
interested in Joss Naylor's view of what had happened to Kenny
Stuart (and Dave Cannon). Joss said simply that, 'Kenny's body
stopped making energy. Steve Birkinshaw has had similar problems since his Wainwrights effort.'

Kenny Stuart seems to partly acknowledge that maybe he
trained too hard. He commented that, 'I preferred to train on
my own. I could come home from work, get my kit on, do it
within an hour or 90 minutes, have a bath (we didn't have a
shower then) and that was your evening. It was like a second
job, if you like. That was the trouble, the better you get and
more ambitious you are the more it seems like a job. It starts
to take over. When Dave Cannon was training me he used to
say to me when we went to races, "it is just a matter of going
and getting the job done". That was the result, even though you
enjoyed it. It took a bit out of you, but that is the way it is. I can
imagine these lads that go out for fun and just decide to have
a run round and run against the course, and enjoy it. I can see

that in it. You don't have to train that hard, don't have to push yourself, it is a different ball game.'

So what is life like now for John Wild and Kenny Stuart? Having recently undergone knee surgery, John now regularly takes in early morning spin-bike sessions at a gym in Stafford to keep fit. As he says, 'I just need that burn. I don't really miss running. I've had my time, but I never wanted to be a running veteran.'

Recently John Wild has been diagnosed with Obstructive Sleep Apnoea. He is happy enough to talk about it. It is a fact of life, as he puts it. He talked through how he found out what the issue was and explained how it has panned out. 'For years Anne would say to me, "you stopped breathing when you were sleeping". She would wait, and if I didn't start again she would dig me and I would grunt and groan. I kept saying I'll do something about it. I always had an MOT at the doctor's in February, around my birthday. I mentioned it because Anne was keeping on about it.' He was referred to Stoke Hospital, and they gave him an oxygen finger monitor to wear for three nights. Then they said they needed more advanced tests, so he had a heart monitor, oxygen monitor and another finger monitor. When he took it back the consultant said, 'that "from the results in front of me I expected somebody morbidly obese with a thick neck". Apparently I stopped breathing 47 times a night, and the longest I stopped breathing was over a minute. I now use Continuous Positive Air Pressure, using a mask, which I have to wear at night. It plugs in, but is mobile if I go away, as long as I have a power supply. When I stop breathing, the kit detects it and it ramps the air pressure up, opening the airways. It is not ideal, but I mention it as it might prompt someone who recognises the symptoms to get it sorted. The consultant said, "if you weren't as fit as you are, I am sure you would have had a mini stroke by now." It is no great grief, but you never get used to it. I do have to sleep on my back now.'

Kenny Stuart lives in a house called *Fellside*, still near where he was born, and says that he is now enjoying his running for the first time in his life. He had given up his previous job to concentrate full time on his running career, so he returned to college to study horticulture, before working as a gardener at the University of Cumbria, and now does the same kind of work on a freelance basis.

Having been something of a running obsessive, Kenny Stuart's lifestyle is a little more relaxed now. 'At the moment I like walking, wild plants, and wild life. I am involved in trail hunting as well. I also used to lay the trails for hound trail events. My son works for Northumbria Wildlife Trust as a red squirrel ranger. As to relaxing, when the garden is done I might sit in the summer house and have a glass of wine. We never went on holiday ['*and still don't*' chipped in Pauline!].'

Kenny Stuart reckoned that his favourite events had to be the local races where he was expected to win but, paradoxically, these could be a bit nerve-racking as well. 'I always found travelling long distances to races boring, so local venues suited me better. Even though I still hold the Ben Nevis record it was never my favourite race. I always found the course demanding, to say the least. My favourite short/medium races would be steep and grassy – Butter Crag, Latrigg, Gategill, Sailbeck, etc., and my favourite long races were Ennerdale and Borrowdale. Both these latter races have long run-offs to the finish line and I could always use a bit of leg speed to finish fast if necessary. I could manage rocky descents if pushed but I have always preferred steep, relatively "clean" ground.'

Kenny feels that his greatest satisfaction from fell running comes from, 'the dedication I achieved from being able to train hard on a daily basis – only now can I fully appreciate the standards of fitness fell runners need to compete at their best. I also had the pleasure of meeting many people from a variety of backgrounds and look forward to meeting them still on occasions.'

Has the sport changed much in the time since they were at their peak, I wondered. Kenny and John were both conscious that some records they set are still unbeaten. I posited the argument that because in their day the best athletes raced against each other, forcing them to go faster. But, it isn't that simple. Pauline Stuart thought that, 'yes, there was far more competition, and more very good runners in quantity.' Kenny's view was that, 'One big difference is that in my time, more so with John Wild but with me as well, was that we could compete at a fairly high level on the flat at the Inter-Counties and the national, but the current crop of fell runners probably couldn't. That might be just an older bloke looking back at it. There are exceptions of course, particularly on the women's side just now.'

I had a short exchange with Kenny and Pauline Stuart about running versus work, particularly in light of the pressure their daughters had to establish their careers, at the expense of their running. Kenny commented that, 'runners now have to choose between a career or the time to train. What do you do?' Pauline retorted that, 'most people who ran in the 1980s had careers', to which Kenny responded that there were, 'a lot on the dole, a lot of good runners.' Pauline looked straight at Kenny, and swiftly closed the conversation with, 'you were a good runner and you worked!'

There is definitely a sense that trail running and mountain running are having a negative impact on fell running, and that successful events like parkrun are affecting participation in road and track events. Kenny Stuart commented, 'I was talking to Ken Jones down at Snowdon the other day. He was saying the top Italian runners won't come over any more for the Snowdon race. There is a circuit out in Europe now that is virtually professional.' Stuart had been invited down to Snowdonia to be part of a piece in the BBC *Countryfile* programme. There were short interviews with Kenny, plus the former Snowdon race organiser (Ken Jones) and the present one, as well as current top fell runner Ben Mounsey. Mounsey was challenged to race the Snowdon train to the summit, as a stunt in the programme. Kenny Stuart explained to me that he was happy to be involved as, 'the *Countryfile* thing was about the link between the race and the way that the community actually hold it themselves, rather than someone coming in and taking the money. It is all voluntary, with tea and cakes made by local people, and run by local committee it is bringing money in.'

Worryingly, Kenny also feels that there is still this attitude about runners (like John Wild), and also about people like myself writing about the sport, who weren't brought up in the Lakes, for instance. I won't pursue the latter statement, as I have aired my views elsewhere. What Kenny says is definitely evident, as the Fell Runners Association (the sport's governing body) is constantly trying to maintain an inward-looking stance, and actually discourages participation in the sport by people from other athletic disciplines, or from what might be termed 'non-athletes'. Safety and environmental impact are usually the excuses used to justify the position. I may be being overly optimistic, but is this stance about to change? The first question in a FRA survey that came to members in March 2016 was: 'The FRA has always had a policy of taking a passive stance in publicising fell running. Should we maintain this policy or be more proactive?'

Before asking John and Kenny to give their thoughts on each other, I asked a couple of their contemporaries to give me their assessment of the two them.

I started by asking Joss Naylor for his assessment of John Wild. Joss thought that John was, 'as good an all-rounder as there was. He wasn't the best at any one thing, but he was up there. He wasn't born in the right spot! If he had been born in Borrowdale, or Wasdale or somewhere, he would have a little bit less fear of coming down. If anything he did hold back a little coming down. He would hang on though, and wasn't shy of jumping things.'

Joss was effusive in discussing Kenny's strengths. 'He was dedicated to training. I tell you what, it is a pity that he just didn't have that little bit extra leg speed when he went on the road. Because the work he put in, he deserved a lot more out of it. He trained hard twice a day, and maybe he did too much. He is just a great bloke, is Kenny. Very quiet, very sincere in everything he does. It hurt me when he couldn't do it anymore. If he could have got away to these training camps they have now he might have been one of the top blokes in the world on the road.'

Joss also commented on the skill of ascending and descending. 'Kenny was better than average, but not the best, at descending. He could fly up though, could the man. Stuart Bland and Billy Bland were two of the best descenders. I liked descending when I was right. It is an art of its own. You have got to be able to line the ground up in front of you, and feel it.'

I also discussed ascending and descending with Billy Bland, who reckoned you could improve your uphill running, but have absolutely minimal chance to improve your downhill. 'It is the fear of falling that stops people doing well. I don't care what anyone says, and they are not being truthful if they don't think this, but what is stopping them running fast downhill is fear. If they cannot accept that then they are wrong.'

My next thought was that maybe it was risk-takers that were the best descenders. Billy thought not. 'It isn't a risk though. It is so natural that there is no risk. I used to be at the bottom of somewhere and think well why can't they do it. My brother Stuart was a real good downhiller, and Andy Styan, Tommy Sedgwick, they all were. Also Bob Whitfield, a good runner who never got the credit he deserved. We didn't think we were gonna fall, we weren't going crazy or we would have been in and out of hospital. We were in more control than others were. You were very fortunate if you were born a descender. You can definitely get fitter and run better uphill though. That was my achilles heel for a few years, but the more I trained, then the better I got at it. I was never as good as Kenny or John at going up, even then.'

Malcolm Patterson had his own take on Kenny Stuart and John Wild's athletic careers. 'It is interesting how much John's cross country and steeplechase pedigree enabled him to progress to elite level on the fells. That is a very different backstory to Kenny's, though in the end Kenny progressed to elite level on the roads.'

When John Wild saw what others had said about his running, his first comment was that he wouldn't quibble with Billy Bland having said that John was 'not a proper fellsman or mountain man' (in an earlier exchange). John added, 'I count Billy as more of a fell runner than me, without a doubt. But I came to the fells with good mileage. I trained harder in 1981 than perhaps I first thought. People made a lot of my early fell stuff – setting several course records and all that. I didn't try and run to beat records, I ran to run. Even though I did good stuff on the fells (and after, though not as good as I wanted), my running career was predominantly before the fells.'

John agreed that Kenny became an outstanding road runner. 'He started as a pro, and didn't do as much cross country as me. For top quality cross country races you needed speed and a change of pace. I look at myself as cross country first, fell second, then track, and then road. That is probably based on both success and in enjoyment. I have some amazing memories.'

Kenny Stuart summarised his thoughts on John Wild, the athlete. 'John was a great cross country runner. He spent a lot of time in Europe doing cross countries in winter. I think when you talk about John Wild, he would have been a lot more recognised if he had been a fell runner from the Lake District for instance, or Lancashire. Because he came from a background of the RAF, track running, Commonwealth Games and steeplechase, he probably isn't as recognised as he should be. There aren't many all-round athletes of the calibre of John Wild, I can tell you. I have run against some good Italian fell runners and none were as good as John Wild. When international fell running started, he was coming towards the end of his fell career, although he was not finished. If he had been running events like the [*mountain running*] World Cup when at his absolute peak he would have dominated that race. He had everything, he could go up hill, he could come down, and he had the speed and tenacity too.'

Warming to his theme, Kenny continued with his analysis, seeming to rue the fact that he might have missed racing against

John at his absolute peak. 'If John had been running the fells when he won the inter-counties and finished in the top 10 in the National he may well have been unbeatable. But it is anybody's guess. That is the thing. When I saw the report about John coming down to the finish when winning the Kentmere race minutes ahead of the field I just thought this bloke is special. If at that time I had thought I could have got anywhere near John I would have pretty happy. So now it was an absolute privilege to have raced against him, maybe not when he was at his absolute peak, but it was great to run against a man of that calibre on the fells.'

Kenny Stuart added that, 'John Wild was a truly tremendous athlete, and has been to an extent forgotten about. Actually, until 10 years ago no-one had bothered to talk to me either. That is the good thing about the *It's a hill, get over it* book, where those early days in the sport, particularly the era of Fred Reeves and Tommy Sedgwick, are documented forever. The same is true of John Wild in this book, he is like a hidden partner in the sport of fell running, and his story needs to be documented too.'

He continued, 'There is quite a difference between our upbringings. Mine is a traditional village life, John has a wider context. The fact that he didn't come from a traditional fell running background as well held that exposure up for him a bit, even at the time. Now, his interests are similar to mine. He is into shooting, as a beater, and he has his dogs. I am into hunting, I have a couple of ferrets up the back shed, and used to do a bit of rabbiting.'

Separately, John Wild noted that, 'Kenny and I both had our fans and enemies. Friends of mine would say "beat that ex-pro". Kenny's friends would say "you have to get that international upstart". We would just laugh it off. In 1983 Kenny and I were absolutely head to head. I was a better descender than him, but he could go uphill better than me. One week in 1983 Kenny was interested in doing one of my speed sessions. I was out on the fells with the dog for 3 hours or so running over rocks and that, then I got down to a sheep track and I twisted my ankle. So I never got to train with Kenny, which is a quite sad.'

Finally, reflecting back on the amazing battle they had throughout the 1983 fell season, Kenny Stuart commented, 'In some races I pushed myself beyond the limit, but then I've consoled myself thinking that if I am going to kill myself I'll be killing a few others at the same time.'

John Wild agreed, 'We've raced each other into the ground.' Kenny Stuart added, 'That is it about fell running. John and I have knocked ourselves up against each other, but still gone out for a few beers.'

Throughout their careers John Wild and Kenny Stuart trained remarkably hard and maintained incredibly high standards of performance across a range of athletic disciplines, including track, cross country, road and the fells. They should be remembered for all their achievements, but especially as two of the finest ever runners to grace the fells, setting as they did an amazing number of course records, some of which have stood the test of time and remain unbeaten. They came together for a couple of years on the fells, and raced each other in the absolutely enthralling rivalry that is at the core of this book. There was no quarter given, nor asked, as they battled through injuries and setbacks to try to secure the title in an amazing season-long challenge. From not really knowing each other at the start of that 1983 season, they had an almighty tussle for the fell championship, and despite their different backgrounds they finished as firm friends.

Index

Note: entries in **bold type** refer to the 1983 fell racing season.